Getting the Love You Want

Harville Hendrix, Ph.D.

GETTING THE

LOVE YOU WANT

a guide for couples

20th Anniversary Edition

REVISED AND UPDATED

With a new foreword by Harville Hendrix, Ph.D.,
and Helen LaKelly Hunt, Ph.D.

ST. MARTIN'S GRIFFIN

NEW YORK

The Library of Congress has cataloged the Henry Holt edition as follows:

Hendrix, Harville.
    Getting the love you want : a guide for couples / Harville Hendrix.
—twentieth-anniversary ed. / rev. and updated, with a new foreward by Harville Hendrix and Helen Lakelly Hunt.
        p. cm.
    Includes index.
    ISBN 978-0-8050-8700-0
    1. Marriage.   2. Love.   I. Title.
HQ734.H49 2008

                                                                2007039617

Originally published in hardcover in 1988 by Henry Holt and Company.

ISBN 978-0-8050-8700-0 (trade paperback)

Twentieth-Anniversary Edition 2008

20   19   18   17   16   15   14   13   12   11

Contents

In Appreciation of Jo Robinson

TWENTY YEARS AGO, after I decided to direct the ideas in this book to the general rather than the professional audience, my editor at Holt suggested that the assistance of a professional writer might be useful. Since this was my first attempt at a popular book, I readily agreed. After interviewing five writers, I was introduced to Jo Robinson. She understood immediately what I was attempting to do. At that time, Jo was the author of *Unplug the Christmas Machine* and *Full House.* In the years that followed, Jo Robinson became a *New York Times* bestselling author and coauthor of many books, including *Hot Monogamy, The Omega Diet, When Your Body Gets the Blues,* and *Pasture Perfect.*

For the first edition of this book, Jo took a lengthy rough manuscript and many transcriptions of lectures and workshops and worked tirelessly to transform a badly organized and somewhat opaque manuscript and much supplementary material into a well organized and finely polished product. When the idea of a second edition of the book was posed, Jo again edited my revisions and integrated them into what became the 2001 edition of *Getting the Love You Want.* For this third incarnation, although she was busy with her own research and writing and preparing for her marriage, she answered the call to help Helen and me organize our new ideas, working tirelessly to integrate them into this heavily revised edition and to help us craft the new foreword. As she did in the beginning, Jo immersed herself in the material by attending a couple's workshop and extensively interviewing Helen and me throughout the writing process.

We owe her a debt of gratitude for her long-term devotion to this project and for her friendship over the past twenty years. Without her intelligence and writing skill, we would all have a difficult time indeed getting the love we want. Thanks, Jo.

Acknowledgments

IN THE PROCESS of writing this book, I have become acutely aware of a truth so aptly stated by the poet John Donne, that "no man is an island," and by Walt Whitman, who said, "I contain multitudes." The pulling together of the ideas and clinical material presented here has deepened my awareness of my dependence upon many resources, persons, and experiences. The new vistas would not have been possible were it not for the intellectual giants upon whose shoulders I stand, and the contributions of many able teachers, stimulating students, trusting couples, supportive friends, and family. To all of them, I want to express my appreciation and ask forgiveness for any unwise liberties I may have taken.

Many special friends gave me much encouragement—some I want to mention by name. Dr. Robert Elliott read early versions of the manuscript and provided loving confrontation when my ideas needed more clarity and accuracy. Dr. Pat Love first introduced my ideas into a graduate school program on marriage and family and provided valuable feedback. Reed and Carolyn Whittle read later drafts of the manuscript and gave valuable advice along the way. Judy McCall graciously consented to read and comment on the final manuscript and helped with the endorsements. Drs. Joan and Robert Thorne opened doors for me to the professional community when I moved to New York and provided emotional support for the whole project.

I also want to express my appreciation for the enthusiasm, support, and stimulation of the many therapists in Dallas and New York who studied at the Institute for Relationship Therapy and helped me test these ideas in their practice of marital therapy.

I am deeply indebted to the many couples who trusted me with their relationship and allowed me to use their stories for research and for the enrichment of this book. I learned most of what I know about couples from them.

I want also to thank Henry Holt and Company for their excitement about the ideas even before they saw a manuscript, and for waiting patiently for its completion long after it should have been due. I especially appreciate the patience and support of my editor at Holt, Channa Taub, who gently but firmly kept my feet to the fire, and my agent, Julian Bach, who shepherded me through the contract process and gave me valuable guidance in the world of publishing. Tamera Allred read several of the last drafts, and made many helpful suggestions. Sharon Morris provided excellent editing assistance. Finally, my thanks to Yvonne Singleton, my secretary, for her typing skills and patience when I wanted sections of the manuscript ready "yesterday."

In the second edition in 2001, I included my appreciation to Barney Karpfinger, who had become my new agent. His support was invaluable for that edition and for all other books published before and after that revision. I am especially grateful for his continuing support for this third edition. Not only is he my agent; he is my friend. His friendship has enriched my life. And for more than two decades he has been a champion for the development of my career as a writer.

My appreciation also goes to the people at Henry Holt and Company who came up with the brilliant idea of publishing this twentieth anniversary edition and working so patiently with me on the revision. I am especially thankful for John Sterling, president and publisher; Sarah Knight, my editor; Claire McKinney, publicity director; Richard Rhorer, marketing director; and Maggie Richards, vp director of sales and marketing.

I continue to feel grateful to Norris Chumley for his excellent direction of the video series for public television and again to Jo Robinson, my writer, who helped with the second edition and answered the call once more for help with the third edition. Sanam Hoon, my assistant for many years, deserves thanks for helping in many capacities including many tedious details for this edition. I also want to thank Meghan Doherty, my personal assistant, for handling all the scheduling details and doing the nitty gritty work of the revised bibliography. Thanks also to Nancy Jones, the first executive director of the Institute for Imago Relationship Therapy, who stabilized Imago institutionally in its early days, and Rick Brown, who helped it grow and expand its services. My deep appreciation also goes to the Board of Imago Relationships International: Tim Atkinson, executive director, and Farrah Daniels and Linda Thompson of the staff, who have been unambivalent in their dedication to Imago and have shepherded its expansion internationally.

My indebtedness to Oprah Winfrey is unlimited. She first exposed Imago to millions of people in 1988, putting *Getting the Love You Want* on the *New York Times* bestseller list. Repeated invitations to be on her show have returned this book to the bestseller list eleven times, and she has rated my second appearance on her show in 1989 among her top twenty shows in her twenty years on television.

Finally, I am deeply indebted to all the couples who have read this book and passed it on to others, to other professionals and friends who have recommended the book, and to all the Imago therapists, especially the Master Trainers and Faculty of the Institute who have helped to develop and deepen Imago Relationship Therapy and make it available in this country and around the world.

Most important, my deepest appreciation goes to my wife, Helen LaKelly Hunt, who has been my partner in this enterprise. Without her support and intellectual contribution, this book and others would not have come into being and Imago Relationship Therapy would not have been born. I also want to thank my six children for their support and patience while the book was written and revised. I also appreciate the lessons I have learned from them over the years. They and Helen have helped me to live the ideas and become a more whole person. They, and I, were all excited for the completion of the second edition, and are now again thrilled that this third edition is done!

Foreword to the Twentieth-Anniversary Edition of *Getting the Love You Want*

With Helen LaKelly Hunt, Ph.D.

> The world is not comprehensible, but it is embraceable:
> through the embracing of one of its beings.
>
> — MARTIN BUBER

I BEGAN AN intense exploration of love relationships in 1975 in response to a question from a student in a marriage and family therapy class that I then taught. I remember the day clearly. It was a Tuesday morning, and I was twenty minutes late. I had just come from the county courthouse where I had been granted a divorce. I was hoping the students would have wandered off by the time I arrived, but when I opened the door I saw that they were all there. I had no choice but to stand in front of them, a living testimony to all that I *did not* know about marriage.

As it turned out, the students knew where I had been, and they greeted me with a surprising amount of compassion. I learned they had spent the last twenty minutes talking about their own relationships, something they had never done before in class. Three of them had already married and divorced, three had never had a serious love relationship, and the remaining six were in troubled relationships. At the end of the class, a recently divorced student asked me this question: "Dr. Hendrix, why do couples have such a hard time staying together?" I thought for a moment and then responded. "I don't have the foggiest notion. That is a great question and I think I'll spend the rest of my career trying to find out."

Two years later I met Helen, and we began a conversation about this question that has lasted to this day. After thirty years of being immersed together in the study of relationship dynamics, we have learned a great deal. Many of our insights can be found in this Twentieth-Anniversary Edition of *Getting the Love You Want.* These pages summarize what we have gleaned from our collaboration, intensive reading, work with thousands of couples in private practice and workshops, and conversation with other psychologists and Imago therapists.

Although this edition brings some very significant additions to the book, which I will discuss later in this essay, much of the basic text is the same as the 2001 revised edition. On the whole, our ongoing research has supported rather than challenged the book's main premises. We have also amassed plentiful evidence that the book "works" in the real world. To date, several millions of couples worldwide have read *Getting the Love You Want,* and thousands of them have taken the time to share their experiences with Helen and me. Recently, a couple told us that they had been edging toward divorce, but decided to give their marriage one last chance. They rented a remote beach cabin, took along enough food and supplies for seven days, and packed a copy of *Getting the Love You Want.* They vowed to read the entire book to each other and practice all the exercises. By the end of the week, they felt closer to each other than they had in ten years. Ultimately, they decided to stay together and create a conscious partnership. Five years later, they continue to enjoy a mutually satisfying relationship. They said, "Your book was exactly what we needed. It saved our marriage and turned our lives around."

WHAT WE CHANGED

WHILE MUCH OF the 2001 text remains, we have made some important revisions. The first revision was to use more inclusive language. Momentous changes in women's rights and same-sex relationships have taken place in the last twenty years. Just as it now seems inappropriate to use the pronoun "he" to describe both men and women, it is outdated to describe all committed love relationships as "marriages" and the two individuals involved as "spouses" or "husbands and wives." The last comprehensive census revealed that the United States has at least 5.5 million households headed by unmarried couples, a seventy-two percent increase from 1990.[1] An estimated one in eight of today's unmarried couples is a same-sex partnership. To reflect these societal changes, we now use the generic terms "partners" and "couples."

Second, we've made Helen's seminal role in developing Imago Relationship Therapy more apparent. The original book reads like a one-man odyssey. In truth, Helen and I have been on a two-person mission to understand love relationships since our first date. In fact, we forged many of the key ideas in Imago Relationship Therapy in the crucible of our own marriage. Without Helen, there would be no book.

Third, the most substantive revision is replacing the original chapter 11 with an entirely new chapter. This chapter used to be titled "Containing Rage," and it was designed to help couples express the anger and frustration they had carried over from childhood. The chapter described an exercise called the "Full Container" that guided each partner in venting his or her anger, while helping the other listen with more compassion. At the time, we believed that this catharsis would reduce the amount of tension in their day-to-day interactions. The opposite proved to be true. We discovered that the more couples practiced the exercise, the angrier they became with each other in their daily lives.

The entirely new chapter 11, now titled "Creating a Sacred Space," presents our new and highly effective strategies for defusing childhood anger left over from childhood—anger than can undermine an otherwise successful relationship. But the intent of this chapter goes far beyond helping couples reduce angry outbursts. It describes a process that helps couples eliminate *all* forms of negativity from their interactions—everything from physical abuse and loud yelling to snide remarks—and thereby cuts anger off at its roots. As I explain at length in the chapter, we now believe that eliminating negativity is the most powerful way to transform a love relationship. Indeed, it is the foundation for lasting love.

Finally, we made numerous smaller additions and deletions throughout the book. In places where we had not described a concept in enough depth, we added more information. When we discovered an idea that had become inconsistent with current IRT theory, we made the appropriate changes. We added four new exercises, making the book an even more useful tool for self-help. All in all, we believe that the readers of this Twentieth-Anniversary Edition will be highly successful at getting the love they want, and that even readers of the earlier editions will find much beneficial new material.

CONNECTION

AS WE THOUGHT about writing this foreword, we realized that we want to do more than simply explain the changes we made to the book. We decided to use this opportunity to talk about some of our overall conclusions about love relationships, conclusions that underlie every word of the text. Helen and I have reached the stage in our lives and our work with couples when a summing up seems appropriate.

At the end of his career, Freud asked the now famous question: "What do women want?" We, too, have been struggling to answer a question: "What do men and women want from their love relationships?" We now believe that the answer to Freud's question and our question—indeed all of humanity's yearning—is one and the same. Above all else, we seek *connection*—with parts of ourselves that we have repressed, with other people, and with the larger universe. We cannot experience life in its fullness unless we have an intimate relationship with another human being and, beyond that, a feeling of connection with the world around us. Using the language of Martin Buber, each person needs a "Thou" to become a fully realized "I."

Looking back, we now see that our life's work has been rooted in helping couples create the hyphen in Buber's "I-Thou" relationship. In this celebrated notation, the hyphen serves as both a link and a space holder. It signifies that the most fulfilling love relationship is one in which two people are intimately connected with each other, yet keep a respectful distance apart by acknowledging each other's "otherness." The nature of this relationship cannot be described by the term "I *and* Thou," or by the collapsed "Ithou." It is an "I-Thou" relationship. The two individuals are separate *and* connected at the same time.

The operative term here is "connection." To us, it is more than a psychological term that describes human experience. From our extensive reading in other disciplines, we have come to believe that the word "connection" describes the universe. Since we, as humans, are an integral part of the universe, it also describes us. As all things are interconnected, so are we; it is our nature to be connected. If we do not *feel* connected, it is because something has happened to us to rupture our awareness of the connection. We may sometimes lose our awareness that we are a part of the whole, but that separateness is just an illusion. We cannot *not* be connected.

RUPTURED CONNECTION

THE ILLUSION OF separateness is what brings most couples into therapy. They don't feel connected to each other, nor do they experience a seamless connection with the world around them or with the universe. They feel disjointed, isolated, and lonely. Their relationship might be characterized as "Me versus You." Our experience has taught us that the primary reason couples fail at creating an I-Thou relationship is that they did not experience it in childhood. Unfortunately, most people experience their first "relationship difficulty" in the first eighteen months of life. Experts in child development call this critical period the "Attachment Stage." Having a close bond with one or more caregivers is important throughout childhood, but it is *essential* in those earliest months.

In order to experience a strong and safe connection with a caregiver, children need what child psychologists call an "attuned" parent. This is a caregiver who is present in both meanings of the word: available to you physically and with warm emotions most of the time. Ideally, this caregiver respects your individuality and turns to you for clues as to what you need in the moment. You are held when you need comfort and physical connection. You are fed when you are hungry. You are soothed when you are irritable, afraid, or in pain. You are put to bed when you are tired. This attuned parent also encourages you to express your full range of emotions—joy and playfulness, frustration and anger. The good, the bad, and the ugly. Rather than deflecting your feelings, your caregiver accepts them and mirrors them: "Happy baby! You are such a happy baby!" "You look mad. Are you angry that you have to stop playing?" All of this is done in a spirit of acceptance, love, and generosity. When you have an attuned parent, you are not a burden to your parent, nor are you the solution to your parent's own unmet needs. You are free to be you and to be emotionally and physically close to a caring person at the same time.

Children raised by attuned parents are more likely to create satisfying love relationships in adulthood. Because they had safe, nurturing bonds with their caregivers, they do not have an exaggerated fear of abandonment or engulfment. They are not likely to choose a partner out of sheer neediness because most of their primary needs were satisfied in childhood. They are not attracted to people who neglect, criticize, or abuse them. Being mistreated feels totally foreign, out of place, and intrinsically wrong. Further, they tend to attract the appropriate mate with relative ease. A person who is emotionally expressive, has a positive self-image, feels relatively secure, and who welcomes intimacy is highly attractive to others.

DESPERATELY SEEKING CONNECTION

REGRETTABLY, MANY OF us had *un*attuned parents, and we bring the resulting unmet needs into our adult relationships. Not only did we experience disconnection from our parents; we began to feel disconnected from parts of ourselves. This inner and outer rupture resulted in a feeling of isolation—both from others and, in the larger context, the universe itself. The rupture was brought about by two fundamental kinds of psychological wounding: neglect or intrusion. In the broadest sense, our parents either neglected us by failing to attend to our needs, or they intruded upon us by trying to meet their own needs through us. Most children suffer both types of wounds because, in many families, one caregiver tends to be intrusive and the other neglectful. This confusing behavior says to the child: "Now I need you. Now I don't."

Helen and I see this ruptured connection in childhood as the source of all human problems, and we believe that *restoring* the awareness of our connection is the source of all healing. We have one diagnosis of unhappy couples—ruptured connection, and we have one goal in therapy: helping them restore awareness of connection with each other. When two people learn how to connect on a very deep level, the pain they experienced in childhood loses its sting. As we discuss in chapter 1, the unconscious mind has great difficulty distinguishing between past and present. When couples repair the ruptured connection in their present day relationship, they simultaneously heal the trauma they felt as young children. Their relationship to each other and the universe is restored. This connection can have the power and quality associated with a spiritual experience. The relationship becomes a sacred space. Heal in the present; heal the past; heal the relation to the whole.

It has also become very clear to us that safety is the number one precondition for connection. Two people cannot connect if they are defending themselves against a barrage of negativity or if they live in fear of being abandoned or overwhelmed by their partners. *For this reason, all of the exercises in Imago are designed to remove negativity and to promote safety and mutual respect.* Reromanticizing, the exercise featured on pages 274–76, is the first example. Reromanticizing encourages couples to act as if they were newly in love with each other, giving each other the same tender attention, gifts, and words of endearment that came effortlessly during romantic love. This playacting is to go on for weeks. Even though many couples begin this exercise with gritted teeth, repetition rewires their neural connections, allowing them to see each other as lovers and friends once again, not enemy combatants. A feeling of safety begins to grow.

The Behavior Change Request described on pages 168–82 instills safety by helping couples satisfy their unmet childhood needs, which is the underlying source of much of their anger. In the first step of this exercise, couples examine the chronic frustrations they have with each other and then identify the childhood wish that is embedded in each frustration. "I'm frustrated that you don't do a thorough job of cleaning the kitchen. My unmet wish is to have the people who care about me to be more responsible. As a child, I felt there was no one to help me." In the second step, the person asks his or her partner for a specific, doable change in behavior that will help satisfy that underlying wish. Because the two individuals unconsciously perceive each other as surrogate parents, the change in behavior is experienced as if it took place in the past, and it heals the original injury. Because childhood pain was the *basis* for the frustration between them, soothing the pain defuses the anger so that it no longer intrudes into the relationship. Removing anger draws couples even closer together.

Safety is further enhanced by the Holding exercise (pages 284–86). At the height of the power struggle, it seems to us that our partners are intentionally withholding love or inflicting pain. We have to strike back or close ourselves off to protect ourselves. But in less than thirty minutes, the Holding exercise helps people see beyond their partners' defenses to the underlying pain that caused them. This evocative exercise instructs couples to cradle each other in their arms as they listen to each other's childhood stories. By the end of the exercise, they can begin to see one another as being "full of hurt" instead of "hurtful" or "bad."

As it promotes safety, the Holding exercise also makes a major contribution to the healing process. The beauty of this exercise is that it deliberately blurs the boundaries between your partner and your parents. Your partner is holding you tenderly as you talk about not getting enough physical affection as a child. Your partner is listening to you with full attention as you talk about being ignored by your caregivers. Your partner is rocking you and making supportive sounds as you recall being a young child alone in your grief. As you bring to mind the pain from the past, your partner's attentiveness and compassion applies the universal balm. You begin to feel more intimately connected with your partner and less anguished about the past.

THE IMAGO DIALOGUE

OF ALL THE exercises in Imago Relationship Therapy, we now regard the Imago Dialogue as being the most effective tool for healing a ruptured connection. This technique is described in chapter 9, and involves three separate steps: mirroring, validation, and empathy. Early in our work with the Imago Dialogue, we viewed it as an effective way to deepen communication. Eventually, we discovered that its power goes far beyond communication and can result in profound healing and growth for both partners. Ultimately, it transforms their perceptions of each other and that transforms the relationship.

In addition to the benefits of the Imago Dialogue as outlined in the previous edition of *Getting the Love You Want,* I'd like to focus here on how and why it is so effective at creating safety and connection. Mirroring, the first step, is designed to help each of you understand what the other is saying. It involves listening to your partner's comments, restating them without altering their meaning, and then asking for confirmation that you "got it." Mirroring is elementary in the dual meaning of the word: It is both simple and basic.

Mirroring alone is a potent tool for creating an I-Thou relationship. To mirror your partner you have to turn down the volume on your own thoughts so that you can listen attentively; you have to switch the channel from "me" to "you." With this shift in focus, you are telling your partner, in effect: "I am no longer the sole person in the universe. I am acknowledging your separate existence. Your thoughts are important to me."

Second, the exercise requires you to be an *accurate* mirror of your partner. You can't be like a fun house mirror and twist your partner's thoughts, leave out important details, or embellish them with your own. If you commit one of these common errors, your partner is to coach you until you get it right: "You got part of it right, but you left out what I said about my feelings." Asking for confirmation is humbling and tedious, but it's the best way to know if you truly understand what your partner is saying.

Just as important, asking for confirmation empowers your partner. He or she gets to persist until you interpret the message correctly. Very few of us had this latitude as young children. Whether or not we were understood was dependent on the mood and presence of mind of the adults around us. They could diminish what we had to say, ignore it, counter with their own views, or shame us for even daring to express it. Sadly, many people perpetuate this pattern in their daily conversations with their partners.

Mirroring stops this destructive pattern in its tracks. When you mirror each other, you both get to experience what it is like to have someone pay close attention to you, understand exactly what you have to say, and honor your uniqueness. But mirroring goes deeper than that. Unbeknownst to you, your old brain, your unconscious mind, pays close attention as you work your way through this exercise. Having no sense of time and unable to make a clear distinction between individuals, your unconscious mind perceives the attention and respect you are receiving as coming from a caretaker, not just from your present-day intimate partner, and vice versa. As a result, a few repair stitches are made in the ruptured connections you both experienced in childhood.

After several years of using this exercise, we discovered that the listening partner can magnify the healing effect of mirroring by asking this question: "Do you have more to say about that?" Or, simply, "Is there more about that?" It's a wonderful feeling to have your partner's full attention and to be asked to reveal even more about what you are thinking and feeling. Very few of us had caretakers who expressed much curiosity about our inner world. We were most visible to them when we excelled or when we caused trouble. Our partner's keen interest in our thoughts helps repair those feelings of neglect from long ago. This, in turn, makes us feel much safer in our partner's presence, and we begin to discover parts of ourselves that have been hidden since childhood. We become more whole.

The second part of the Imago Dialogue, validation, continues the reparation process. Once you have listened to your partner and fully understood what they have to say, you then strive to see how their thoughts make sense to *them*. You do not have to agree with your partner. You need to see them as they *are*, not as you wish them to be. Many people spend much of their time trying to get their partners to think the same way they do—this is a common obstacle to restoring connection—but it is important that you affirm the logic of your partner's thinking—to see your partner as an "other" and no longer an extension of yourself: "You are not crazy. From all that I'm learning about you, I can see why you think that way." Many of us had parents who could not transcend their own worldviews. If we didn't agree with them or heed their advice, they ignored us or implied that we were stupid, misguided, rebellious, disrespectful, or crazy. The fact that two quite different points of view could be equally valid—especially opposing views between a parent and child—was beyond their comprehension. Validation establishes the fact that there are two realities; both are correct.

Empathy is the final step in the Imago Dialogue. Once you have been reassured that you received your partner's messages exactly as they were intended, you strive to understand the feelings behind them: "Now that I really listen to you and understand what you're saying, I'm wondering if you might feel threatened." Or "Wow! I think I understand how much your new job means to you. You must be feeling thrilled!" The word "empathy" comes from the German term *"Einfuhlung,"* which means "to feel as one with." When you and your partner are empathic with each other, you are as emotionally close as two people can be. As the poet Rumi said: "Out beyond ideas of wrong doing and right doing, there is a field. I will meet you there."

"Love heals all" is a well known sentiment. And it can. It can even heal the deepest emotional wound of all—the ruptured connection between you and your parents. But it needs to be a specific kind of love. It needs to be a mature, patient love that is free of manipulation and distortion, and it needs to take place within the context of an intimate relationship. Receiving empathy from a friend may be very moving, but it does not reach all the way down into your psyche. In order to heal the wounds of the past, you need to receive love from a person whom your unconscious mind has merged with your childhood caregivers.

WALKING THE WALK

WHEN HELEN AND I first contemplated writing a book about love relationships over twenty years ago, we saw it as text without exercises. We would explain the principles of creating a lasting, intimate bond, but we would not provide any explicit instructions. Today, we are glad that we changed our minds and decided to write a "how to" book. We've learned that people can understand all the principles we've just outlined and still have a troubled relationship if they don't do the exercises.

Helen's research in the field of epistemology, the science of "how we know what we know," helps explain why. There are two different types of knowing: "Separate Knowing" and "Connected Knowing." Here's an illustration of the differences between the two. You have a "separate" or intellectual knowing of an apple if you can recognize a picture of the fruit, understand that it contains the seeds of the plant, or talk about its health benefits. You have a "connected" or more *experiential* knowing of an apple when you hold one in your hand, feel the waxy texture of the skin, smell it, and taste it. Separate knowing is abstract. Connected knowing is concrete. Combining these two ways of knowing can give you a more comprehensive level of understanding. You learn about the apple *and* you taste it.

The Holding exercise that I described earlier fosters *connected* knowing. Intellectually, you may accept the fact that creating a safe connection with your partner helps heal the ruptured connection that you had with your parents. It makes sense, especially when you factor in your old brain's tendency to blur the boundaries between people. But when you actually lie in your partner's arms and tell your life story, you begin to react to your partner as if he or she were indeed merged with your caregivers. Then you begin to *experience* the actual healing process. You feel more loving toward your partner. You feel less anguished about your past. Healing is no longer an intellectual concept; it's a spine-tingling experience.

Helen was the first one to realize that she and I had not integrated our intellectual understanding of relationships with our daily behavior. We were great at teaching the concepts of Imago Relationship Therapy, and we could work wonders with other couples, but we were not reaping all its benefits in our own marriage. When we followed our own advice and stopped all criticism of each other, and then began spending more time practicing the Imago exercises, especially the Imago Dialogue, we were able to connect with each other on a much more intimate level. We were talking the talk *and* walking the walk.

The Essence of a Conscious Partnership

IF HELEN AND I were to take all the insights we've gained about love relationships in the past thirty years and reduce them to their essence, we would summarize them in the following five sentences:

1. Accept the reality that your partner is not you.
2. Be an *advocate* for your partner's separate reality and potential.
3. Make your relationship a sacred space by removing all negativity.
4. Always honor your partner's boundaries.
5. Practice the Imago Dialogue until it becomes second nature and you can interact spontaneously once again.

Eventually, you will not have to "work" on your relationship anymore. The changes will become stable. You will have rewired your brain so that your new way of relating is far more comfortable to you than your old way. You will begin living in a different reality—the reality of sustained connection. You will look for ways to spend more time together, not less. You will begin to experience your differences of opinion as creative tension, as an opportunity to move beyond your isolated points of view. Your desire for sameness will disappear, and you will begin to revel in your partner's "otherness." If you happen to slip back into negativity, the pain will be acute. "Why on earth did we do that?" But the moment typically passes, and you will find it easy to get back on track and restore the sacred nature of your relationship. Your relationship will have become self-sustaining, self-organizing, and self-healing.

One reason that this relationship will feel so "right" to you is that it allows you to participate in one of the fundamental facts about the universe. Much of nature has a "dyadic" or two-part structure. According to quantum physics, each particle that comes into being is paired with another particle. Furthermore, each particle is both a point and a wave depending upon how it is viewed, which is why some physicists now refer to particles as "wavicles." Sexual reproduction in the majority of species we know involves two entities; Noah included one of each on the ark. Our DNA splits into two and then generates the missing half. Our cells divide into two. Anthropologists tell us that in the creation stories in most cultures, people are first introduced as a couple, not as separate individuals. Physiologists tell us that our brains are complementary—right and left brain. Our language is binary: up and down, black and white, etc. Our blood circulates in oscillation between the right and left sides of our body.

A recent discovery in astronomy gives us another example of the dyadic nature of the universe, one that is especially appropriate for our view of love relationships. We now know that most stars in the sky are not solitary stars like our sun. Most of them have a "companion star." The two stars are attracted to each other by a strong gravitational force but are kept from collapsing into each other by an opposing centrifugal force. Helen and I like to think of two people in a conscious love relationship as companion stars. Each person is a unique individual ablaze with potential. One is just as important as the other, and each has a unique and equally valid view of the universe. Yet, together, they form a greater whole, kept connected by the pull of mutual love and respect. They mirror the interconnected universe.

New Jersey, July 2007

Preface to the 2001 Edition

by Harville Hendrix and Helen LaKelly Hunt

IN THE INTRODUCTION to the first edition of this book written in 1988, I reported that *Getting the Love You Want* was born out of the dissolution of my first marriage, a breakup that compelled me to explore the mysteries of love relationships. In this introduction, written thirteen years later, I am happy to report a very different reality. Helen LaKelly Hunt and I have been married for nineteen years, and relying on the ideas described in this book, we have achieved its promise of "passionate friendship." As we have been pleased to discover, being in a close and loving relationship is far easier than being in a strained or distant one. These days, our life together is surprisingly peaceful. But, paradoxically, it also resonates with a new energy, an energy fueled by our close connection. Even our middle-aged bodies feel more alive!

In addition to having a passionate friendship, Helen and I also have what we call a "passionate partnership" because we are allies in our professional lives as well. Indeed, Helen has influenced my work from our very first date. We began to court each other in 1977, two years after my divorce. Helen was completing her master's degree in counseling, and I was a professor at the Perkins School of Theology. On our first night out together, I remember telling her that I wanted to leave Perkins and move on to something else, but I wasn't sure what I wanted to do. I talked about some options I was considering, which included an in-depth exploration of the psychology of the couple. I wanted to know why couples were having such a difficult time staying together and why they were so devastated when their relationship fell apart. Nothing that I had read in the professional literature seemed to give an adequate explanation. Helen was drawn to this possibility above all the others I mentioned and encouraged me to share my half-formed ideas with her. Fifteen minutes into our conversation she said, "The way you're talking about the centrality of relationships brings to my mind the 'I-Thou' of Martin Buber." Then she quoted a passage from Fyodor Dostoyevsky that she had committed to memory as a young woman: "The man who desires to see the living God face-to-face does not seek God in the empty firmament of his mind, but in human love." "No, no," I said, failing to see the obvious connection between my thinking and Buber's philosophy of relationship or Dostoyevsky's spirituality, "I don't think my thoughts have much to do with either one of them."

Then, as now, Helen had sensed where I was headed, even when I did not.

In the years that followed, Helen developed her own passions, but she continued to be actively involved in my work. To some degree, she played the traditional supporting role—caring for the family, offering financial help, and being a sympathetic ear. But there were many times when she stepped outside those bounds and strategically intervened in ways that would prove to be pivotal. When others would accept my ideas at face value, she would question my thinking or, more often, challenge me to deepen my understanding. What I valued most, however, is that she always cared enough about me and my work to be willing to enlarge my view with her own truth. I can honestly say that every idea in this book was forged within the crucible of our relationship. So when I was asked to write a new introduction to this revised edition of *Getting the Love You Want,* it was only natural that I ask Helen to write it with me. It was time to make her role as cocreator more visible.

As Helen and I began to reflect on what to write, we found ourselves overcome with a wave of nostalgia. We recalled the long years of research, thinking, and talking that had gone into the first edition. In the beginning, we had debated whether to start with a book for couples or write a more academic book for therapists. Once we had decided to write a book for the general public, we discussed whether or not to include exercises in the book. If so, which ones? The writing itself took several years. We remembered with admiration our writer, Jo Robinson, who helped give order to our thoughts and wrote with a lyricism and simplicity that remains one of the keys to the book's success. We recalled our euphoria when the book was finally published in 1988 and then, to our great surprise, was featured on the *Oprah Winfrey Show.* Oprah's enthusiastic support propelled the book to the *New York Times* bestseller list, far exceeding our expectations. The readership for the book continued to grow over the years, until by now the book has sold over a million and a half copies and has been translated into more than thirty languages.

Helen and I also reflected on the groundswell of interest in Imago Therapy, the name for the couple's therapy that is described in this book. Starting in the late 1980s, a growing number of therapists began expressing an interest in being trained in this new way of working with couples. Today, there is a thriving international Imago community of about 1,500 therapists practicing in thirteen countries. More than 150 presenters conduct approximately 400 Imago workshops each year. Twenty faculty members of the Institute for Imago Relationship Therapy train a steady stream of new therapists in a dozen cities. The combination of all this talent and energy has transformed

Imago into a movement that should become a significant force for social transformation.

As Helen and I replayed these wondrous events, we realized that, at times, we feel more like onlookers than creators. We set the process in motion, but we do not feel wholly responsible for its continued success. We feel like parents who helped a child learn to ride a bike by giving a push and running alongside, but now watch in awe as that adult child finishes first in a race. We were there at the beginning; we gave the initial push. But the child has attained a degree of proficiency for which we are only partly responsible.

To what, then, do we credit the success of *Getting the Love You Want* and the burgeoning growth of the Imago community? The simplest way to put it is that we have managed to further a dynamic that was already in place. In the second half of the twentieth century, the old notion of marriage was no longer working for many couples. In unprecedented numbers, people were deciding they would rather go through the pain and stigma of divorce than put up with an unhappy or stultifying relationship. In the 1960s and 1970s, marriage itself came into question as couples began experimenting with "open marriages" and cohabitation, hoping that they could create something more meaningful by transcending the restrictions of traditional relationships.

But many of the people in conventional marriages were also searching for a relationship that was larger, deeper, and more meaningful than what their parents and grandparents had. Thousands of couples sought that "something more" in couple's therapy. But the type of therapy that was offered at the time focused on the psyche of the individual, not on relationship dynamics. The underlying theory was that working on each person's issues would create two healthy, self-actualized people. These two people could then come together and—with little additional effort or insight—create a satisfying love relationship.

This traditional form of therapy had a limited success rate—if one defines success simply as keeping couples from getting divorced. About two-thirds of the couples would fail to reconcile their differences and decide to go their separate ways. But even some of those who managed to stay together would express a need for more support and insight than they'd been given. Counseling had given them a better understanding of their own issues and had improved their communication skills, but their relationship itself remained a bit of a mystery. Despite all the knowledge they'd gained, they continued to act in self-defeating ways. What's more, they sensed that their relationship held out a promise of healing and wholeness that they could not define, much less realize.

One of the reasons that *Getting the Love You Want* and Imago Therapy had something to offer these couples is that I, too, had experienced the frustration of being in a relationship that had not lived up to its potential. As I began to construct my own theory and practice of couple's therapy, it was critical to me that I answer the questions that had arisen from my own failed marriage. One of my main realizations was that the two individuals in a relationship need to let go of the illusion that they are the center of the universe and learn to see each other as equal partners. (I think of that old saying, "You and I are one, and I am the one.") There are indeed two people in the relationship. When two individuals surrender their centrality, something unexpected occurs—the relationship itself becomes the center. Once that fundamental shift occurs, they can begin to work with the unconscious purpose of their relationship, not against it. They can begin to accept the fact that being in an intimate love relationship calls forth all the unresolved issues of their childhood, and that they can learn how to work together to resolve them. We are born in relationship, we are wounded in relationship, and we can be healed in relationship. Indeed, we cannot be fully healed outside of a relationship. This is the idea that resonated with so many couples.

DETHRONING THE MARITAL THERAPIST

WITH HINDSIGHT, HELEN and I can see another reason for the success of *Getting the Love You Want.* It challenges another fundamental tenet of couple's therapy, which is that the therapist is the source of the healing. In Imago Therapy, the therapist is transformed into a facilitator of the healing process. This does not make the therapist unimportant; in fact, the need for a competent therapist is increased. It's somewhat like requiring an obstetrician to take on the additional role of a midwife. The obstetrician becomes a highly skilled aide to a natural process rather than a remote authority figure with all of the answers.

Interestingly, even though transferring authority from the therapist to the couple was a monumental change, we were not fully aware that this is what was happening until after *Getting the Love You Want* was written. Once again, it was Helen who first had the insight: "You're dethroning the therapist," she said to me one day. "You're shifting the emphasis to the relationship between the couple, not the relationship between client and therapist." I immediately saw she was right. Once the idea had been verbalized, we began to understand the significance of the shift. In traditional therapy, one of the primary healing mechanisms involves "transference." Transference is when you assign to someone else either characteristics that belong to you (which is called "projective" transference), or characteristics that belong to somebody else: "You're like my mother." Once transference occurs between client and therapist, the therapist can use that misidentification in a positive way to help the client resolve issues from the past. Thus transference is a fundamental part of the therapy. The therapy is successful when the client "works through" the transference and begins to see the therapist as a distinct individual once again.

As you will see as you read this book, transference also occurs between couples in a love relationship. In fact, there's no way to avoid it. During the romantic love stage, this is a positive transference. You imagine that your partner has many of your own good qualities and also the positive traits of the people who influenced you most deeply in childhood. Later on, as conflict emerges, you begin to project negative traits onto your partner. This is typically when marriages fall apart. "You've changed. You're not the person I married," you say to each other. In reality, what has changed is not your partner, but the nature of the information you're projecting onto your partner. Imago Therapy helps you use this transference as a source of healing. This is very similar to the psychodynamics of traditional therapy, only in this context, the transference is between you and your partner, not between you and a therapist.

Some couples are able to resolve the transference without outside help. But like most people, you may need to work with a structured set of exercises or a competent therapist. The exercises or the therapist help create a zone of safety and provide the step-by-step instructions to guide you through the process. Like the millions of people who have read this book before you, you will find that reading the text and practicing the exercises will do this for you. If you require additional help, we are glad to say there are now many more trained therapists available to give you a hand.

CHANGES IN THE REVISED EDITION

WHEN WE REALIZED that this revised edition of *Getting the Love You Want* gave us the opportunity to make changes in the body of the text as well as write a new introduction, we read the book carefully, looking for flaws in the theory or changes that needed to be made in the therapy process. We were surprised to discover that most of what we've learned in the intervening thirteen years has been an extension, rather than a correction, of what we stated in the first edition. One of the gratifying extensions is that the partnership dynamics we described in heterosexual couples applies to all intimate partnerships, regardless of their sexual preference. We are excited about our new insights, of course, and will be elaborating on them in a forthcoming book. But we want to reassure you that the center still holds.

The only changes we felt obliged to make in this edition were to clarify some points about closing exits in chapter 7 and to enlarge upon an exercise in chapter 9 that was originally referred to as the Mirroring exercise. Regarding exits, we have learned how important it is to understand "closing an exit" as a process that takes time, rather than a particular action. The Mirroring exercise is now called the Imago Dialogue, and it has been expanded to include two additional steps—validation and empathy—which we had not discovered when the original edition was published. As will be explained in more detail in chapter 9, "mirroring," or paraphrasing your partner, is an essential first step in exploring your partner's reality. But by itself, it may not be sufficient to establish a profound sense of connection. If you can go on to confirm the validity of your partner's view ("You make sense to me. You're not crazy.") and then empathize with his or her feelings ("I can see why you feel angry."), you deepen the bond between you. Or, as I say to couples, you go beyond mere contact to connection and then, ultimately, to communion.

In our own relationship, Helen and I have been privileged to experience this transcendent state. We have also seen it manifested in the lives of couples who have been through Imago Therapy. We'd like to close this introduction by sharing some of their comments with you. A man who read *Getting the Love You Want* expressed his new understanding this way: "I've learned that my view of the world is no more true than my wife's point of view. In fact, when we combine our views, we create something more valid than either one of us can create alone. We both give something up, only to gain a great deal more. It's been a profound change in our marriage." A couple that attended a weekend seminar wrote to us to say that "issues that have baffled us for years make perfect sense to us now, and we can truly empathize with each other. Perhaps for the first time in our relationship of almost twenty-eight years, we feel safe. This is what we have always dreamed for our relationship, and we can hardly believe it is coming true!" Echoing their thoughts, another couple wrote, "What we have learned in your workshops and your books has been nothing short of transformational. We are in love again and marveling that this is so."

As so many other couples have discovered, if you take this book to heart and embrace the seemingly mundane exercises described herein, you, too, will attain a more loving, support-ive, and deeply satisfying relationship. Imago Therapy is not just a theory of wishful thinking, it is a tried and true way to create the passionate friendship you've always wanted. As you will see, marriage is therapy—provided you honor its uncon-scious intent.

New Jersey, April 2001

Introduction to the 1988 Edition

IN TODAY'S SOCIETY, you are encouraged to view marriage as a box. First you choose a mate. Then you climb into a box. Once you've had a chance to settle in, you take your first close look at your boxmate. If you like what you see, you stay put. If you don't, you climb out of the box and scout around for another mate. In other words, marriage is viewed as an unchanging state, and whether or not it works depends upon your ability to attract a good partner. The common solution to an unhappy marriage, the one chosen by nearly fifty percent of all couples, is to divorce and start all over again with a new and, it is hoped, better mate.

The problem with this solution is that there is a lot of pain involved in switching boxes. There is the agony of dividing up children and possessions and putting aside treasured dreams. There is the reluctance to risk intimacy again, fearing that the next relationship, too, might fail. And there is the emotional damage to the other inhabitants of the box—the children—who grow up feeling responsible for the divorce and wonder if they will ever experience lasting love.

Unfortunately, the only alternative many people see to divorce is to stay in the box, tighten the lid, and put up with a disappointing relationship for the rest of their lives. They learn to cope with an empty marriage by filling themselves up with food, alcohol, drugs, activities, work, television, and romantic fantasies, resigned to the belief that their longing for an intimate love will never be realized.

In this book I propose a more hopeful and, I believe, more accurate view of love relationships. Marriage is not a static state between two unchanging people. Marriage is a psychological and spiritual journey that begins in the ecstasy of attraction, meanders through a rocky stretch of self-discovery, and culminates in the creation of an intimate, joyful, lifelong union. Whether or not you realize the full potential of this vision depends not on your ability to attract the perfect mate, but on your willingness to acquire knowledge about hidden parts of yourself.

PERSONAL HISTORY

WHEN I BEGAN my career as a therapist, I counseled both individuals and couples. My preference was to work with one person at a time. My training was geared toward individuals, and when I saw clients singly, I felt competent and effective. Not so when a couple walked into my office. A marriage relationship introduced a complex set of variables that I was not trained to deal with. I ended up doing what most therapists did—problem-oriented, contractual marriage counseling. When this approach didn't work, I'd split up the couple and assign them to separate groups or counsel them individually.

In 1967 my confusion about the psychology of love relationships was compounded when I began to have problems with my own marriage. My wife and I were deeply committed to our relationship and had two young children, so we gave our marriage eight years of intensive examination, working with numerous therapists. Nothing seemed to help, and in 1975 we decided to divorce.

As I sat in the divorce court waiting my turn to see the judge, I felt like a double failure, a failure as a husband and as a therapist. That very afternoon I was scheduled to teach a course on marriage and the family, and the next day, as usual, I had several couples to counsel. Despite my professional training, I felt just as confused and defeated as the other men and women who were sitting beside me, waiting for their names to be called.

In the year following my divorce, I woke up each morning with an acute sense of loss. When I went to bed at night, I stared at the ceiling, trying to find some explanation for our failed marriage. Sure, both my wife and I had our ten reasons for divorcing, just as everyone else did. I didn't like this about her; she didn't like that about me; we had different interests; we had different goals. But beneath our litany of complaints, I could sense that there was a central disappointment, an underlying cause of our unhappiness, that had eluded eight years of probing.

Time passed, and my despair turned into a compelling desire to make sense out of my dilemma; I was not going to walk away from the ruins of my marriage without gaining some insight. I began to focus my efforts exclusively on learning what I could about relationship therapy. As I researched the professional books and journals, I was surprised to find few meaningful discussions of marriage, and the material that I did find was invariably slanted toward the psychology of the individual and the family. There seemed to be no comprehensive theory to explain the intricacies of the male-female relationship. No satisfactory explanation of the powerful emotions that can destroy a marriage. And there was nothing that explained what I found so painfully missing in my first marriage.

To fill in the gaps, I worked with hundreds of couples in private practice and thousands more in workshops and seminars. Out of my research and clinical observations, I gradually developed a theory of marital therapy called Imago (ih-mah-go) Relationship Therapy. My approach was eclectic. I brought together depth psychology, the behavioral sciences, the Western spiritual tradition, and added some elements of Transactional Analysis, Gestalt psychology, systems theory, and cognitive therapy. In my view, each of these schools of thought made a unique and important contribution to the understanding of the psychology of the individual, but it was only when they were all brought together in a new synthesis that they illuminated the mystery of love relationships.

When I began implementing my ideas, my work with couples became immensely rewarding. The divorce rate in my practice sharply declined, and the couples who stayed together reported a much deeper satisfaction in their marriages. As my work became more visible, I began to lecture to both singles and couples. Eventually I developed an introductory workshop for couples, called Staying Together. In 1981 I began a training course for professionals. To date, more than thirty thousand people have been exposed to my ideas through counseling, workshops, and seminars.

ABOUT THIS BOOK

MY PURPOSE IN writing this book is twofold: to share with you what I have learned about the psychology of love relationships, and to help you transform your relationship into a lasting source of love and companionship. In short, it's a book about the theory and practice of becoming passionate friends.

The book is divided into three parts. In Part I, I chronicle the fate of most relationships: attraction, romantic love, and the power struggle. As I describe the familiar details of married life, I invite you to see them as an emerging psychological drama. I call this drama "The Unconscious Marriage," and by that I mean a marriage that includes all the hidden desires and automatic behaviors that are left over from childhood and that inexorably lead couples into conflict.

In Part II, I explore a radically different kind of marriage, "The Conscious Marriage,"[1] a marriage that helps you satisfy your unmet childhood needs in positive ways. First, I will explain a proven technique for rekindling romantic love. This process restores a spirit of cooperation and gives you the motivation to work on your underlying problems. Next I will show you how to replace confrontation and criticism, tactics learned in childhood, with a healing process of mutual growth and support. Finally, I will describe how to convert your pent-up frustration into empathy and understanding.

Part III takes all these ideas and packages them into a unique, ten-week course in relationship therapy. Through a series of proven, step-by-step exercises that you can do in the privacy of your home, you will not only gain insight into your marital problems, you will be able to resolve them—perhaps without the expense of a marital therapist.

This book can help you create a more loving and supportive relationship, and it is within this revitalized marriage that you will find peace and joy.

part I

THE UNCONSCIOUS
PARTNERSHIP

THE MYSTERY OF ATTRACTION

The type of human being we prefer
reveals the contours of our heart.
—ORTEGA Y GASSET

WHEN COUPLES COME to me for relationship therapy, I
usually ask them how they met. Maggie and Victor, a couple in
their mid-fifties who were contemplating divorce after twenty-
nine years of marriage, told me this story:

"We met in graduate school," Maggie recalled. "We were
renting rooms in a big house with a shared kitchen. I was cooking breakfast when I looked up and saw this man—Victor—
walk into the room. I had the strangest reaction. My legs
wanted to carry me to him, but my head was telling me to stay
away. The feelings were so strong that I felt faint and had to sit
down."

Once Maggie recovered from shock, she introduced herself
to Victor, and the two of them spent half the morning talking.
"That was it," said Victor. "We were together every possible
moment for the next two months, and then we eloped."

"If those had been more sexually liberated times," added Maggie, "I'm sure we would have been lovers from that very first week. I've never felt so intensely about anyone in my entire life."

Not all first encounters produce seismic shock waves. Rayna and Mark, a couple ten years younger, had a more tepid and prolonged courtship. They met through a mutual friend. Rayna asked a friend if she knew any single men, and her friend said she knew an interesting man named Mark who had recently separated from his wife. She hesitated to introduce him to Rayna, however, because she didn't think that they would be a good match. "He's very tall and you're short," the friend explained; "he's Protestant and you're Jewish; he's very quiet and you talk all the time." But Rayna said none of that mattered. "Besides," she said, "how bad could it be for one date?"

Against her better judgment, the friend invited Rayna and Mark to an election-night party. "I liked Mark right away," Rayna recalled. "He was interesting in a quiet sort of way. We spent the whole evening talking in the kitchen." Rayna laughed and then added, "I suspect that I did most of the talking."

Rayna was certain that Mark was equally attracted to her, and she expected to hear from him the next day. But three weeks went by, and she didn't hear a word. Eventually she prompted her friend to find out if Mark was interested in her. With the friend's urging, Mark invited Rayna to the movies. That was the beginning of their courtship, but it was never a torrid romance. "We dated for a while, then we stopped for a while," said Mark. "Then we started dating again. Finally, three years later, we got married."

"By the way," added Rayna, "Mark and I are still married, and the friend who didn't want to introduce us is now divorced."

Those contrasting stories raise some interesting questions. Why do some people fall in love with such intensity, seemingly at first glance? Why do some couples ease into a love relationship with a levelheaded friendship? And why, as in the case of

Rayna and Mark, do so many couples seem to have opposite personality traits? When we have the answers to these questions, we will also have our first clues to the hidden psychological desires that underlie intimate love relationships.

UNRAVELING THE MYSTERY OF ROMANTIC ATTRACTION

IN RECENT YEARS, scientists from various disciplines have labored to deepen our understanding of romantic love, and valuable insights have come from each area of research. Some biologists contend that there is a certain "bio-logic" to courtship behavior. According to this broad, evolutionary view of love, we instinctively select mates who will enhance the survival of the species. Men are drawn to classically beautiful women—ones with clear skin, bright eyes, shiny hair, good bone structure, red lips, and rosy cheeks—not because of fad or fashion but because these qualities indicate youth and robust health, signs that a woman is in the peak of her childbearing years.

Women select mates for slightly different biological reasons. Because youth and physical health aren't essential to the male reproductive role, women instinctively favor mates with pronounced "alpha" qualities, the ability to dominate other males and bring home more than their share of the kill. The assumption is that male dominance ensures the survival of the family group more than youth or beauty. Thus a fifty-year-old chairman of the board—the human equivalent of the silver-backed male gorilla—is as attractive to women as a young, handsome, virile, but less successful male.

If we can put aside, for a moment, our indignity at having our attractiveness to the opposite sex reduced to our breeding and food/money-gathering potential, there is some validity to this theory. Whether we like it or not, a woman's youth and physical appearance and a man's power and social status do play a role in mate selection, as a quick scan of the personal messages in the classified ads will attest: "Successful forty-five-year-old S.W.M. with private jet desires attractive, slim, twenty-year-old S.W.F.," and so on. But even though biological factors play a key role in our amorous advances, there's got to be more to love than this.

Let's move on to another field of study, social psychology, and explore what is known as the "exchange" theory of mate selection.[1] The basic idea of the exchange theory is that we select mates who are more or less our equals. When we are on a search-and-find mission for a partner, we size each other up as coolly as business executives contemplating a merger, noting each other's physical appeal, financial status, and social rank, as well as various personality traits such as kindness, creativity, and a sense of humor. With computer-like speed, we tally up each other's scores, and if the numbers are roughly equivalent, the trading bell rings and the bidding begins.

The exchange theory gives us a more comprehensive view of mate selection than the simple biological model. It's not just youth, beauty, and social rank that interests us, say the social psychologists, but the whole person. For example, the fact that a woman is past her prime or that a man has a low-status job can be offset by the fact that he or she is a charming, intelligent, compassionate person.

A third idea, the "persona" theory, adds yet another dimension to the phenomenon of romantic attraction.[2] The persona theory maintains that an important factor in mate selection is the way a potential suitor enhances our self-esteem. Each of us has a mask, a persona, which is the face that we show to other people. The persona theory suggests that we select a mate who will enhance this self-image. The operative question here is: "What will it do to my sense of self if I am seen with this person?" There appears to be some validity to this theory. We have all experienced some pride and perhaps some embarrassment because of the way we believe our mates are perceived by others; it does indeed matter to us what others think.

Although these three theories help explain some aspects of romantic love, we are still left with our original questions. What accounts for the intensity of romantic love—as in the case of Maggie and Victor—those feelings of ecstasy that can be so overpowering? And why—as in the case of Rayna and Mark—do so many couples have complementary traits?

In fact, the more deeply we look at the phenomenon of romantic attraction, the more incomplete these theories appear to be. For example, what accounts for the emotional devastation that frequently accompanies the breakup of a relationship, that deadly undertow of feelings that can drown us in anxiety and self-pity? One client said to me as his girlfriend was leaving him: "I can't sleep or eat. My chest feels like it's going to explode. I cry all the time, and I don't know what to do." The theories of attraction we've looked at so far suggest that a more appropriate response to a failed romance would be simply to plunge into another round of mate selection.

There is another puzzling aspect of romantic attraction: we seem to have much more discriminating tastes than any of these theories would indicate. To see what I mean, take a moment to reflect on your own dating history. In your lifetime you have met thousands of people; as a conservative estimate, let's suppose that several hundred of them were physically attractive enough or successful enough to catch your eye. When we narrow this field by applying the social-exchange theory, we might come up with fifty or a hundred people out of this select group who would have a combined "point value" equal to or greater than yours. Logically, you should have fallen in love with scores of people. Yet most people have been deeply attracted to only a few individuals. In fact, when I counsel single people, I hear again and again that "there just aren't any good men (or women) out there!" The world is littered with their rejects.

Furthermore—and this is a curious fact—those few individuals that people are attracted to tend to resemble one another quite closely. Take a moment and think about the personality traits of the people that you have seriously considered as mates. If you were to make a list of their predominate personality traits, you would discover a lot of similarities, including, surprisingly, their negative traits.

From my vantage point as a relationship therapist, I see the unmistakable pattern in my clients' choice of relationship partners. One night, in a group-therapy session, I was listening to a man who was three months into his second marriage. When his first marriage broke up, he had vowed to the group that he would never be involved with a woman like his first wife. He thought she was mean, grasping, and selfish. Yet he confessed during the session that the day before he had "heard" the voice of his ex-wife coming from the lips of his new partner. With a sense of panic he realized that the two women had nearly identical personalities. *It appears that each one of us is compulsively searching for a mate with a very particular set of positive and negative personality traits.*

Plumbing the Depths of the Unconscious Mind

FOR THIS HIGH degree of selectivity to make any sense, we need to understand the role that the unconscious mind plays in mate selection. In the post-Freudian era, most people have become quite adept at rummaging around in the unconscious for explanations of daily events. We talk knowledgeably about "Freudian slips," analyze our dreams, and look for ways in which the unconscious might be influencing our daily behavior. Even so, most of us vastly underestimate the scope of the unconscious mind. There is an analogy that might give a better appreciation for its pervasive influence. In the daytime, we can't see the stars. We talk as if they "come out" at night, even though they are there all the time. We also underestimate the sheer number of stars. We look up at the sky, see a smattering of dim stars, and assume that's all there is. When we travel far away from city lights, we see a sky strewn with stars and are over-whelmed by the brilliance of the heavens. But it is only when we study astronomy that we learn the whole truth: the hundreds of thousands of stars that we see on a clear, moonless night in the country are only a fraction of the stars in the universe, and many of the points of light that we assume to be stars are in fact entire galaxies. So it is with the unconscious mind: the orderly, logi-cal thoughts of our conscious mind are but a thin veil over the unconscious, which is active and functioning at all times.

Let's take a brief look at the structure of the brain, that mys-terious and complex organ with many different subdivisions. For simplicity's sake, I like to use neuroscientist Paul McLean's model and divide the brain into three concentric layers.[3]

The brain stem, which is the inner and most primitive layer, is that part of the brain that oversees reproduction, self-preservation, and vital functions such as the circulation of blood, breathing, sleeping, and the contraction of muscles in response to external stimulation. Located at the base of the skull, this portion of the brain is sometimes referred to as the "reptilian brain," because all vertebrates from reptiles to mammals share this portion of the anatomy. For the purpose of this discussion, let's think of the brain stem as the source of physical action.

Flaring like a wishbone around the top of the brain stem is the portion of the brain called the limbic system, whose func-tion seems to be the generation of vivid emotions. Scientists can surgically stimulate the limbic system of laboratory animals and create spontaneous outbursts of fear and aggression. In this book I use the term "old brain" to refer to the portion of the brain that includes both the brain stem and the limbic system. Think of the old brain as being hard-wired and determining most of your automatic reactions.

The final area of the brain is the cerebral cortex, a large, convoluted mass of brain tissue that surrounds the two inner sections and is itself divided into four regions or lobes. This portion of the brain, which is most highly developed in *Homo sapiens,* is the site of most of our cognitive functions. I refer to the cerebral cortex as the "new brain" because it appeared most recently in evolutionary history. Your new brain is the part of you that is conscious, alert, and in contact with your daily surroundings. It's the part of you that makes decisions, thinks, observes, plans, anticipates, responds, organizes information, and creates ideas. The new brain is inherently logical and tries to find a cause for every effect and an effect for every cause. To a degree, it can moderate some of the instinctual reactions of your old brain.[4] By and large, this analytical, probing, questioning part of your mind is the part that you think of as being "you."

Old-Brain Logic

IN SHARP CONTRAST to the new brain, you are unaware of most of the functions of your old brain. Trying to comprehend this part of your being is a maddening task, because you have to turn your conscious mind around to examine its own underbelly. Scientists who have subjected the old brain to this kind of scrutiny tell us that its main concern is self-preservation. Ever on the alert, the old brain constantly asks the primeval question: "Is it safe?"

As it goes about its job of ensuring your safety, your old brain operates in a fundamentally different manner from your new brain. One of the crucial differences is that the old brain appears to have only a hazy awareness of the external world. Unlike the new brain, which relies on direct perception of outside phenomena, the old brain derives its incoming data from the images, symbols, and thoughts produced by the new brain.

This reduces its data to very broad categories. For example, while your new brain easily distinguishes John from Suzy from Margaret, your old brain summarily lumps these people into six basic categories. The only thing your old brain seems to care about is whether a particular person is someone to: (1) nurture, (2) be nurtured by, (3) have sex with, (4) run away from, (5) submit to, or (6) attack.[5] Subtleties such as "this is my neighbor," "my cousin," "my mother," or "my wife" slide right on by.

The old brain and the new brain, different in so many ways, are constantly exchanging and interpreting information. Here is how this takes place. Let's suppose that you are alone in your house, and all of a sudden, person A walks through the door. Your new brain automatically creates an image of this creature and sends it to your old brain for scrutiny. The old brain receives the image and compares it with other, stored images. Instantly there is a first observation: "This humanoid is not a stranger." Apparently encounters with this creature have been recorded before. A millisecond later there is a second observation: "There are no dangerous episodes associated with this image." Out of all the interactions you have had with this mystery guest, none of them has been life-threatening. Then, rapidly, a third observation: "There have been numerous *pleasurable* episodes associated with this image." In fact, the records seem to suggest that A is someone who is nurturing. Having reached this conclusion, the limbic system sends an all-clear signal to the reptilian brain, and you find yourself walking toward the intruder with open arms. Operating out of your new brain, you say, "Aunt Mary! What a pleasure to see you!"

All of this has taken place outside your awareness in only a fraction of a second. To your conscious mind, all that has happened is that your beloved Aunt Mary has walked in the door. Meanwhile, as you visit with your aunt, the data-gathering process continues. This latest encounter produces more thoughts, emotions, and images, which are sent to the limbic system to be stored in the part of the brain reserved for Aunt Mary. These new data will be a part of the information scanned by the old brain the next time she comes to visit.

Let's look at a slightly different situation. Let's suppose that the person who walked in the door was not Aunt Mary but her sister, Aunt Carol, and instead of greeting her with open arms, you found yourself resenting the interruption. Why such a different reaction to these two sisters? Let's pretend that when you were eighteen months old you spent a week with Aunt Carol while your mother was in the hospital having another baby. Your parents, trying to prepare you in advance for this visit, explained to you that "Mommy is going bye-bye to the hospital to bring home a little brother or sister." The words "hospital," "brother," and "sister" had no meaning to you, but "Mommy" and "bye-bye" certainly did. Whenever they mentioned those two words together, you felt anxious and sucked your thumb. Weeks later, when your mother went into labor, you were lifted out of your crib in a sound sleep and transported to Aunt Carol's house. You woke up alone in a strange room, and the person who came to you when you cried was not your mother or father but Aunt Carol.

You dwelled in anxiety for the next few days. Even though Aunt Carol was loving and kind to you, you felt abandoned. This primal fear became associated with your aunt, and for years the sight of her or the smell of her perfume sent you running from the room. In later years you had many pleasurable or neutral experiences with Aunt Carol; nonetheless, thirty years later, when she walks into the room, you feel the urge to run away. It is only with great discipline that you rise to greet her.

No Time Like the Present

THIS STORY ILLUSTRATES an important principle about the old brain: it has no sense of linear time. Today, tomorrow, and yesterday do not exist; everything that was, still is. Understanding this basic fact about the nature of your unconscious may help explain why you sometimes have feelings within your relationship that seem alarmingly out of proportion to the events that triggered them. For example, imagine that you are a thirty-five-year-old woman, a lawyer in a prestigious firm. One day you are sitting in your office thinking warm, loving thoughts about your husband and decide to call him. You dial his number, and his secretary informs you that he is out of the office and can't be reached. Suddenly your loving thoughts vanish, and you feel a surge of anxiety: where is he? Your rational mind knows that he's probably calling on a client or enjoying a late lunch, but another part of you feels—let's be honest—abandoned. There you are, a sophisticated, capable woman, and just because your husband isn't available you feel as vulnerable as you did when your mother left you all day with an unfamiliar babysitter. Your old brain is locked in an archaic perspective.

Or let's suppose that you are a middle-aged man, a middle manager in a large company. After a hectic day at work, where you manage to placate important clients and put the finishing touches on a multimillion-dollar budget, you drive home, eager to share your successes with your partner. When you walk in the door, you see a note from your partner saying that she will be late coming home from work. You stop dead in your tracks. You had counted on her being there! Do you recover from the disappointment and relish the time to yourself? Do you use the time to do a final check on the budget? Yes. But not before you head straight for the freezer and consume two bowlfuls of bland, sweet vanilla ice cream, as close a substitute for mother's milk as you can possibly find. The past and the present live side by side within your mind.

Now that we've spent some time pondering the nature of the unconscious mind, let's return to our original discussion of mate selection. How does this information about the old brain add to our understanding of romantic attraction? The curious phenomenon I noted earlier in this exploration was that we seem to be *highly selective* in our choice of mates. In fact, we appear to be searching for a "one and only" with a very specific set of positive and negative traits.

What we are doing, I have discovered from years of theoretical research and clinical observation, is looking for someone who has the predominant character traits of the people who raised us. Our old brain, trapped in the eternal now and having only a dim awareness of the outside world, is trying to re-create the environment of childhood. And the reason the old brain is trying to resurrect the past is not a matter of habit or blind compulsion but of a compelling need to heal old childhood wounds.

The ultimate reason you fell in love with your mate, I am suggesting, is not that your mate was young and beautiful, had an impressive job, had a "point value" equal to yours, or had a kind disposition. You fell in love because your old brain had your partner confused with your parents! Your old brain believed that it had finally found the ideal candidate to make up for the psychological and emotional damage you experienced in childhood.

CHILDHOOD WOUNDS

Age is no better, hardly so well,
qualified for an instructor as youth,
for it has not profited so much as it has lost.

— HENRY DAVID THOREAU

WHEN YOU HEAR the words "psychological and emotional damage of childhood," you may immediately think about serious childhood traumas such as sexual or physical abuse or the suffering that comes from having parents who divorced or died or were alcoholics. And for many people this is the tragic reality of childhood. However, even if you were fortunate enough to grow up in a safe, nurturing environment, you still bear invisible scars from childhood, because from the very moment you were born you were a complex, dependent creature with a never-ending cycle of needs. Freud correctly labeled us "insatiable beings." And no parents, no matter how devoted, are able to respond perfectly to all of these changing needs.

Before we explore some of the subtler ways in which you may have been wounded and how this affects your love relationships, let's take a look at what you were like when you first came into the world, because this state of "original wholeness" contains an important clue to the hidden expectations you bring to your partner.

Original Wholeness

THERE HAVE BEEN no miracle babies born with the ability to reveal to us the dark mysteries of life before birth, but we do know something about the physical life of the fetus. We know that its biological needs are taken care of instantly and automatically by an exchange of fluids between it and its mother. We know that a fetus has no need to eat, breathe, or protect itself from danger, and that it is constantly soothed by the rhythmical beat of its mother's heart. From these simple biological facts and from observations of newborns, we can surmise that the fetus lives a tranquil, floating, effortless existence. It has no awareness of boundaries, no sense of itself, and no recognition that it is encased in a sac inside its mother. There is a widely held belief that when a baby is inside its mother's womb, it experiences a sense of oneness, an Edenic experience free from desire. Martin Buber, a Jewish theologian, put it this way: "in fetal existence, we were in communion with the universe."[1]

This idyllic existence comes to an abrupt end as the mother's contractions forcibly expel the baby from the womb. But for the first few months, a developmental stage called the "autistic period," the baby still makes no distinction between itself and the rest of the world.[2] Early in the second year of our marriage, Helen and I became parents again, and we have clear memories of when our daughter Leah was in this stage. When all her physical needs were taken care of, she would nestle in our arms and look around her with the contentment of Buddha. Like all babies, she had no awareness of herself as a separate being and no internal divisions between thoughts, feelings, and actions. To our eyes, she was experiencing a primitive spirituality, a universe without boundaries. Although she was immature and utterly dependent on Helen and me for survival, she was nonetheless a vital, complete human being—in some ways more entire than she would ever be again.

As adults, we seem to have a fleeting memory of this state of original wholeness, a sensation that is as hard to recapture as a dream. We seem to recall a distant time when we were more unified and connected to the world. This feeling is described over and over again in the myths of all cultures, as if words could lend it more reality. It is the story of the Garden of Eden, and it strikes us with compelling force.

But what does this have to do with marriage? For some reason, we enter marriage with the expectation that our partners will magically restore this feeling of wholeness. It is as if they hold the key to a long-ago kingdom, and all we have to do is persuade them to unlock the door. Their failure to do so is one of the main reasons for our eventual unhappiness.

You and I Are One

THE FEELING OF unity that a child experiences in the womb and in the first few months of life gradually fades, giving way to a drive to be a distinct self. The essential state of unity remains, but there is a glimmer of awareness of the external world. It is during this stage of development that the child makes the monumental discovery that its mother, the gentle giant who holds it and feeds it and makes such comforting sounds, is not always there. The child still feels connected to its mother but has a primitive awareness of self.

When babies are in this symbiotic stage, development psychologists tell us that they experience a yearning to be connected with their caretakers. They label this the drive for attachment. The child's life energy is directed outward toward the mother in an effort to recapture its earlier sense of physical and spiritual union. A term that describes this yearning is "eros," a Greek word that we normally equate with romantic or sexual love but that originally had the broader meaning of "the life force."[3]

A child's success at feeling both distinct from and connected to its mother has a profound impact on all later relationships. If the child is fortunate, he will be able to make clear distinctions between himself and other people but still feel connected to them; he will have fluid boundaries that he can open or close at will. A child who has painful experiences early in life will either feel cut off from those around him or will attempt to fuse with them, not knowing where he leaves off and others begin. This lack of firm boundaries will be a recurring problem in marriage.

As a child grows older, eros is directed not only to the mother but also to the father, siblings, and the world as a whole. I remember when my daughter Leah was three years old and wanted to explore everything around her. She had so much vitality that she could run all day long and not be tired. "Run with me, Daddy! Somersault!" She twirled in circles and got so dizzy that she would fall down and laugh and laugh. She would chase fireflies, talk to leaves, swing from her knees on the monkey bars, and pet every dog she saw. Like Adam, she enjoyed naming objects, and developed a keen ear for words. When I looked at Leah, I saw eros, the full pulsation of life. I envied her and yearned for what I had lost.

Helen and I strive to keep eros alive in Leah, to sustain the brightness of her eyes and the thrill of her contagious laughter. But, despite our best intentions, we do not meet all of her needs. Sometimes it seems as if life itself is making her turn inward. Once she was frightened by a large dog and learned to be wary of strange animals. One day she slipped in a pool and developed a fear of water. But sometimes Helen and I are more directly to blame. We have five other children besides Leah, and there are times when she feels left out. There are days when

we come home from work too tired to listen to what she is saying, too distracted to understand what she wants. Tragically, we
also wound her by unwittingly passing on our own childhood
wounds, the emotional inheritance of generations. We either
overcompensate for what we didn't get from our parents or
blindly re-create the same painful situations.

For whatever reasons, when Leah's desires are not satisfied a
questioning look comes over her face; she cries; she is afraid.
She no longer talks to leaves or notices the fireflies darting
about the bushes. Eros is blunted and turns in on itself.

THE PERILOUS PILGRIMAGE

LEAH'S STORY IS my story and your story. We all started out
life whole and vital, eager for life's adventures, but we had
a perilous pilgrimage through childhood. To one degree or
another, we were all wounded by our caretakers' intrusiveness
or neglect. In fact, some of that wounding took place in the first
few months of our lives. Think for a moment about the cease-
less demands of an infant. When an infant wakes up in the
morning, it cries to be fed. Then its diapers are wet and it cries
to be changed. Then the baby wants to be held, a physical craving as powerful as its need for food. Then the baby is hungry
again and once more cries to be fed. A bubble of gas forms in its
stomach, and the baby cries out in anguish. It signals distress
the only way it knows how—with an undifferentiated cry—
and if its caretakers are perceptive enough, the infant is fed,
changed, held, or rocked, and experiences momentary satisfaction. But if the caretakers can't figure out what is wrong, or if
they withhold their attentions for fear of spoiling the baby, the
child experiences a primitive anxiety: the world is not a safe
place. Since it has no way of taking care of itself and no sense of
delayed gratification, it believes that getting the outside world

to respond instantly to its needs is truly a matter of life and death.

Although you and I have no recollection of these first few months of life, our old brains are still trapped in an infantile perspective. Although we are now adults, capable of keeping ourselves fed and warm and dry, a hidden part of us still expects the outside world to take care of us. When our partners are hostile or merely unhelpful, a silent alarm is triggered deep in our brains that fills us with the fear of death. As you will soon see, this automatic alarm system plays a key role in intimate love relationships.

As a child grows out of infancy, new needs emerge, and each new need defines a potential area of wounding. When a baby is about eighteen months old, for example, it has a clearer sense of where it leaves off and others begin. This is a stage of development referred to as the stage of "autonomy and independence." In this period the child has a growing interest in exploring the world beyond its primary caretaker. If a toddler had an adult's command of language, he would say something like this: "I'm ready to spend some time off your lap now. I'm ready to let go of the nipple and wander away by myself. I'm a little insecure about leaving you, however, and I'll be back in a few minutes to make sure you haven't disappeared." But since the child has only a limited vocabulary, he simply climbs down from his mother's lap, turns his back, and toddles out of the room.

Now, ideally, the mother smiles and says something like this: "Bye, sweetie. Have a good time. I'll be right here when you need me." And when the toddler comes back a few minutes later, suddenly aware of how dependent he really is, his mother says, "Hi! Did you have fun? Come sit in my lap for a minute." She lets the child know that it is OK to leave her side and venture off on his own, yet she is available whenever he needs her. The little boy learns that the world is a safe, exciting place to explore.

FUSERS AND ISOLATERS

MANY CHILDREN ARE frustrated at this crucial stage of development. Some have a caretaker who thwarts their independence. The mother or father is the one who feels insecure when the child is out of sight, not the child. For some reason— one that is rooted in the parent's own childhood—the parent needs the child to remain dependent. When a little girl wanders out of the room, her insecure mother might call out, "Don't go into the next room! You might get hurt!" The child dutifully comes back to her mother's lap. But inside her shell of conformity she is afraid. Her inner drive for autonomy is being denied. She fears that, if she always comes running back to her mother, she will be engulfed; she will be trapped in a symbiotic union forever.

Without the child's knowing it, this fear of engulfment becomes a key part of her character, and in later years she becomes what I call an "isolater," a person who unconsciously pushes others away. She keeps people at a distance because she needs to have "a lot of space" around her; she wants the freedom to come and go as she pleases; she doesn't want to be "pinned down" to a single relationship. All the while underneath this cool exterior is a two-year-old girl who was not allowed to satisfy her natural need for independence. When she marries, her need to be a distinct "self" will be on the top of her hidden agenda.

Some children grow up with the opposite kind of parents, ones who push them away when they come running to them for comfort: "Go away, I'm busy." "Go play with your toys." "Stop clinging to me!" The caretakers are not equipped to handle any needs but their own, and their children grow up feeling emotionally abandoned. Eventually they grow up to become what I call "fusers," people who seem to have an insatiable need for closeness. Fusers want to "do things together" all the time. If people fail to show up at the appointed time, they feel abandoned. The thought of divorce fills them with terror. They crave physical affection and reassurance, and they often need to stay in constant verbal contact. Underneath all this clinging behavior is a young child who needed more time on a parent's lap.

Ironically, for reasons I will explore in later chapters, fusers and isolaters tend to grow up and marry each other, thus beginning an infuriating game of push and pull that leaves neither partner satisfied.

AS YOU JOURNEYED through childhood, you went through one developmental stage after another, and the way your caretakers responded to your changing needs greatly affected your emotional health. More than likely, they coped with one stage of your growth better than another. They may have taken excellent care of you when you were an infant, for example, but fallen apart at your first temper tantrum. Or they may have been delighted by your inquisitive nature as a toddler but been threatened by your attraction to your opposite-sex parent when you were five or six. You may have grown up with caretakers who met most of your needs, or only some of them, but, like all children, you grew up knowing the anguish of unmet needs and these needs followed you into your love relationships.

THE LOST SELF

WE HAVE NOW explored one important feature of the vast hidden world I call the "unconscious partnership," and that is our storehouse of unmet childhood needs, our unfulfilled desire to be nurtured and protected and allowed to proceed unhindered along a path to maturity. Now we will turn to another kind of childhood wound, an even subtler kind of psychic injury called "socialization," all those messages we receive from our caretakers and from society at large that tell us who we are and how we have to behave. These, too, play a compelling but hidden role in your relationship with your partner.

At first it may seem strange to equate socialization with emotional injury. To help explain why this is so, I want to describe one of my clients. (As is true for most of the people I mention in this book, names and certain identifying characteristics have been changed to preserve anonymity.) Sarah is an attractive, personable woman in her mid-thirties. A main concern in her life is her apparent inability to think clearly and logically. "I can't think," she has told me over and over again, "I just can't think." She is a lower-level manager in a computer firm, where she has worked diligently for fifteen years. She would have advanced much further in the company if she were an effective problem-solver, but whenever she is presented with a difficult situation, she panics and runs to her supervisor for support. Her supervisor gives her sage advice, reinforcing Sarah's belief that she is incapable of making decisions on her own.

It didn't take much probing to discover part of the reason for Sarah's anxiety. From a very early age, she received from her mother the explicit message that she was not very intelligent. "You're not as smart as your older brother," her mother would say, and "You'd better marry a smart man, because you're going to need a lot of help. But I doubt if a smart man would marry you." As blatant as these messages were, they didn't fully account for Sarah's perceived inability to think. Amplifying her mother's message was the prevalent view of the 1950s that little girls were sweet, pretty, and compliant, but not especially bright; the girls in Sarah's grade school dreamed of being wives, nurses, and teachers, not executives, astronauts, and doctors.

Another influence on Sarah's problem-solving capacity was the fact that her mother had very little confidence in her own reasoning ability. She managed the house and took care of her children's needs, but she deferred all major decisions to her husband. This dependent, passive model defined "womanhood" for Sarah.

When Sarah was fifteen, she was fortunate enough to have a teacher who recognized her natural abilities and encouraged her to work harder on her schoolwork. For the first time in her life, Sarah came home with a report card that was mostly As. She will never forget her mother's reaction: "How on earth did that happen? I bet you can't do that again." And Sarah couldn't, because she finally gave in and put to sleep the part of her brain that thinks calmly and rationally.

The tragedy was not only that Sarah lost her ability to reason, but also that she acquired the unconscious belief that thinking was dangerous. Why was that? Since Sarah's mother had strongly rejected her intellectual capabilities, she believed that if she were to think clearly she would be defying her mother; she would be contradicting her mother's definition of her. She couldn't risk alienating her mother, because she was dependent on her mother for survival. It was dangerous, therefore, for Sarah to know that she had a mind. Yet she couldn't fully disown her intelligence. She envied people who could think, and when she married she chose a man who was exceptionally bright, an unconscious ploy to make up for the psychological damage of childhood.

Like Sarah, we all have parts of ourselves that we have hidden from consciousness. I call these missing elements the "lost self." Whenever we complain that we "can't think" or that we "can't feel anything" or "can't dance" or "can't have orgasms" or "aren't very creative," we are identifying natural abilities, thoughts, or feelings that we have surgically removed from our awareness. They are not gone; we still possess them. But for the moment they are not a part of our consciousness, and it is as if they do not exist.

As in Sarah's case, our lost self was formed early in childhood—largely as a result of our caretakers' well-intentioned efforts to teach us to get along with others. Each society has a unique collection of practices, laws, beliefs, and values that children need to absorb, and mothers and fathers are the main conduit through which they are transmitted. This indoctrination process goes on in every family in every society. There seems to be a universal understanding that, unless limits are placed on the individual, the individual becomes a danger to the group. In the words of Freud, "The desire for a powerful and uninhibited ego may seem to us intelligible, but, as is shown by the times that we live in, it is in the profoundest sense antagonistic to civilization."

But even though our parents often had our best interests at heart, the overall message handed down to us was a chilling one. There were certain thoughts and feelings we could not have, certain natural behaviors that we had to extinguish, and certain talents and aptitudes we had to deny. In thousands of ways, both subtly and overtly, our parents gave us the message that they approved of only a part of us. In essence, we were told that we could not be whole and exist in this culture.

BODY TABOOS

ONE OF THE areas in which we were most restricted was our bodies. At a very young age, we were taught to cover our bodies in gender-specific ways and not to talk about or touch our genitals. These prohibitions are so universal that we tend to notice them only when they are broken. A friend of mine told me a story that illustrates how startling it can be when parents fail to pass on these unspoken taboos. A friend of hers named Chris and her eleven-month-old son happened to drop by her house one day. Soon my friend and Chris and the baby were sitting out on the back deck, sipping ice tea. Since the May sunshine was pleasantly warm, Chris took off the baby's clothes so he could sunbathe. The two women chatted while the little boy crawled around on the deck, happily digging his fingers into the warm soil of the flowerpots. After about half an hour, the baby became hungry, and Chris put him to her breast. My friend noticed that as the baby nursed he developed a miniature erection. Apparently nursing was such a sensual experience that he felt pleasure throughout his body. Instinctively, the little boy reached down to touch his genitals. Unlike most mothers, Chris did not pull his hand away. Her baby was allowed to feel the warm sun on his naked skin, nurse from his mother's breasts, have an erection, and add to his pleasure by holding on to his penis.

It is normal and natural for an infant to want to have those good feelings, but we rarely allow it. Think about all the rules his mother was breaking. First of all, society tells us that women can nurse their babies but that if they do so it should be discreetly, so that no one might catch a fleeting glimpse of a naked breast. Second, infants should be clothed at all times—at least in a diaper—even when they are outside and the day is mild and sunny. Third, little boys and girls should not experience any form of genital arousal, but if for some reason they do they should not be permitted to enjoy it. By allowing her baby to revel in all of his senses, Chris was violating three potent taboos.

It is not my purpose to attack or defend society's prohibitions against bodily pleasure. That would be an entire book in itself. (Nor do I want to simplify the problem that having a body, much less enjoying it, has been in the Western world.) But to understand the hidden desires that permeate your relationship, it's important to know this simple fact: when you were young, there were many, many times when limits were placed on your sensuality. Like most children growing up in this culture, you were probably made to feel embarrassed or guilty or naughty that you had a body that was capable of exquisite sensation. To be a "good" boy or girl, you had to psychologically cut off or disown that part of yourself.

FORBIDDEN FEELINGS

YOUR EMOTIONS WERE another prime candidate for socialization. Some feelings, of course, were not just permitted, they were encouraged. Oh, how hard your parents worked to get you to smile when you were an infant! And a few weeks later, when you laughed out loud, everyone had a marvelous time. Anger, however, was another matter. Temper tantrums are noisy and unpleasant, and most parents try to discourage them. They do this in a number of ways. Some parents tease their children: "You look so cute when you're mad. I see a smile coming on. Give us a smile." Others discipline them: "You stop that right now! Go to your room. I'll have none of this back talk!" Insecure parents often give in to their children: "OK. Have it your way. But the next time you'd better behave!"

It is the rare parent who validates a child's anger. Imagine a little girl's relief if her parents were to say something like this: "I can see that you're mad. You don't want to do what I ask. But I am the parent and you are the child and you need to do what I say." Having her anger acknowledged would contribute to her sense of self. She would be able to tell herself, "I exist. My parents are aware of my feelings. I may not always get my way, but I am listened to and respected." She would be allowed to stay in touch with her anger and retain an essential aspect of her wholeness.

But such is not the fate of most children. The other day I was in a department store and happened to witness how abruptly a child's anger can be put off—especially when it's anger directed at a parent. A woman was doing some clothes shopping while her little boy, about four years old, tagged along. She was preoccupied, and the little boy kept up an insistent monologue in an effort to get her attention. "I can read these letters," he said, pointing to a sign, "M-A-D-E." He got no reaction. "Are you going to try on more clothes?" he asked. No response. The whole time I was watching, she gave him only a few seconds of attention, and when she did she sounded annoyed and depressed. Finally I heard him say loud and clear to a store clerk, "My mommy was hurt in a car crash. She got killed." This pronouncement got his mother's instant attention. She shook her son by the shoulders, spanked him, and forcibly shoved him down on a chair. "What do you mean? I wasn't killed in a car crash! Stop talking like that. Go over and sit on that chair and be quiet. Not another word out of you." The boy was white-faced and sat without moving until his mother was done with her shopping.

Inside his head, the little boy's anger at his mother had been transformed into a vengeful fantasy in which she was killed in a highway accident. He hadn't been the one to hurt her. At four, he had already been taught to disown his angry thoughts and feelings. Instead he imagined that she had simply gotten in the way of a car driven by somebody else.

When you were young, there were probably many times when you, too, were angry at your caretakers. More than likely, it was a sentiment that got little support. Your angry feelings, your sexual feelings, and a host of other "antisocial" thoughts and feelings were pushed deep inside of you and were not allowed to see the light of day.

A few parents take this invalidation process to the extreme. They deny not only their children's feelings and behaviors, but the entire child as well. "*You* do not exist. You are not important in this family. Your needs, your feelings, your wishes are not important to us." I worked with one young woman I'll call Carla whose parents denied her existence to the point where they made her feel invisible. Her mother was an immaculate housekeeper, and her instructions to her daughter were to "clean up after yourself so well that no one can tell you live here." Plastic runners placed on the carpets determined where Carla could walk. The professionally landscaped yard had no room for tricycles or swings or sandboxes. Carla has a strong memory of sitting in the kitchen one day when she was about ten years old, feeling so depressed she wanted to die. Her mother and father walked in and out of the kitchen numerous times without even acknowledging her presence. Carla began to feel that she had no bodily reality. It is no wonder that when she turned thirteen she complied with her parents' unspoken directive to disappear and became anorexic, literally trying to starve herself out of existence.

TOOLS OF REPRESSION

IN THEIR ATTEMPTS to repress certain thoughts, feelings, and behavior, parents use various techniques. Sometimes they issue clear-cut directives: "You don't really think that." "Big boys don't cry." "Don't touch yourself there!" "I never want to hear you say that again!" "We don't act like that in this family!" Or, like the mother in the department store, they scold, threaten, or spank. Much of the time, they mold their children through a subtler process of invalidation—they simply choose not to see or reward certain things. For example, if parents place little value on intellectual development, they give their children toys and sports equipment but no books or science kits. If they believe that girls should be quiet and feminine, and boys should be strong and assertive, they only reward their children for gender-appropriate behavior. For example, if their little boy comes into the room lugging a heavy toy, they might say, "What a strong little boy you are!" But if their daughter comes in carrying the same toy, they might caution, "Be careful of your pretty dress."

The way that parents influence their children most deeply, however, is by example. Children instinctively observe the choices their parents make, the freedoms and pleasures they allow themselves, the talents they develop, the abilities they ignore, and the rules they follow. All of this has a profound effect on children: "This is how we live. This is how to get through life." Whether children accept their parents' model or rebel against it, this early socialization plays a significant role in mate selection and, as we will soon see, is often a hidden source of tension in married life.

A CHILD'S REACTION to society's edicts goes through a number of predictable stages. Typically, the first response is to hide forbidden behaviors from the parents. The child thinks angry thoughts but doesn't speak them out loud. He explores his body in the privacy of his room. He teases his younger sibling when his parents are away. Eventually the child comes to the conclusion that some thoughts and feelings are so unacceptable that they should be eliminated, so he constructs an imaginary parent in his head to police his thoughts and activities, a part of the mind that psychologists call the "superego." Now, whenever the child has a forbidden thought or indulges in an "unacceptable" behavior, he experiences a self-administered jolt of anxiety. This is so unpleasant that the child puts to sleep some of those forbidden parts of himself—in Freudian terms, he represses them. The ultimate price of his obedience is a loss of wholeness.

THE FALSE SELF

TO FILL THE void, the child creates a "false self," a character structure that serves a double purpose: it camouflages those parts of his being that he has repressed and protects him from further injury. A child brought up by a sexually repressive, distant mother, for instance, may become a "tough guy." He tells himself, "I don't care if my mother isn't very affectionate. I don't need that mushy stuff. I can make it on my own. And another thing—I think sex is dirty!" Eventually he applies this patterned response to all situations. No matter who tries to get close to him, he erects the same barricade. In later years, when he overcomes his reluctance to getting involved in a love relationship, it is likely that he will criticize his partner for her desire for intimacy and her intact sexuality: "Why do you want so much contact and why are you so obsessed with sex? It's not normal!"

A different child might react to a similar upbringing in an opposite manner, exaggerating his problems in the hope that someone will come to his rescue: "Poor me. I am hurt. I am deeply wounded. I need someone to take care of me." Yet another child might become a hoarder, striving to hold on to every bit of love and food and material goods that comes his way out of the certain knowledge that there is never enough. But, whatever the nature of the false self, its purpose is the same: to minimize the pain of losing part of the child's original, God-given wholeness.

The Disowned Self

AT SOME POINT in a child's life, however, this ingenious form of self-protection becomes the cause of further wounding as the child is criticized for having these negative traits. Others condemn him for being distant or needy or self-centered or fat or stingy. His attackers don't see the wound he is trying to protect, and they don't appreciate the clever nature of his defense: all they see is the neurotic side of his personality. He is deemed inferior; he is less than whole.

Now the child is caught in a bind. He needs to hold on to his adaptive character traits, because they serve a useful purpose, but he doesn't want to be rejected. What can he do? The solution is to deny or attack his critics: "I'm not cold and distant," he might say in self-defense, "what I really am is strong and independent." Or "I'm not weak and needy, I'm just sensitive." Or "I'm not greedy and selfish, I'm thrifty and prudent." In other words, "That's not me you're talking about. You're just seeing me in a negative light."

In a sense, he is right. His negative traits are not a part of his original nature. They are forged out of pain and become a part of an assumed identity, an alias that helps him maneuver in a complex and sometimes hostile world. This doesn't mean, however, that he doesn't have these negative traits; there are any number of witnesses who will affirm that he does. But in order to maintain a positive self-image and enhance his chances for survival, he has to deny them. These negative traits became what is referred to as the "disowned self," those parts of the false self that are too painful to acknowledge.

Let's stop for a moment and sort out this proliferation of self parts. We have now succeeded in fracturing your original wholeness, the loving and unified nature that you were born with, into three separate entities:

1. Your "lost self," those parts of your being that you had to repress because of the demands of society.
2. Your "false self," the facade that you erected in order to fill the void created by this repression and by a lack of adequate nurturing.
3. Your "disowned self," the negative parts of your false self that met with disapproval and were therefore denied.

The only part of this complex collage that you were routinely aware of was the parts of your original being that were still intact and certain aspects of your false self. Together these elements formed your "personality," the way you would describe yourself to others. Your lost self was almost totally outside your awareness; you had severed nearly all connections with these repressed parts of your being. Your disowned self, the negative parts of your false self, hovered just below your level of awareness and was constantly threatening to emerge. To keep it hidden, you had to deny it actively or project it onto others: "I am *not* self-centered," you would say with great energy. Or "What do you mean, I'm lazy? *You're* lazy."

PLATO'S ALLEGORY

ONE DAY WHEN Helen and I were talking about all the splits in the psyche, she recalled an allegory in Plato's *Symposium* that serves as a mythical model for this state of split existence.[4] Human beings, the story goes, were once composite creatures that were both male and female. Each being had one head with two faces, four hands and four feet, and both male and female genitals. Being unified and whole, our ancestors wielded tremendous force. In fact, so magnificent were these androgynous beings that they dared to attack the gods. The gods, of course, would not tolerate this insolence, but they didn't know how to punish the humans. "If we kill them," they said to one another, "there will be no one to worship us and offer up sacrifices." Zeus pondered the situation and finally came up with a solution. "Men shall continue to exist," he decreed, "but they will be cut in two. Then they will be diminished in strength so we need not fear them." Zeus proceeded to split each being in two, asking Apollo's help to make the wounds invisible. The two halves were then sent in opposite directions to spend the rest of their lives searching frantically for the other half-creature, the reunion with whom would restore their wholeness.

Just like Plato's mythical creatures, we, too, go through life truncated, cut in half. We cover our wounds with healing ointment and gauze in an attempt to heal ourselves, but despite our efforts an emptiness wells up inside us. We try to fill this emptiness with food and drugs and activities, but what we yearn for is our original wholeness, our full range of emotions, the inquisitive mind that was our birthright, and the Buddha-like joy that we experienced as very young children. This becomes a spiritual yearning for completion, and, as in Plato's myth, we develop the profound conviction that finding the right person—that perfect mate—will complete us and make us whole. This special person can't be just anyone. It can't be the first man or woman who comes along with an appealing smile or a warm disposition. It has to be someone who stirs within us a deep sense of recognition: "This is the one I've been looking for! This is the one who will make up for the wounds of the past!" And for reasons we will explore in greater depth in the next chapter, this person is invariably someone who has both the positive and the negative traits of our parents!

YOUR IMAGO

In literature, as in love, we are astonished
at what is chosen by others.

—ANDRÉ MAUROIS

MANY PEOPLE HAVE a hard time accepting the idea that they
have searched for partners who resembled their caretakers. On
a conscious level, they were looking for people with only positive traits—people who were, among other things, kind, loving,
good-looking, intelligent, and creative. In fact, if they had an
unhappy childhood, they may have deliberately searched for
people who were radically different from their caretakers. They
told themselves, "I'll never marry a drunkard like my father,"
or "There's no way I'm going to marry a tyrant like my
mother." But, no matter what their conscious intentions, most
people are attracted to mates who have their caretakers' positive *and* negative traits, and, typically, the negative traits are
more influential.

I came to this sobering conclusion only after listening to
hundreds of couples talk about their partners and then sharing

my insights with Helen. Helen is also trained in counseling and therapy and has been invaluable in helping me process my experiences with couples. At some point during the course of therapy, just about every person would turn angrily to his or her partner and say, "You treat me just the way my mother did!" Or "You make me feel just as helpless and frustrated as my stepfather did!" This idea gained further validity when I assigned all my clients an exercise that asked them to compare the personality traits of their partners with the personality traits of their primary caretakers. In most cases, there was a close correlation between parents and partners, and with few exceptions *the traits that matched up the most closely were the negative traits!* (You will be able to do this exercise yourself when you turn to Part III of this book, which includes all the exercises mentioned in this chapter and those that follow. I suggest that you read all of the text before you attempt the written work.)

Why do negative traits have such an appeal? If people chose mates on a logical basis, they would look for partners who compensated for their parents' inadequacies, rather than duplicated them. If your parents wounded you by being unreliable, for example, the sensible course of action would be to marry a dependable person, someone who would help you overcome your fear of abandonment. If your parents wounded you by being overprotective, the practical solution would be to look for someone who allowed you plenty of psychic space so that you could overcome your fear of absorption. The part of your brain that directed your search for a mate, however, was not your logical, orderly new brain; it was your time-locked, myopic old brain. And what your old brain was trying to do was recreate the conditions of your upbringing, in order to correct them. Having received enough nurturing to survive but not enough to feel satisfied, it was attempting to return to the scene of your original frustration so that you could resolve your unfinished business.[1]

SEARCH FOR THE LOST SELF

WHAT ABOUT YOUR other unconscious drive, your need to recover your lost self, those thoughts and feelings and behaviors that you had to repress to adapt to your family and to society? What kind of person would help you regain your sense of wholeness? Would it be someone who actively encouraged you to develop these missing parts? Would it be someone who shared your weaknesses and therefore made you feel less inadequate? Or, on the other hand, would it be someone who complemented your weaknesses? To find the answer, think for a minute about some part of your being that you feel is deficient. Maybe you feel that you lack artistic talent, or strong emotions, or, like Sarah in the last chapter, the ability to think clearly and rationally. Years ago, when you were around people who were especially strong in these areas, you probably were even more aware of your shortcomings. But if you managed to form an intimate relationship with one of these "gifted people," you experienced quite a different reaction. Instead of feeling awestruck or envious, you suddenly felt more complete. Being emotionally attached to this person—this is "my" boyfriend or "my" girlfriend—made his or her attributes feel a part of a larger, more fulfilled you. It was as if you had merged with the other person and become whole.

Look around you, and you will find ample evidence that people choose mates with complementary traits. Dan is glib and talkative; his wife, Gretchen, is thoughtful and introverted. Janice is an intuitive thinker; her husband, Patrick, is very logical. Rena is a dancer; her boyfriend, Matthew, has a stiff and rigid body. What people are doing in these yin/yang matches is trying to reclaim their lost selves by proxy.

THE IMAGO

TO GUIDE YOU in your search for the ideal mate, someone who both resembled your caretakers and compensated for the repressed parts of yourself, you relied on an unconscious image of the opposite sex that you had been forming since birth. Helen and I decided that a good name for this inner picture is "imago," which is the Latin word for "image."[2] Essentially, your imago is a composite picture of the people who influenced you most strongly at an early age. This may have been your mother and father, one or more siblings, or maybe a babysitter, nanny, or close relative. But whoever they were, a part of your brain recorded everything about them—the sound of their voices, the amount of time they took to answer your cries, the color of their skin when they got angry, the way they smiled when they were happy, the set of their shoulders, the way they moved their bodies, their characteristic moods, their talents and interests. Along with these impressions, your brain recorded all your significant interactions with them. Your brain didn't interpret these data; it simply etched them onto a template.

It may seem improbable that you have such a detailed record of your caretakers somewhere inside your head when you have only a dim recollection of those early years. In fact, many people have a hard time remembering anything that happened to them before the age of five or six—even dramatic events that should have made a deep impression. But scientists report that we have incredible amounts of hidden information in our brains. Neurosurgeons discovered this fact while performing brain surgery on patients who were under local anesthesia.[3] They stimulated portions of the patients' brains with weak electrical currents, and the patients were suddenly able to recall hundreds of forgotten episodes from childhood in astonishing detail. Our minds are vast storehouses of forgotten information. There are those who suggest that everything that we have ever experienced resides somewhere in the dark, convoluted recesses of our brains.

Not all of these experiences are recorded with equal intensity, however. The most vivid impressions seem to be the ones that we formed of our caretakers early in life. And of all the interactions that we had with these key people, the ones that were most deeply engraved were the ones that were the most wounding, because these were the encounters that seemed to threaten our existence. Gradually, over time, these hundreds of thousands of bits of information about our caretakers merged together to form a single image. The old brain, in its inability to make fine distinctions, simply filed all this information under one heading: the people responsible for our survival. You might think of the imago as a silhouette with few distinguishing physical characteristics but with the combined character traits of all of your primary caretakers.

To a large degree, whether or not you have been romantically attracted to someone depended on the degree to which that person matched your imago. A hidden part of your brain ticked and hummed, coolly analyzing that person's traits, and then compared them with your rich data bank of information. If there was little correlation, you felt no interest. This person was destined to be one of the thousands of people who come and go in your life with little impact. If there was a high degree of correlation, you found the person highly attractive.

This imago-matching process bears some resemblance to the way soldiers were trained to identify flying aircraft during World War II. The soldiers were given books filled with silhouettes of friendly and enemy aircraft. When an unidentified plane came into view, they hurriedly compared the plane with these illustrations. If it turned out to be a friendly plane, they relaxed and went back to their posts. If it was an enemy aircraft, they leaped into action. Unconsciously you have compared every man or woman that you have met to your imago. When you identified a close match, you felt a sudden surge of interest.

As with all aspects of the unconscious mind, you had no awareness of this elaborate sorting mechanism. The only way you can glimpse your imago is in dreams. If you reflect on your dreams, one thing you will notice is that your old brain capriciously merges people together. A dream that starts out with one person playing a part suddenly has another person filling that role; the unconscious has little regard for corporeal boundaries. You may be able to recall a dream where your partner suddenly metamorphosed into your mother or father, or a dream in which your partner and a parent played such similar roles or treated you in such a similar manner that they were virtually indistinguishable. This is the closest you will ever come to directly verifying the existence of your imago. But when you do the exercises in Part III and have a chance to compare the dominant character traits of your mate with the dominant character traits of your primary caretakers, the parallel that your unconscious mind draws between partners and caretakers will become unmistakably clear.

The Imago and Romantic Love

LET'S TAKE THIS information about the imago and see how it adds to our earlier theories of romantic attraction. As an illustration, let me tell you about a client named Lynn and her search for love. Lynn is forty years old and has three school-age children. She lives in a mid-sized New England town, where she works for the city government. Peter, Lynn's husband, is a graphics designer.

In the initial counseling sessions I had with Lynn and Peter, I learned that Lynn's father had had a profound influence on her. Apparently he was a good provider and spared no expense in her behalf. But he could also be very insensitive. When he was, Lynn felt angry and threatened. She told me about the relentless way he would tickle her, even though he knew she hated it.

When she finally broke down and cried, he would laugh at her and call her a crybaby. An incident that she will never forget is the time he threw her into a river to "teach her how to swim." When Lynn told me this story, her throat was tight and her hands gripped the seat of her chair. "How could he have done that?" she asked. "I was only four years old! I remember looking at my daughter when she was four years old and being amazed that he could have done that to me. It's such a trusting, vulnerable age."

Although she wasn't aware of it, Lynn had much earlier images of her father stored deep in her unconscious, ones that affected her even more deeply. As a hypothetical example, let's suppose that, when she was an infant, her father would neglect to warm the bottle when it was his turn to feed her, and she learned to associate lying in his arms with the shock of cold milk. Or maybe, when she was a few months old, he would toss her high into the air, misreading her frantic cries as an indication of excitement. She has no memory of incidents like these, but every one of her significant experiences with her father is recorded somewhere in her mind.

Lynn's mother was an equally potent source of images. On the plus side, she was generous with her time and attention and consistent with her discipline. Unlike Lynn's father, she was sensitive to her daughter's feelings. When she tucked Lynn into bed at night, she would ask her about her day and was sympathetic if Lynn reported any emotional difficulties. But Lynn's mother was also overly critical. Nothing Lynn said or did seemed to be quite good enough. Her mother was always correcting her grammar, combing her hair, double-checking her homework. Lynn felt on stage around her, and she had the feeling that she was always flubbing her lines.

Another important thing about her mother was that she was not comfortable with her own sexuality. Lynn remembers that her mother always wore long-sleeved blouses buttoned up to the top button and covered the blouses with loose, concealing sweaters. She never allowed anyone in the bathroom with her, even though the house had only one bathroom. When Lynn was a teenager, her mother never talked to her about menstruation, boyfriends, or sex. It's not surprising that one of Lynn's problems is that she is sexually inhibited.

Other people had a strong influence on Lynn, too, and one of them was her older sister, Judith. Judith, only fourteen months older, was her idol. Tall and talented, she seemed to succeed at everything she did. Lynn admired her older sister and wanted to spend as much time as possible around her, but when she did she always felt inferior.

Gradually the personality traits of these key people—Lynn's mother, her father, and her older sister—merged together in Lynn's unconscious mind to form a single image, her imago. Her imago was a picture of someone who was, among other things, affectionate, devoted, critical, insensitive, superior, and generous. The character traits that stood out in bold relief were the negative ones—the tendency to be critical, insensitive, and superior—because these were the ones that had wounded her; this is where she had unfinished business.

Lynn first met Peter at a friend's house. Her main memory of this meeting is that, when she was introduced to him, she looked in his face and felt as if she already knew him. It was a curious sensation. The next week she kept finding excuses to go over to her friend's house, and she was glad when Peter was there. Gradually she became aware of an even stronger attraction, and realized that she wasn't really happy unless she was around him. In these first encounters, Lynn wasn't consciously comparing Peter with anyone she knew—certainly not with her parents or her sister—she just found him a wonderfully appealing person who seemed easy to talk to.

In the course of their therapy, I grew to appreciate what a good imago match Peter was for Lynn. He was outgoing and confident, traits that he shared with Lynn's father and sister. But he also had a critical nature, like Lynn's mother. He kept telling Lynn that she should lose weight, loosen up, and be more playful at home—especially in bed—and be more assertive at work. The parent trait that was most marked in him, however, was his lack of compassion for her feelings, just like Lynn's father. Lynn had frequent bouts of depression, and Peter's advice to her was "Talk less and do more. I'm tired of hearing about your problems!" This was consistent with his own approach to unhappy feelings, which was to cover them up with frantic activity.

Another reason Lynn was attracted to Peter was that he was so at home in his body. When I looked at the two of them, I was often reminded of the words of one of my professors: "If you want to know what kind of person a client is married to, imagine his or her opposite." Lynn would sit with her arms and legs crossed, while Peter would sprawl in his chair with complete abandon. Sometimes he would kick off his shoes and sit cross-legged. Other times he would swing one leg up and hook it across the arm of the chair. Lynn wore tailored clothes buttoned to the top button, or a business suit with a silk scarf knotted securely around her neck. Peter wore loose-fitting corduroy pants, shirts open at the neck, and loafers without socks.

Now we have some clues to why Lynn was attracted to Peter. Why was Peter attracted to Lynn? The fact that she had an emotional nature was one of the reasons. Although his parents had accepted Peter's body, they had rejected his feelings. When he was with Lynn, he felt more connected to his repressed emotions; she helped him regain contact with his lost self. In addition, she had numerous character traits that reminded him of his parents. Her sense of humor reminded him of his mother, and her dependent, self-effacing manner reminded him of his father. Because Lynn matched Peter's imago and Peter matched Lynn's, and because they had numerous complementary traits, they had "fallen in love."

The question that I'm frequently asked when I talk about

the unconscious factors in mate selection is this: how can people tell so much about each other so quickly? While certain characteristics may be right on the surface—Peter's sexuality, for example, or Lynn's sense of humor—others are not so apparent.

The reason that we are such instant judges of character is that we rely on what Freud called "unconscious perception." We intuitively pick up much more about people than we are aware of. When we meet strangers, we instantly register the way they move, the way they seek or avoid eye contact, the clothes they wear, their characteristic expressions, the way they fix their hair, the ease with which they laugh or smile, their ability to listen, the speed at which they talk, the amount of time it takes them to respond to a question—we record all of these characteristics and a hundred more in a matter of minutes.

Just by looking at people, we can absorb vast amounts of information. When I walk to work each morning, I automatically appraise the people on the crowded Manhattan sidewalks. My judgment is instantaneous: this person is someone I wish I knew; that person is someone I have no interest in. I find myself attracted or repulsed with only a superficial glance. When I walk into a party, one glance around the room will often single out the people that I want to meet. Other people report similar experiences. A truck driver told me that he could tell whether or not he wanted to pick up a particular hitchhiker even though he was cruising at sixty-five miles an hour. "And I'm rarely wrong," he said.

Our powers of observation are especially acute when we are looking for a mate, because we are searching for someone to satisfy our fundamental unconscious drives. We subject everyone to the same intense scrutiny: is this someone who will nurture me and help me recover my lost self? When we meet someone who appears to meet these needs, the old brain registers instant interest. In all subsequent encounters, the unconscious mind is fully alert, searching for clues that this might indeed be the perfect mate. If later experiences confirm the imago match, our interest climbs even further. On the other hand, if later experiences show the match to be superficial, our interest plummets, and we look for a way to end or reduce the importance of the relationship.

Unbeknown to them, this was the psychological process that Lynn and Peter were engaged in when they met that day at a friend's house. Because Peter seemed to match Lynn's imago, she went out of her way to see him again. Because Lynn, in turn, was a reasonably good imago match for Peter, her interest was returned; this was not just another case of unrequited love. After a few weeks, Peter and Lynn had accumulated enough data about each other to realize that they were in love.

Not everyone finds a mate who conforms so closely to the imago. Sometimes only one or two key character traits match up, and the initial attraction is likely to be mild. Such a relationship is often less passionate and less troubled than those characterized by a closer match. The reason it is less passionate is that the old brain is still looking for the ideal "gratifying object," and the reason it tends to be less troubled is that there isn't the repetition of so many childhood struggles. When couples with weak imago matches terminate their relationships, it's often because they feel little interest in each other, not because they are in great pain. "There wasn't all that much going on," they say. Or "I just felt restless. I knew that there was something better out there."

AT THIS POINT in our discussion of love relationships, we have a more complete understanding of the mystery of romantic attraction. To the biological theory and the exchange theory and the persona theory discussed in chapter 1, we have added the idea of the unconscious search for a person who matches our imago. Our motivation for seeking an imago match is our urgent desire to heal childhood wounds. We also have new insight into marital conflict: if the primary reason we select our mates is that they resemble our caretakers, it is inevitable that they are going to reinjure some very sensitive wounds. But before we sink into this quagmire of pain and confusion called "the power struggle," I would like to focus on the ecstasy of romantic love, those first few months or years of a relationship when we are filled with the delicious expectation of wish fulfillment.

ROMANTIC LOVE

We two form a multitude.

— OVID

I KNOW FROM my own experience with Helen, and from listening to others, that lovers believe their time together is special and separate from the experiences of all the other people of the world. It is a time they savor and return to in their memories again and again. When I ask couples to describe these idyllic first days to me, they describe a world transformed. People seemed friendlier, colors were brighter, food tasted better— everything around them shimmered with a pristine newness, just as it did when they were young.

But the biggest change was in the way they felt about themselves. Suddenly they had more energy and a healthier outlook on life. They felt wittier, more playful, more optimistic. When they looked in the mirror, they had a new fondness for the face that looked back at them—maybe they were worthy of their lovers' affection, after all. Some people felt so good about themselves that for a time they were even able to give up their substitute forms of gratification. They no longer needed to indulge themselves with sweets or drugs or alcohol, or tranquilize themselves with TV, or spice up their lives with recreational sex. Working overtime lost its appeal, and scrabbling after money and power seemed rather pointless. Life had meaning and substance, and it was standing right there beside them.

At the peak of their love relationships, these intense good feelings radiated outward, and people felt more loving and accepting of everyone. Some were even blessed with a heightened spiritual awareness, a feeling of inner unity and a sense of being connected with nature that they hadn't experienced since childhood. For a brief time, they saw the world not through the fractured lens of their split-off state but through the smooth, polished lens of their original nature.[1]

Lynn and Peter, the couple I introduced to you at the end of the previous chapter, told me that, when they were very much in love, they spent a day sightseeing in New York City. After dinner they impulsively took the elevator to the top of the Empire State Building so they could see the sun set from the observation deck. They held hands and looked down on the thousands of people milling below them with a feeling of compassion—how tragic that these people were not sharing their moment of ecstasy.

This timeless sentiment is beautifully expressed in a letter from Sophia Peabody to Nathaniel Hawthorne, dated December 31, 1839:[2]

Best Beloved,—
. . . What a year has this been to us! My definition of Beauty is, that it is love, and therefore includes both truth and good. But those only who love as we do can feel the significance and force of this.

My ideas will not flow in these crooked strokes. God be with you. I am very well, and have walked far in Danvers this cold morning. I am full of the glory of the day. God bless you this night of the old year. It has proved the year of our nativity. Has not the old earth passed away from us?—are not all things new?

Your Sophie

THE CHEMISTRY OF LOVE

WHAT CAUSES THE rush of good feeling that we call romantic love? Psychopharmacologists have learned that lovers are literally high on drugs—natural hormones and chemicals that flood their bodies with a sense of well-being.[3] During the attraction phase of a relationship, the brain releases dopamine and norepinephrine, two of the body's many neurotransmitters. These neurotransmitters help contribute to a rosy outlook on life, a rapid pulse, increased energy, and a sense of heightened perception. During this phase, when lovers want to be together every moment of the day, the brain increases its production of endorphins and enkephalins, natural narcotics, enhancing a person's sense of security and comfort. Dr. Michael R. Liebowitz, associate professor of clinical psychiatry at Columbia University, takes this idea one step further and suggests that the mystical experience of oneness that lovers undergo may be caused by an increase in the production of the neurotransmitter serotonin.

But, as intriguing as it is to look at love from a pharmacological point of view, scientists can't explain what causes the release of these potent chemicals, or what causes them to diminish. All they can do is document the fact that romantic love is an intense physical experience with measurable biological components. To gain additional insight, we need to return to the field of psychology, and to the view that romantic love is a creation of the unconscious mind.[4]

The Universal Language of Love

IN THE PREVIOUS chapter, I offered an explanation of romantic love. The reason we have such good feelings at the beginning of a relationship, I asserted, is that a part of the brain believes that finally we have been given a chance to be nurtured and to regain our original wholeness. If we look in the right places, we can find plenty of evidence that this is indeed what happens. One place to look is in the universal language of lovers. By listening to popular songs, reading love poems, plays, and novels, and listening to hundreds of couples describe their relationships, I have come to the conclusion that all the words exchanged between lovers since time began can be reduced to four basic sentences—the rest is elaboration. And these four sentences offer a rare glimpse into the unconscious realm of romantic love.

The first of these sentences occurs early in a relationship, maybe during the first or second encounter, and it goes something like this: "I know we've just met, but somehow I feel as though I already know you." This isn't just a line lovers hand each other. For some unaccountable reason, they feel at ease with each other. They feel a comfortable resonance, almost as if they had known each other for years. *I call this the "phenomenon of recognition."*

Somewhat later, lovers get around to the second significant exchange of information. "This is peculiar," they say to each other, "but even though we've only been seeing each other for a short time, I can't remember when I didn't know you." Even though they met only a few days or weeks ago, it seems as though they've always been together; their relationship has no temporal boundaries. *I call this the "phenomenon of timelessness."*

When a relationship has had time to ripen, lovers look in each other's eyes and proclaim the third meaningful sentence: "When I'm with you, I no longer feel alone; I feel whole, complete." One of my clients, Patrick, expressed the feeling in these words: "Before I knew Diane, I felt as though I had been spending all of my life wandering around in a big house with empty rooms. When we met, it was like opening a door and finding someone home." Being together seemed to put an end to his relentless search for completion. He felt fulfilled, filled up. *I call this the "phenomenon of reunification."*

Finally, at some point, lovers utter a fourth and final declaration of love. They tell each other: "I love you so much, I can't live without you." They have become so involved with each other that they can't imagine a separate existence. *I call this the "phenomenon of necessity."*

Whether lovers actually say words like these or merely experience the feelings behind them, they underscore what I have been saying so far about romantic love and the nature of the unconscious.

The first sentence—in which lovers report an eerie sense of recognition—loses some of its mystery when we recall that the reason people "choose" their lovers is that the lovers resemble their caretakers. No wonder they have a sense of déjà vu, a feeling of familiarity. On an unconscious level, they feel connected once again with their caretakers, only this time they believe their deepest, most fundamental, most infantile yearnings are going to be satisfied. Someone is going to take care of them; they are no longer going to be alone.

The second statement, "I can't remember when I didn't know you," is a testimony to the fact that romantic love is an old-brain phenomenon. When people fall in love, their old brain fuses the image of their partners with the image of their caretakers, and they enter the realm of the eternal now. To the unconscious, being in an intimate love relationship is very much like being an infant in the arms of your mother. There is the same illusion of safety and security, the same total absorption.

In fact, if we could observe a pair of lovers at this critical juncture of their relationship, we would make an interesting observation: the two of them are taking part in an instinctual bonding process that mimics the way mothers bond with their newborn infants. They coo, prattle, and call each other diminutive names that they would be embarrassed to repeat in public. They stroke, pet, and delight in every square inch of each other's bodies—"What a cute little navel!" "Such soft skin!"—just the way a mother adores her baby. Meanwhile, they add to the illusion that they are each other's surrogate parents by saying, "I'm going to love you the way nobody ever has," which the unconscious mind interprets to mean "more than Mommy and Daddy." Needless to say, the old brain revels in all of this delightfully regressive behavior. The lovers believe they are going to be healed—not by hard work or painful self-realization—but by the simple act of merging with someone the old brain has confused with their caretakers.

What about the third sentence—that feeling of wholeness and oneness that envelops lovers? When lovers tell each other, "When I'm with you, I feel whole, complete," they are acknowledging that they have unwittingly chosen someone who manifests the very parts of their being that were cut off in childhood; they have rediscovered their lost self. A person who grew up repressing his or her feelings will choose someone who is unusually expressive. A person who was not allowed to be at ease with his or her sexuality will choose someone who is sensual and free. When people with complementary traits fall in love, they feel as if they've suddenly been released from repression. Like Plato's truncated, androgynous beings, each of them had been half a person; now they are whole.

And what about that last sentence—the feeling that lovers have that they will die if they part? What can this tell us about the nature of romantic love? First, it documents the fact that lovers unknowingly transfer responsibility for their very survival from their parents to their partners. This same marvelous being who has awakened eros is now going to protect them from thanatos, the ever-present fear of death. By attending to their unmet childhood needs, their partners are going to become allies in their struggle for survival. On a deeper level, this sentence reveals the fear that, if the lovers were to part, they would lose their rediscovered sense of wholeness. They would once again be fractured, half-whole creatures, separated from the fullness of existence. Loneliness and anxiety would well up inside them, and they would no longer feel connected to the world around them. Ultimately, to lose each other would be to lose their new sense of self.

A BRIEF INTERLUDE

FOR A WHILE, however, these fears are held at bay, and to the lovers it seems as though romantic love is actually going to heal them and make them whole. Companionship alone is a soothing balm. Because they are spending so much time together, they no longer feel lonely or isolated. And as their level of trust increases, they deepen their level of intimacy. They may even talk about some of the pain and sorrow of their childhood, and if they do they are rewarded for their openness by their lovers' heartfelt sympathy: "Oh, I feel so sad that you had to go through that." "How awful that you had to suffer so much." They feel as if no one, not even their own parents, has cared so deeply about their inner world. As they share these intimacies, they may even experience moments of true empathic communion and become absorbed in each other's world. During these rare moments, they aren't judging each other, or interpreting what their lovers are saying, or even comparing their various experiences. They are doing much more: for a short time, they are letting go of their lifelong self-absorption and sharing in the reality of another human being.

But romantic love brings more than kind words and empathic moments to heal their wounds. With a sixth sense that is often lamentably lacking in later stages of a relationship, lovers seem to divine exactly what their partners are lacking. If the partner needs more nurturing, they gladly play the role of Mommy or Daddy. If the partner wants more freedom, they grant him or her independence. If the partner needs more security, they become protective and reassuring. They shower each other with spontaneous acts of caring that seem to erase their earlier, childhood deprivations. Being in love is like suddenly becoming the favored child in an idealized family.

FOSTERING AN ILLUSION

FOR A WHILE, lovers cling to the illusion of romantic love. However, this requires a good deal of unconscious playacting. One bit of make-believe in which virtually all lovers engage is trying to appear to be more emotionally healthy than they really are. After all, if you don't appear to have many needs of your own, your partner is free to assume that your goal in life is to nurture, not to be nurtured, and this makes you very desirable indeed. One woman, Louise, described to me the efforts she went to to appear to be the perfect mate for her future husband, Steve. A few weeks after they met, Louise invited Steve over to her house for dinner. "I wanted to display my domestic talent," she said. "He saw me as a career woman, and I wanted him to see I could cook, too." To make her life seem as simple and uncomplicated as possible, she arranged to have her eleven-year-old son from a previous marriage stay the night with a friend—no reason to reveal all of life's complexities at this stage of the game. Then she thoroughly cleaned the house, planned the menu around the only two things she could cook really well—quiche and Roquefort salad—and arranged fresh flowers in all the rooms. When Steve walked into the house, dinner was ready, her makeup was fresh, and classical music was on the stereo. Steve, in turn, came as his most charming, helpful self, and when dinner was over he insisted on washing the dishes and fixing the broken porch light. That night they declared their love for each other, and for several months they were both able to orchestrate their lives so that they had few, if any, needs of their own.

This degree of make-believe is quite common; most of us go to a lot of trouble in the early stages of a relationship to appear to be ideal mates. In some cases, however, the deception is more extreme.

One of my clients, a woman I'll call Jessica, had a history of becoming involved with unreliable men. She had two failed marriages and a string of painful relationships. The relationship that finally convinced Jessica she needed therapy was with Brad, a man who at first seemed totally devoted to her. Once he had gained her trust, she told him all about her previous difficulties with men. Brad was sympathetic and assured her that he would never leave her. "If anyone leaves, it will be you," he said. "I will always be here." He seemed for all the world like a stable, trustworthy mate.

The two of them were together constantly for about six months, and Jessica began to relax into the security of the relationship. Then, one day, she came home from work to find a note from Brad pinned to the door. In the note he explained that he had been offered a higher-paying job in another town and couldn't turn it down. He had wanted to tell her about it in person, but he had been afraid she'd be too upset. He hoped that she would understand.

When Jessica recovered from shock, she called Brad's best friend and demanded that he tell her what he knew. As she listened to him talk, a shockingly different portrait of Brad began to emerge. Apparently he never stayed in one place very long. In the previous fifteen years, he had moved six times and been married three times. All this was news to Jessica. Sensing her need for security, Brad had done his best to appear to be a reliable lover. This is a psychological process known as "projective identification." He had unconsciously identified himself with Jessica's vision of the ideal man. My suspicion is that at first his subterfuge was well intentioned. He probably didn't begin the relationship with the purpose of gaining her trust and affection and then leaving her; he just couldn't keep up the charade.

When Brad left her, Jessica had every reason to fly into a rage, but instead she fabricated an illusion that he was planning to send for her as soon as he saved up some money. She stayed by the phone for hours in case he called, and waited anxiously for a letter. But she never heard from him again. "And I'm glad I didn't," she told me one day, "because I would have taken him back—no matter what he had done. That's how badly I needed him."

Jessica was demonstrating a classic case of denial; she was refusing to believe that Brad was in fact an immature, unreliable man. Her memory of the role he had obligingly played for her was more real to her than the truth of his actual behavior.

DENIAL

TO SOME DEGREE, we all use denial as a coping tool. Whenever life presents us with a difficult or painful situation, we have a tendency to want to ignore reality and create a more palatable fantasy. But there is no time in our lives when our denial mechanism is more fully engaged than in the early stages of our love relationships.

John, a man in his thirties who came to me for counseling, was particularly adept at denial. He was a computer programmer who had designed a software program that was so successful he used it to start his own company. For the first ten or fifteen minutes of each session, he would talk about his company and how well it was doing. Then the conversation would grind to a halt, he would avert his eyes, and he would get around to the real topic of conversation, which was Cheryl, the woman he loved. He was utterly bewitched by her and would marry her in a second if she would only say yes. But Cheryl kept refusing to make a commitment.

When John first met Cheryl, she appeared to be everything he wanted in a woman. She was attractive, intelligent, and delightfully sensual. But, a few months into the relationship, he began to be aware of some of her negative traits. When they went out to dinner, for example, he noticed that she always complained about the food or the service, no matter how good it was. He also noticed that she would complain endlessly about her job but would do nothing to improve her working conditions.

To avoid being put off by these negative traits, John engaged in strenuous mental gymnastics. When he went out to dinner with her, he would focus on her discriminating tastes, not on her complaining attitude. When she ranted and raved about her job, he thought about what a trooper she was to put up with such terrible working conditions. "Other people would have quit long ago," he told me with a note of pride.

The only thing that really bothered him about Cheryl was her unavailability. She always seemed to be pushing him away. The situation worsened after they had been seeing each other for about six months, when Cheryl demanded that he not see her during the week so that she could have "a little breathing room." John reluctantly agreed to her terms, even though he knew that one of the reasons she wanted this time off was so that she could date other men. She made it clear to him that he had no choice but to grant her more freedom.

As compensation, John started spending time with a woman named Patricia, who was very unlike Cheryl. Devoted, compliant, and patient, she was crazy about him. "She'd marry me in a minute," John told me one day, "just the way I'd marry Cheryl in a minute. But I don't care that much about Patricia. Even though she's nicer to be around, I never think about her when I'm away from her. It's almost as if she doesn't exist.

Sometimes I feel that I'm taking advantage of her, but I don't like to be alone. She fills up the hole." Meanwhile, unavailable, critical Cheryl occupied his every waking moment. "Whenever I'm not thinking about work," he told me, "I'm dreaming about Cheryl."

Why was John so immune to Patricia's charms and so willing to overlook Cheryl's faults? It should come as no surprise that John's mother had a critical, distant nature, very much like Cheryl's. A worried look would often come over his mother's face, and she would tune him out. John had no idea what was going on in her mind. Like all children, he had no knowledge of—or interest in—his mother's subjective state. All he knew was that she was frequently unavailable to him and this filled him with anxiety. When he recognized that distracted look, he would become angry and strike out at her. She would push him away and send him to his room. If he became very angry at her, she would spank him and not talk to him for hours.

Eventually John learned to suffer in silence. He has a vivid memory of the day he learned to adopt a stoical attitude. His mother had yelled at him and spanked him with a hairbrush. He doesn't remember what had made her so angry. All he remembers is that he felt his punishment was unjustified, and he ran sobbing to his room. When he got to his room, he went into his closet and closed the door. The closet had a mirror on the inside of the door, and he remembers turning on the light and staring at his tear-streaked face. "Nobody cares that I'm in here crying," he told himself. "What good is it to cry?" After a while, he stopped crying and wiped away his tears. The remarkable thing is that he never cried again. That very day he began to cover over his sadness and his anger with an unchanging mask.

John's childhood experiences help explain his mysterious attraction to Cheryl. When Cheryl ignored his advances by going out with other men or by asking him not to call her for a few days, he was filled with the same primitive yearning for closeness that he had experienced with his mother. In fact, there was so much in common between the two women that on an unconscious level he could not distinguish between them. Cheryl's coldness activated in him the same intense longing he had felt for his mother. As far as his old brain was concerned, Cheryl was his mother, and his efforts to win her favor were a grown-up version of the crying and yelling he had done as a child to attract his mother's attention. The psychological term for this case of mistaken identity is "transference," taking the attributes of one person and overlaying them on another. It is especially easy for people to transfer their feelings about their parents onto their partners, because, through a process of unconscious selection, they have chosen partners who resemble their caretakers. All they have to do is exaggerate the similarities between them and diminish the differences.

John had other reasons to be drawn to Cheryl besides her resemblance to his mother. Another source of his attraction was that she had an artistic flair. Since he was a rather "dull businessman" (his own words), her refined sense of aesthetics opened up whole new dimensions to him. "We'll be driving in the car and I'll have my head full of business plans," he told me, "and Cheryl will draw my attention to an interesting building or a beautiful tree, and it will suddenly materialize before my eyes. I wouldn't have seen it at all if she hadn't called it to my attention. It's almost as if she creates it. When I'm alone, my world seems gray and two-dimensional."

Something else about Cheryl that attracted him—though he would have vehemently denied it—was the fact that she had a caustic, critical nature. This dark side of her personality appealed to him for two reasons. First, as we've already discussed, it reminded him of his mother, who was an angry, emotional person. Second, and perhaps more important, Cheryl's bad temper helped him get in touch with his own denied emotions. Even though he had just as much anger as Cheryl, he had learned to mask his hostility behind a compliant, accepting manner. In childhood this had been a useful adaptation, because it protected him from his mother's temper. But now that he was an adult, this repression left him half a person. Without being able to feel and express strong emotions, he felt empty inside. He discovered that, when he was with Cheryl, he experienced a much-needed emotional catharsis. He didn't have to be angry himself—that would have aroused his superego, the parent-cop inside his head, which carried on his mother's prohibitions. Instead he could have the illusion of being a whole person once again just by associating himself with her.

HOME MOVIES

"PROJECTION" IS THE term that describes the way John took a hidden part of himself—his anger—and attributed it to his lover. He projected his repressed anger onto Cheryl's visible anger. Like John, we project whenever we take a part of the disowned self or the lost self and send it out like a picture onto another person. We project all the time, not just in our primary love relationships. I remember one time in Dallas, when I was sharing a suite with a psychiatrist whose first name was James. We had an extra room, and we were looking for another person to share the rent. James had a friend who had finished medical school and was going into private practice, so he suggested that we consider him for a suite mate. Since that sounded fine to me, James agreed to invite his friend over so I could meet him.

A few days later, I opened my office door and happened to see a man walking down the hall. He was walking away from me, so all I saw was his back, but there was something about his walk that I found extremely irritating. He was swinging his hips and his head as if he owned the whole world. He sauntered instead of walked. "That has got to be one of the most arrogant men in the world," I told myself. "I wonder who that is. He must be a client of James's."

I went back into my room and forgot about the incident. A little while later, there was a knock at my door. It was James, and with him was the very man I had seen walking down the hall. "Harville," James said, "this is Robert Jenkins. He's the psychiatrist friend that I told you about who would like to rent the extra room. I thought that you and he might like to go out to lunch together."

I took a look at Robert and saw a man with a smiling, pleasant face. He had neatly trimmed hair, a well-groomed salt-and-pepper beard, horn-rimmed glasses, and large brown eyes. He reached out his hand to me. "Hello, Harville. I've heard so much about you. I hear you're involved in some really interesting things. I'd love to talk with you about it."

Such a nice, humble speech, I thought. Could this be the same man that I thought was so arrogant? Robert and I went out to lunch, and we had an interesting conversation. Later that day, I told James that I thought Robert would be an excellent person to share the suite with us. Eventually Robert became a good friend and a trusted colleague. Although he did have his prideful moments—just like me and everyone else I knew—the negative trait that had seemed so intense when I first saw him was really a part of me. I had taken the part of me that is arrogant—the part of me that does not fit with my image of myself as a sensitive, caring therapist—and thrust it onto Robert.

People in love are masters at projection. Some couples go through their whole lives together as if they were strangers sitting in a darkened movie theater, casting flickering images on each other. They don't even turn off their projectors long enough to see who it is that serves as the screen for their home movies. In just such a way, John projected his repressed anger onto Cheryl. Although she was indeed an angry person, he was also seeing in her a part of his own nature, a part of his being that was "ego-dystonic"—that is, incompatible with his self-image.

Romantic Love Defined

IF WE WERE to translate John's love for Cheryl into dry psychological terms, it could be described as a mixture of denial, transference, and projection. John was "in love with Cheryl" because:

1. He had transferred his feelings about his mother onto her.
2. He had projected his hidden rage onto her visible rage.
3. He was able to deny the pain that she caused him.

He thought he was in love with a person, when in fact he was in love with an image projected upon that person. Cheryl was not a real person with needs and desires of her own; she was a resource for the satisfaction of his unconscious childhood longings. He was in love with the idea of wish fulfillment and— like Narcissus—with a reflected part of himself.

Psyche and Eros

THE ILLUSORY NATURE of romantic love is beautifully illustrated in the myth of Psyche and Eros, an archetypal legend that was first recorded in the second century A.D.[5] According to this legend, the goddess Aphrodite was jealous of a beautiful young mortal named Psyche, and resented the adoration shown her by her countrymen. In a fit of pique, Aphrodite decreed that Psyche be carried to the top of a mountain, where she was to become the bride of a horrible monster (in some versions of the myth, this monster is called Death). Psyche's parents and the local villagers sadly escorted the young virgin up the mountain, chained her to a rock, and left her to her fate. But before Psyche could be claimed by the monster, the West Wind took pity on her and gently wafted her down the mountain to a valley that happened to be the home of Aphrodite's son, Eros, the god of love.

Psyche and Eros promptly fell in love, but Eros did not want Psyche to know that he was a god, so he kept his true identity concealed by coming to her only in darkness. At first Psyche agreed to this strange condition and enjoyed her new love, the splendid palace, and the beautiful grounds. Then, one day, her two sisters paid her a visit and, envious of her good fortune, began to ask prying questions about Eros. When Psyche couldn't answer them, they planted the suspicion in her mind that her lover might be a loathsome serpent intent on devouring her.

That night, before Eros came to her, Psyche hid a lamp and a sharp knife under their bed. If her lover turned out to be an evil creature, she was determined to lop off his head. She waited until Eros was sound asleep, then quietly lit the lamp. But as she leaned over to get a closer look at him, a drop of hot oil spilled from the lamp onto his shoulder. Eros quickly awoke and, when he saw the lamp and the knife, flew out the open window, vowing to punish Psyche for discovering the truth by leaving her forever. In anguish, Psyche ran after him, crying out his name, but she couldn't keep up with him and tripped and fell. Instantly the heavenly palace and the exquisite countryside vanished, and she was once more chained to a rock on the lonely, craggy mountaintop.

As with all fairy tales, there is truth to this legend. Romantic love does indeed thrive on ignorance and fantasy. As long as lovers maintain an idealized, incomplete view of each other, they live in a Garden of Eden. But the myth also contains some fiction. When Psyche lit the lamp and saw Eros clearly for the first time, she discovered that he was a magnificent god with golden wings. When you and I lit our lamps and took our first objective look at our lovers, we discovered that they weren't gods at all—they were imperfect humans, full of warts and blemishes, all those negative traits that we had steadfastly refused to see.

THE POWER STRUGGLE

I can't live either without you or with you.

— OVID

WHEN DOES ROMANTIC love end and the power struggle begin? As in all attempts to map human behavior, it's impossible to define precisely when the stages occur. But for most couples there is a noticeable change in the relationship about the time they make a definite commitment to each other. Once they say, "Let's get married" or "Let's get engaged" or "Let's be primary lovers, even though we still see other people," the pleasing, inviting dance of courtship draws to a close, and lovers begin to want not only the expectation of need fulfillment—the illusion that was responsible for the euphoria of romantic love—but the reality as well. Suddenly it isn't enough that their partners be affectionate, clever, attractive, and fun-loving. They now have to satisfy a whole hierarchy of expectations, some conscious, but most hidden from their awareness.

What are some of these expectations? As soon as they start living together, most people assume that their mates will conform to a very specific but rarely expressed set of behaviors. For example, a man may expect his new bride to do the housework, cook the meals, shop for groceries, wash the clothes, arrange the social events, take on the role of family nurse, and buy everyday household items. In addition to these traditional role expectations, he has a long list of expectations that are peculiar to his own upbringing. On Sundays, for example, he may expect his wife to cook a special breakfast while he reads the Sunday paper, and then join him for a leisurely stroll in the park. This is the way his parents spent their Sundays together, and the day wouldn't feel "right" unless it echoed these dominant chords.

Meanwhile, his wife has an equally long, and perhaps conflicting, set of expectations. In addition to wanting her husband to be responsible for all the "manly" chores, such as taking care of the car, paying the bills, figuring the taxes, mowing the lawn, and overseeing minor and major home repairs, she may expect him to help with the cooking, shopping, and laundry as well. Then, she, too, has expectations that reflect her particular upbringing. An ideal Sunday for her may include going to church, going out to a restaurant for brunch, and spending the afternoon visiting relatives. Since neither of them shared expectations before getting married, these could develop into a significant source of tension.

But far more important than these conscious or semiconscious expectations are the unconscious ones people bring to their love relationships, and the primary one is that their partners, the ones they've winnowed out of long lists of candidates, are going to love them the way their parents never did.[1] Their partners are going to do it all—satisfy unmet childhood needs, complement lost-self parts, nurture them in a consistent and loving way, and be eternally available to them. These are the same expectations that fueled the excitement of romantic love, but now there is less of a desire to reciprocate. After all, people don't enter into relationships to take care of their partner's needs—they do so to further their own psychological and emotional growth. Once a relationship seems secure, a psychological switch is triggered deep in the old brain that activates all the latent infantile wishes. It is as if the wounded child within takes over. Says the child, "I've been good enough long enough to ensure that this person is going to stay around for a while. Let's see the payoff." So the two partners take a big step back from each other and wait for the dividends of togetherness to start rolling in.

The change may be abrupt or gradual, but at some point they wake up to discover that they've migrated to a colder climate. Now there are fewer back rubs; shorter, more cryptic love notes; less lovemaking. Their partners have stopped looking for excuses to be with them and are spending more time reading, watching television, socializing with friends, or just plain daydreaming.

WHY HAVE YOU CHANGED?

THIS BLEAK RATIONING of love is partly the result of a disturbing revelation. At some point in their relationships, most people discover that some aspect of their partners' character, a personality trait they once thought highly desirable, is beginning to annoy them. A man finds that his wife's conservative nature—one of the primary reasons he was attracted to her—is now making her seem staid and prudish. A woman discovers that her partner's tendency to be quiet and withdrawn—a trait she once thought was an indication of a spiritual nature—is making her feel lonely and isolated. A man finds his partner's impulsive, outgoing personality—once so refreshing—is now making him feel invaded.

What is the explanation for these disturbing reversals? If you will recall, in our desire to be spiritually whole—to be as complete and perfect as God had intended—we chose partners who made up for the parts of our being that were split off in childhood. We each found someone who compensated for our lack of creativity or inability to think or to feel. Through union with our partners, we felt connected to a hidden part of ourselves. At first this arrangement seemed to work. But as time passed, our partners' complementary traits began to stir up feelings and attributes in us that were still taboo.

To see how this drama plays out in real life, let's continue with the story of John, the successful businessman from the previous chapter who was spending time with Patricia but desperately wanting to be with Cheryl. John came in for a therapy session one day in an ebullient mood. This time he didn't spend the customary fifteen minutes talking about his software business; he plunged right in and told me his good news. Cheryl, in a rare, conciliatory gesture, had decided to let him move in with her for a six-month trial period. This was the answer to his dreams.

John's euphoria lasted several months, during which time he decided that he no longer needed therapy. (As is true for most of my clients, he had little interest in working on his problems as long as he was feeling happy.) But one day he called and asked for an appointment. When he came in he reported that he and Cheryl were beginning to have difficulties. One of the things he mentioned was that Cheryl's vibrant personality was beginning to grate on him. He could tolerate her "emotional excesses" (as he now described them) when she directed them at others—for example, when she was berating a clerk or talking excitedly with a girlfriend—but when she beamed her high-voltage emotions at him, he had a fleeting sensation of panic. "I feel like my brain is about to short-circuit," he told me.

The reason John was feeling so anxious around Cheryl was that she was beginning to stir his own repressed anger. At first, being around her had given him the comforting illusion that he was in touch with his feelings. But after a time her free emotional state stimulated his own feelings to such a degree that they threatened to emerge. His superego, the part of his brain that was carrying out his mother's injunction against anger, sent out frantic error messages warning him to keep his repression intact. John tried to reduce his anxiety by dampening Cheryl's personality: "For God's sake, Cheryl! Don't be so emotional! You're behaving like an idiot." And "Calm down, and then talk to me. I can't understand a word that you're saying." The very character trait that had once been so seductive to him was now perceived by his own brain as a threat to his existence.

In a similar way, there probably came a time in your relationship when you began to wish that your partner was less sexy or less fun-loving or less inventive—somehow less whole—because these qualities called forth repressed qualities in you, and your hidden self was threatening to make an unscheduled reappearance. When it did, it ran headlong into the internal police force that had severed those self parts in the first place, and you were filled with anxiety. This was such an unpleasant experience that you may have tried to repress your partner the same way your parents repressed you. In an effort to protect your existence, you were trying to diminish your partner's reality.

Your growing discomfort with your partner's complementary traits was only part of the rapidly brewing storm. Your partner's negative traits, the ones that you had resolutely denied during the romantic phase of your relationship, were also beginning to come into sharp focus. Suddenly your partner's chronic depression or drinking problem or stinginess or lack of responsibility became evident. This gave you the sickening realization that not only were you not going to get your needs met, but your partner was destined to wound you in the very same way you were wounded in childhood!

A Glimpse at a Painful Reality

I MADE THIS painful discovery early on in my first marriage—in fact, on the second day of our honeymoon. My new bride and I were spending a week on an island off the shores of South Georgia. We were walking along the beach. I was poking through piles of driftwood, and my wife was down by the water, two or three hundred feet in front of me, head down, totally absorbed in the task of looking for shells. I happened to glance up and saw her silhouetted against the rising sun. To this day I can remember exactly what she looked like. She had her back to me. She was wearing black shorts and a red top. Her shoulder-length blonde hair was blowing in the wind. As I gazed at her, I noticed a slight droop to her shoulders. At that instant I felt a jolt of anxiety. This was immediately followed by the sick, sinking realization that I had married the wrong person. It was a strong feeling—I had to check an impulse to run back to the car and drive away. While I was standing there transfixed, my wife turned to me, waved, and smiled. I felt as though I were awakening from a nightmare. I waved back and rushed up to meet her.

It was as if a veil had lifted for a moment, and then dropped back down. It took me years to figure out exactly what had happened. The connection was finally made one day while I was in therapy. My therapist was guiding me through a regression exercise, an exercise designed to take me back to my childhood, and with his help I was able to picture myself playing on the floor in my mother's kitchen. I was only one or two years old. I visualized my mother busy at the stove, with her back to me. This must have been a typical scene, because I was her ninth child, and she probably spent four or five hours a day in the kitchen, cooking and cleaning. I could see my mother's back quite clearly. She was standing at the stove wearing a print dress, and she had apron strings tied around her waist. She was tired and depressed and her shoulders sagged.

As an adult viewing this imaginary scene, I was flooded with the awareness that she didn't have any physical or emotional energy for me. My father had died only a few months before from a head injury, and she was left alone with her grief, very little money, and a houseful of children to look after. I felt like an unwanted child. Not that my mother didn't love me—she was an affectionate, caring woman—but she was physically and emotionally worn out. She was so wrapped up in her own worries, she could only look after me mechanically.

This was a new discovery for me. Until that point in my therapy, I had attributed my anxiety to the fact that both my parents had died by the time I was six years old. But that day I learned that my feelings of abandonment had started much earlier. In my regressed state, I called to my mother, but she would not answer. I sat in the psychiatrist's office and cried in deep pain. Then I had a second revelation. I suddenly realized what had happened to me that day on my honeymoon. When I had seen my wife so far away from me, so absorbed in herself, and with the same slump to her shoulders, I had had the eerie premonition that my marriage was going to be a repetition of my early days with a depressed mother. The emptiness of the early days of my childhood was going to continue. It had been too much for me to absorb, and I had quickly drawn the curtain.

At some point in their love relationships, most people discover that something about their partners awakens strong memories of childhood pain. Sometimes the parallels are obvious. A young woman with abusive parents, for example, may discover a violent streak in her boyfriend. A man with alcoholic parents may wake up to find himself married to an incipient alcoholic or drug addict. A woman who grew up in a contorted Oedipal relationship with her parents may be enraged to discover that her partner is having a secret affair.

But the similarities between parents and partners are often subtler. This was the case for Bernard and Kathryn, clients of mine who had been married for twenty-eight years. Bernard was a manager of a public utility; Kathryn was going back to school to get a degree in counseling. They had three children and one grandchild.

One evening as they walked into my office for their weekly appointment, they both looked downtrodden and defeated. I guessed right away that they had recently had one of the "core" scenes, a fight that they had had over and over again throughout the last twenty years of their marriage in countless subtle variations. Most couples have such a core scene, a fight they have so many times that they know their parts by heart.

They told me that the fight had taken place while they were decorating the house for Christmas. Bernard had been characteristically quiet, absorbed in his own thoughts, and Kathryn had been issuing orders. All three of their children and their spouses were coming to stay for the holidays, and Kathryn wanted everything to be perfect. Bernard dutifully performed whatever task was asked of him and went on pondering his own thoughts. After an hour or so, his silence became deafening to Kathryn, and she tried to involve him in a conversation about their children. He volunteered only a few sentences. She became more and more annoyed with him. Finally she lashed out at him for the way he was hanging the lights on the tree: "Why don't you pay attention to what you're doing? I may as well do it myself!" Bernard let her tirade wash over him, then calmly turned and walked out the back door.

Kathryn went to the kitchen window. As she watched the garage door close behind Bernard, she was filled with two primal emotions: fear and anger. Anger was uppermost: this time she wasn't going to let him retreat. She marched out after him and threw open the garage door. "For God's sake! Why don't you help me? You're always locked up in the garage. You never help me when I need you. What's the matter with you?"

To a therapist, Kathryn's use of global words like "always" and "never" would have been a clear indication that she was in a regressive state. Young children have a hard time distinguishing between past and present; whatever is happening at this moment has always happened in the past and will always happen in the future. But Bernard was not a therapist. He was her beleaguered husband, and he had just escaped from a torrent of criticism in the hopes of finding peace and quiet. His old brain responded to her attack—which in reality was nothing more than an adult version of the infant's cry—with a counter-attack. "Maybe I'd help you more if you weren't so bitchy!" he retorted. "You're always hounding me. Can't I be alone for five minutes?" He seethed with anger, and Kathryn burst into tears.

As an outsider, I could easily see the step-by-step evolution of their arguments. The trigger for the fights was almost always the fact that Bernard was withdrawn. Trying to get some response from him, Kathryn would nag. Bernard would pay no attention to her until he had had all that he could stand; then he would go to another room to try to find peace and quiet. At that point Kathryn would explode in rage and Bernard would respond in kind. Finally Kathryn would burst into tears.

When they were through recounting this latest episode, I asked Kathryn to remember exactly how she had felt working on the holiday preparations with her unresponsive husband. She sat quietly for a moment, struggling to recall her feelings. Then she looked up at me with a puzzled expression and said, "I felt scared. It scared me that he wouldn't talk to me." For the first time she realized that she was actually afraid of his silences.

"What were you afraid of, Kathryn?" I asked her.

She answered quickly. "I was afraid he was going to hurt me."

Bernard looked over at her with wide-open eyes. I said, "Let's check this out with Bernard. Bernard, were you standing in the kitchen thinking about hurting Kathryn?"

"Hurting her?" he said, his surprise evident. "Hurting her?! I have never touched her in my life. I was just thinking my own thoughts. If I remember correctly, I was worrying about the fact that we would need to put a new roof on the house in the spring because of the leak. And I was probably thinking about something at the office."

"Really?" asked Kathryn. "You weren't mad at me that day?"

"No! Sure, I got annoyed when you kept criticizing me, but all I wanted to do was get away. I kept thinking about how nice it would be to be out in the garage working on my own projects instead of being nagged at all the time."

"Well, the way I see it, you're always angry at me, and eventually you can't hold it in any longer, so you blow up."

"I do blow up, but it takes about two or three hours of your nagging before I do! Anybody would get angry at that. I don't start out being angry at you."

This checked out with me. Bernard did not seem to be a violent man.

"Kathryn," I said to her, "for a moment I want you to close your eyes and think some more about what makes you afraid when Bernard doesn't respond to you."

After half a minute she replied, "I don't know. It's just the silence." She was having a hard time coming up with additional insight.

"Well, stay with that thought for a moment and try to recall something about silence in your childhood. Close your eyes."

The room was quiet. Then Kathryn gasped and opened her eyes. "It's my father! I've never seen that before. He used to sink into a deep depression and not talk for weeks. Whenever he was in one of those moods, I knew not to bother him because, if I did one thing wrong, he would hit me. When I saw him start to sink into a depression, I would panic. I knew that I was in for a hard time."

Kathryn's father and her husband shared an important personality trait—they both were prone to long periods of silence—and this undoubtedly was one of the reasons that Kathryn was attracted to Bernard. She had chosen someone who resembled her father so she could resolve her childhood fear of being abused. She didn't marry a talkative, outgoing person—she found someone who had her father's *negative traits* so she could re-create her childhood and continue her struggle for consistent love and kindness. But Bernard resembled Kathryn's father only superficially. He was silent because he was an introvert, not because he was depressed and given to anger. It was Kathryn's constant nagging that provoked her husband.

I have found this phenomenon in many of my clients. They react to their partners as if they were carbon copies of their parents, even though not all of their traits are the same. In their compelling need to work on unfinished business, they project the missing parental traits onto their partners. Then, by treating their partners as if they actually had these traits, they manage to provoke the desired response. A colleague of mine claims that people either "pick imago matches, project them, or provoke them."

Home Movies, Part II

SO FAR IN this chapter, we've talked about two factors that fuel the power struggle:

1. Our partners make us feel anxious by stirring up forbidden parts of ourselves.
2. Our partners have or appear to have the same negative traits as our parents, adding further injury to old wounds and thereby awakening our unconscious fear of death.

Now there is a third and final aspect of the power struggle that deserves our attention. In the previous chapter, I talked about the fact that many of our joyful feelings of romantic love come from projecting positive aspects of our imago onto our partners; in other words, we look at our partners and see all the good things about Mom and Dad and all the good but repressed parts of our own being. In the power struggle, we keep the movie projectors running, only we switch reels and begin to project our own denied negative traits!

In chapter 2, I defined these denied negative traits as the "disowned self." If you will recall, I talked about the fact that all people have a dark side to their nature, a part of their being that they try to ignore. For the most part, these are creative adaptations to childhood wounds. People also acquire negative traits by observing their parents. Even though they may not like certain things about their parents, they "introject" these traits through a process called "identification." A father's judgmental nature and a mother's tendency to belittle herself, for example, become traits passed on to the children. But as the children become more self-aware, they recognize that these are the very traits they dislike in their parents, and they do their best to deny them.

Now, this is where it gets interesting. Not only do the children manifest these negative traits themselves—although disowned and thus out of awareness—but when they grow up they also look for these traits in potential mates, for they are an essential part of their imagos. *The imago is not only an inner image of the opposite sex; it is also a description of the disowned self.*

A case history might help you understand this curious and complex psychological phenomenon. I spent many years working with a young woman named Lillian. Lillian's parents divorced when she was nine years old, and her mother gained custody of both Lillian and her twelve-year-old sister, June. A year after the divorce, her mother married a man who did not get along with June. The stepfather yelled at her constantly, punishing even the smallest transgression. Several times a week his rage would escalate, and he would take the girl into her room and spank her with a belt. Lillian would stand outside the door, listening to the blows from the belt and shaking with anger and fear. She detested her stepfather. Yet, to Lillian's dismay, when she was left alone with her sister, she began to treat her with almost equal disdain. She would even call her some of the very same hurtful names she heard her stepfather use.

The fact that she was capable of hurting her sister was so painful to Lillian that she repressed these episodes. It was only after a year of therapy that she could remember those times, and it was even longer before she trusted me enough to tell me about them. When she did, I was able to help her see that it was human nature for her to absorb both the positive *and the negative* traits of her stepfather. He was the dominant influence in the household, and her unconscious mind registered the fact that the person who was most angry happened to be the most powerful. Anger and derision, therefore, must be a valuable survival skill. Gradually this character trait wormed its way into Lillian's basically kind nature.

When Lillian grew up and married, it was inevitable that she would fall in love with someone who had some of her step-father's characteristics, notably his violent anger, because this was the part of him that had been so threatening to her. In fact, the reason she came in for therapy was that her husband had physically abused her.

After two years of therapy, she was able to see that the anger she had found so detestable in her stepfather was one of the unconscious factors behind her attraction to her husband, and—even more alarming—was also a denied part of her own personality. This particular imago trait, therefore, was not only a description of her husband but also a description of a dis-owned part of herself.

I see a similar tendency in virtually every love relationship. People try to exorcise their denied negative traits by projecting them onto their mates. Or, to put it another way, they look at their partners and criticize all the things they dislike and deny in themselves. Taking a negative trait and attributing it to their partners is a remarkably effective way to obscure a not-so-desirable part of the self.

Now we have defined the three major sources of conflict that make up the power struggle. As the illusion of romantic love slowly erodes, the two partners begin to:

1. Stir up each other's repressed behaviors and feelings.
2. Reinjure each other's childhood wounds.
3. Project their own negative traits onto each other.

All of these interactions are unconscious. All people know is that they feel confused, angry, anxious, depressed, and unloved. And it is only natural that they blame all this unhappiness on their partners. *They* haven't changed—they're the same people they used to be! It's their partners who have changed!

WEAPONS OF LOVE

IN DESPAIR, PEOPLE begin to use negative tactics to force their partners to be more loving. They withhold their affection and become emotionally distant. They become irritable and critical. They attack and blame: "Why don't you . . . ?" "Why do you always . . . ?" "How come you never . . . ?" They fling these verbal stones in a desperate attempt to get their partners to be warm and responsive—or to express whatever positive traits are in their imagos. They believe that, if they give their partners enough pain, the partners will return to their former loving ways.

What makes people believe that hurting their partners will make them behave more pleasantly? Why don't people simply tell each other in plain English that they want more affection or attention or lovemaking or freedom or whatever it is that they are craving? I asked that question out loud one day as I was conducting a couples workshop. It wasn't just a rhetorical question; I didn't have the answer. But it just so happened that, a few minutes before, I had been talking about babies and their instinctual crying response to distress. All of a sudden I had the answer. Once again our old brains were to blame. When we were babies, we didn't smile sweetly at our mothers to get them to take care of us. We didn't pinpoint our discomfort by putting it into words. We simply opened our mouths and screamed. And it didn't take us long to learn that, the louder we screamed, the quicker they came. The success of this tactic was turned into an "imprint," a part of our stored memory about how to get the world to respond to our needs: "When you are frustrated, provoke the people around you. Be as unpleasant as possible until someone comes to your rescue."

This primitive method of signaling distress is characteristic of most couples immersed in a power struggle, but there is one example that stands out in my mind. A few years ago I was seeing a couple who had been married about twenty-five years. The husband was convinced that his wife was not only selfish but also vindictive. "She never thinks of me," he complained, listing numerous ways his wife ignored him. Meanwhile, his wife sat in her chair and shook her head in mute disagreement. As soon as he was through, she leaned forward in her chair and said to me in a strong and earnest voice, "Believe me, I do everything I can to please him. I spend more time with him; I spend less time with him. I even learned how to ski this winter, thinking that would make him happy—and I hate the cold! But nothing seems to work."

To help end the stalemate, I asked the husband to tell his wife one specific thing that she could do that would make him feel better—one practical, doable, measurable activity that would help him feel more loved. He hemmed and hawed and then said with a growl, "If she's been married to me for twenty-five years and still doesn't know what I want, then she hasn't been paying any attention! She just doesn't care about me!"

This man, like the rest of us, was clinging to a primitive view of the world. When he was an infant lying in the cradle, he experienced his mother as a large creature leaning over him, trying to intuit his needs. He was fed, clothed, bathed, and nurtured, even though he could not articulate a single need. A crucial lesson learned in the preverbal stage of his development left an indelible imprint on his mind: other people were supposed to figure out what he needed and give it to him without his having to do anything more than cry.[2] Whereas this arrangement worked fairly well when he was a child, in adulthood his needs were a great deal more complex. Furthermore, his wife was not a devoted mother hovering over his crib. She was an equal, with—much to his surprise—needs and expectations of her own. And although she wanted very much to make him happy, she didn't know what to do. Lacking this information, she was forced to play a grown-up version of pin-the-tail-on-the-donkey: "Is this what you want? Is this?"

When partners don't tell each other what they want and constantly criticize each other for missing the boat, it's no wonder that the spirit of love and cooperation disappears. In its place comes the grim determination of the power struggle, in which each partner tries to force the other to meet his or her needs. Even though their partners react to these maneuvers with renewed hostility, they persevere. Why? Because in their unconscious minds they fear that, if their needs are not met, they will die. This is a classic example of what Freud called the "repetition compulsion," the tendency of human beings to repeat ineffective behaviors over and over again.

Some couples stay in this angry, hostile state forever. They hone their ability to pierce each other's defenses and damage each other's psyches. With alarming frequency, the anger erupts into violence.

STAGES OF THE POWER STRUGGLE

WHEN YOU ARE immersed in the power struggle, life seems chaotic. You have no reference points. You have no sense of when it all started or how it will end. But from a distant perspective the power struggle can be seen to follow a predictable course, one that happens to parallel the well-documented stages of grief in a dying or bereaved person.[3] But this death is not the death of the real person; it's the death of the illusion of romantic love.

First comes the shock, that horrifying moment of truth when a window opens and a wrenching thought invades your consciousness: "This is not the person I thought I had married." At that instant you assume that married life is going to be a continuation of the loneliness and pain of childhood; the long-anticipated healing is not to be.

After the shock comes denial. The disappointment is so great that you don't allow yourself to see the truth. You do your best to see your partner's negative traits in a positive light. But eventually the denial can no longer be sustained, and you feel betrayed. Either your partner has changed drastically since the days when you were first in love, or you have been deceived all along about his or her true nature. You are in pain, and the degree of your pain is the degree of the disparity between your earlier fantasy of your partner and your partner's emerging reality.

If you stick it out beyond the angry stage of the power struggle, some of the venom drains away, and you enter the fourth stage, bargaining. This stage goes something like this: "If you will give up your drinking, I will be more interested in sex." Or "If you let me spend more days sailing, I will spend more time with the children." Relationship therapists can unwittingly prolong this stage of the power struggle if they help couples negotiate behavioral contracts without getting to the root of the problem.[4]

The last stage of the power struggle is despair. When couples reach this final juncture, they no longer have any hopes of finding happiness or love within the relationship; the pain has gone on too long. At this point, approximately half the couples withdraw the last vestiges of hope and end the relationship. Most of those who stay together create what is called a "parallel" relationship and try to find all their happiness outside the partnership. A very few, perhaps as few as five percent of all couples, find a way to resolve the power struggle and go on to create a deeply satisfying relationship.[5]

FOR THE SAKE of clarity, I would like to reduce the discussion in these first five chapters to its simplest form. First of all, we choose our partners for two basic reasons: (1) they have both the positive and the negative qualities of the people who raised us, and (2) they compensate for positive parts of our being that were cut off in childhood. We enter the relationship with the unconscious assumption that our partner will become a surrogate parent and make up for all the deprivation of our childhood. All we have to do to be healed is to form a close, lasting relationship.

After a time we realize that our strategy is not working. We are "in love," but not whole. We decide that the reason our plan is not working is that our partners are deliberately ignoring our needs. They know exactly what we want, and when and how we want it, but for some reason they are deliberately withholding it from us. This makes us angry, and for the first time we begin to see our partners' negative traits. We then compound the problem by projecting our own denied negative traits onto them. As conditions deteriorate, we decide that the best way to force our partners to satisfy our needs is to be unpleasant and irritable, just as we were in the cradle. If we yell loud enough and long enough, we believe, our partners will come to our rescue. And, finally, what gives the power struggle its toxicity is the underlying unconscious belief that, if we cannot entice, coerce, or seduce our partners into taking care of us, we will face the fear greater than all other fears—the fear of death.

What may not be immediately apparent in this brief summary is this: there is really very little difference between romantic love and the power struggle. On the surface, these first two stages of a love relationship appear to be worlds apart. A couple's delight in each other has turned to hatred, and their goodwill has degenerated into a battle of wills. But what's important to note is that the underlying themes remain the same. Both individuals are still searching for a way to regain their original wholeness, and they are still holding on to the belief that their partners have the power to make them healthy and whole. The main difference is that now, in the power struggle, the partner is perceived as withholding love. This requires a switch in tactics, and the two people begin to hurt each other, or deny each other pleasure and intimacy, in hopes of having their partners respond with warmth and love.

What is the way out of this labyrinth of confusion? What lies beyond the power struggle? In the next chapter, "Becoming Conscious," we will talk about a new kind of relationship, "the conscious partnership," and show how it helps two people in a love relationship begin to satisfy each other's childhood longings.

part II

THE CONSCIOUS
PARTNERSHIP

BECOMING CONSCIOUS

Seldom or never does a marriage develop into
an individual relationship smoothly without crisis.
There is no birth of consciousness without pain.

— C. G. JUNG

SCANNING THE FIRST five chapters, it would be easy to get
the impression that the old brain is the cause of most of our
relationship problems. It's the old brain that prompts us to
choose partners who resemble our caretakers. It's the old brain
that is the source of all our elaborate defenses—the projections,
transferences, and introjections—that obscure the reality of
ourselves and our partners. And it's the old brain that is
responsible for our infantile response to frustration, the "cry-
or-criticize" response that causes further alienation.

But the old brain also plays a positive role in love relationships. Although some of the tactics of the old brain may be
self-defeating, its fundamental drives are essential to our well-
being. Our unconscious drive to repair the emotional damage
of childhood is what allows us to realize our spiritual potential as human beings, to become complete and loving people

capable of nurturing others. And even though our projections and transferences may temporarily blind us to our partners' reality, they're also what binds us to them, setting up the preconditions for future growth.

The problem with the old brain is that it's unguided; it's like a blind animal trying to find its way to the watering hole. To achieve the valid and important objectives of the old brain, we need to enlist the aid of the new brain—the part of us that makes choices, exerts will, knows that our partners are not our parents, that today is not always, and that yesterday is not today. We need to take the rational skills that we use in other parts of our lives and bring them to bear on our love relationships. Once we forge a working alliance between the powerful, instinctual drives of the old brain and the discriminating, cognitive powers of the new brain, we can begin to realize our unconscious goals. Through the marriage of old-brain instincts and new-brain savvy, we can gradually leave the frustrations of the power struggle behind us.

NEW BRAIN-OLD BRAIN MERGER

HOW WOULD LOVE relationships be different if the new brain played a more active role? Here's an example of a typical interaction between a couple and how it might be handled in an unconscious partnership, a typical love relationship dominated by old-brain reactivity, and in a conscious partnership, a relationship where the old brain is tempered by reason.

Imagine that you are happily eating breakfast, and your partner suddenly criticizes you for burning the waffles. Your old brain, the perpetual guardian of your safety, instantly prompts you to fight or flee. It cares not that the person who criticized you is your partner; all it cares about is that you're under attack. Unless you interfere with your automatic old-brain response, you will immediately return your partner's critical remark with a scathing rejoinder—"Well, I may have burned the waffles, but you spilled the syrup!" Or, on the other hand, you might attempt to flee the encounter altogether by leaving the room or burying your head in the newspaper. Depending on your approach, your partner will feel either attacked or abandoned and will most likely lash out again. A perpetual-emotion machine will be set in gear, and you will have defeated the desired outcome, which is to have a pleasant, intimate breakfast together.

This is precisely the kind of situation in which the new brain could be pressed into service to come up with a less provocative response. One approach (an approach that we will explore in detail in a later chapter) might be to paraphrase your partner's statement in a neutral tone of voice, acknowledging the anger but not rushing to your own defense. For example, you might say something like this: "You're really upset that I burned the waffles again." Your partner might then respond: "Yes, I am! I'm tired of all the wasted food around here. Next time be more careful!" And, still relying on new-brain tact, you could respond once again in the same nondefensive manner: "You're right. Food does get wasted around here. I'll get an extension cord and bring the waffle iron into the dining room, where we can keep a closer eye on it." Your partner, disarmed by your rational tone of voice and your ability to think of an alternative solution, will probably calm down and become more tractable: "Good idea. And thanks for not getting upset. I guess I'm a little edgy this morning. I'm behind at work and I don't know how I'm going to manage." Because you were willing to risk a creative response to anger, you have suddenly become a trusted confidant, not a sparring partner.

Once you become skilled in this nondefensive approach to criticism, you will make an important discovery: *in most inter-actions with your partner, you are actually safer when you lower your defenses than when you keep them engaged, because your partner becomes an ally, not an enemy.* By relying on your new

brain, which, unlike your old brain, recognizes that being criticized for burning the waffles is not the same thing as being
attacked with the bread knife, you learn to moderate your
instinctual fight/flight response. Paradoxically, you do an even
better job of satisfying the underlying purpose of this automatic defense, which is to keep yourself safe and unharmed.

This is only one example of how greater reliance on the flexi-
bility and discriminating powers of the conscious brain can help
you achieve your unconscious goals. Let's move on to the larger
picture and get a comprehensive view of what I mean by "a conscious partnership." Let's start with a definition: a conscious
partnership is a relationship that fosters maximum psychological
and spiritual growth; it's a relationship created by becoming conscious and cooperating with the fundamental drives of the
unconscious mind—to be safe, to be healed, and to be whole.[1]

What are some of the differences when you become conscious? The following list highlights some of the essential differences in attitude and behavior:

Ten Characteristics of a Conscious Partnership

1. *You realize that your love relationship has a hidden
   purpose—the healing of childhood wounds.* Instead of
   focusing entirely on surface needs and desires, you learn
   to recognize the unresolved childhood issues that underlie them. When you look at relationships with this X-ray
   vision, your daily interactions take on more meaning.
   Puzzling aspects of your relationship begin to make sense
   to you, and you have a greater sense of control.

2. *You create a more accurate image of your partner.* At the
   very moment of attraction, you began fusing your lover
   with your primary caretakers. Later you projected your
   negative traits onto your partner, further obscuring your
   partner's essential reality. As you move toward a con-

scious relationship, you gradually let go of these illusions and begin to see more of your partner's truth. You see your partner not as your savior but as another wounded human being, struggling to be healed.

3. *You take responsibility for communicating your needs and desires to your partner.* In an unconscious partnership, you cling to the childhood belief that your partner automatically intuits your needs. In a conscious partnership, you accept the fact that, in order to understand each other, you have to develop clear channels of communication.

4. *You become more intentional in your interactions.* In an unconscious partnership, you tend to react without thinking. You allow the primitive response of your old brain to control your behavior. In a conscious partnership, you train yourself to behave in a more constructive manner.

5. *You learn to value your partner's needs and wishes as highly as you value your own.* In an unconscious partnership, you assume that your partner's role in life is to take care of your needs magically. In a conscious partnership, you let go of this narcissistic view and divert more and more of your energy to meeting your partner's needs.

6. *You embrace the dark side of your personality.* In a conscious partnership, you openly acknowledge the fact that you, like everyone else, have negative traits. As you accept responsibility for this dark side of your nature, you lessen your tendency to project your negative traits onto your mate, which creates a less hostile environment.

7. *You learn new techniques to satisfy your basic needs and desires.* During the power struggle, you cajole, harangue, and blame in an attempt to coerce your partner to meet your needs. When you move beyond this stage, you realize that your partner *can indeed be a resource for you—* once you abandon your self-defeating tactics.

8. *You search within yourself for the strengths and abilities you are lacking.* One reason you were attracted to your

partner is that he or she had strengths and abilities that you lacked. Therefore, being with your partner gave you an illusory sense of wholeness. In a conscious partnership, you learn that the only way you can truly recapture a sense of oneness is to develop the hidden traits within yourself.

9. *You become more aware of your drive to be loving and whole and united with the universe.* As a part of your God-given nature, you have the ability to love unconditionally and to experience unity with the world around you. Social conditioning and imperfect parenting made you lose touch with these qualities. In a conscious partnership, you begin to rediscover your original nature.

10. *You accept the difficulty of creating a lasting love relationship.* In an unconscious partnership, you believe that the way to have a good relationship is to pick the right partner. In a conscious partnership you realize you have to *be* the right partner. As you gain a more realistic view, you realize that a good relationship requires commitment, discipline, and the courage to grow and change; creating a fulfilling love relationship is hard work.

Let's take a closer look at number ten, the need to accept the difficulty involved in creating a conscious partnership, because none of the other nine ideas will come to fruition unless you first cultivate your willingness to grow and change.

Becoming a Lover

WE ALL HAVE an understandable desire to live life as children. We don't want to go to the trouble of raising a cow and milking it; we want to sit down at the table and have someone hand us a cool glass of milk. We don't want to plant seeds and tend a grapevine; we want to walk out the back door and pluck a handful of grapes. This wishful thinking finds its ultimate expression in relationships. We don't want to accept responsibility for getting our needs met; we want to "fall in love" with a superhuman mate and live happily ever after. The psychological term for this tendency to put the source of our frustrations and the solutions to our problems outside ourselves is "externalization," and it is the cause of much of the world's unhappiness.

I remember the day when a client whom I will call Walter came in for his appointment with slumped shoulders and a sad expression.

"What's the matter?" I asked Walter. "You look very unhappy today."

"Harville," he said to me as he slumped into the chair, "I feel really terrible. I just don't have any friends."

I was sympathetic with him. "You must be very sad. It's lonely not having any friends."

"Yeah. I can't seem to . . . I don't know. There are just no friends in my life. I keep looking and looking, and I can't find any."

He continued in a morose, complaining voice for some time, and I had to suppress a growing annoyance with his regressed, childlike state. He was locked into a view of the world that went something like this: wandering around the world were people on whose foreheads were stamped the words "Friend of Walter," and his job was merely to search until he found them.

"Walter," I said with a sigh, "do you understand why you don't have any friends?"

He perked up. "No. Tell me!"

"The reason you don't have any friends is that there aren't any friends out there."

His shoulders slumped.

I was relentless. "That's right," I told him. "There are no friends out there. What you want does not exist." I let him stew in this sad state of affairs for a few seconds. Then I leaned forward in my chair and said, "Walter—listen to me! All people in the world are *strangers*. If you want a friend, you're going to have to go out and make one!"

Walter was resisting the idea that creating a lasting friendship takes time and energy. Even though he was responsible and energetic in his job, he retained the childlike notion that all he had to do to establish intimacy was to bump up against the right person. Because he hadn't acknowledged that a friendship evolves slowly over time and requires thoughtfulness, sensitivity, and patience, he had been living a lonely life.

The passive attitude Walter brought to his friendships was even more pronounced in his love life: he couldn't seem to find the ideal woman. Recovering from a painful divorce (in a bitter legal battle, his wife had gotten custody of their son), he was desperately trying to find a new lover.

The specific problem that had plagued Walter in his relationship was that he was caught up in concepts and ideas, not feelings. He hid his vulnerability behind his formidable intellect, which prevented any genuine intimacy. He had been coming to group-therapy sessions for about six months, and at each session he would hear from the group the same message that he had been hearing from his wife—that he wasn't sharing his feelings, that he was emotionally distant. One evening a member of the group finally broke through to him. "When you talk about your pain," she said, "I can't see any suffering. When you hug me, I can't feel your hugs." Walter finally realized that there was some basis to his ex-wife's complaints. "I thought she was just being bitchy and critical," he confessed. "It never occurred to me that maybe she was right. That I could learn something about myself from listening to her."

When Walter had time to absorb this awareness, he developed more enthusiasm for the therapeutic process and was able to work on dismantling his emotional barriers. As he became more alive emotionally, he was finally able to have a satisfying relationship with a new woman friend. During his last session with me, he shared his feelings about therapy. "You know," he said, "it took me two years to learn one simple fact: that, in order to have a good relationship, you have to be willing to grow and change. If I had known this ten years ago, I would still be living with my wife and son."

Walter can't be blamed for wanting to believe that relationships should be easy and "natural." It's human nature to want a life without effort. When we were infants, the world withheld and we were frustrated; the world gave and we were satisfied. Out of thousands of these early transactions, we fashioned a model of the world, and we cling to this outdated model even at the expense of our relationships. We are slow to comprehend that, in order to be loved, we must first become lovers. And I don't mean this in sentimental terms. I don't mean sending flowers, writing love notes, or learning new lovemaking techniques—although any one of these activities might be a welcome part of a loving relationship. To become a lover, we must first abandon the self-defeating tactics and beliefs that I've discussed in the first five chapters and replace them with more constructive ones. We must change our ideas about love relationships, about our partners, and, ultimately, about ourselves.

The Fear of Change

STANDING IN THE way of the changes we need to make in order to have a more satisfying relationship is our fear of change. A fear of change is also basic to human nature. We can feel anxious even when we're undergoing a positive change, such as getting promoted, moving into a new home, or going on vacation. Anything that breaks us out of our comfortable or not-so-comfortable routines sets off an alarm in our old brain. The old brain is alerting us to the fact that we are entering territory that has not been mapped or surveyed, and that danger may lurk around every corner.

I see a wish to cling to well-worn paths even in young children. When our daughter, Leah, was two and a half years old, her younger brother, Hunter, had outgrown the bassinet, and Helen and I decided it was time to move her into a youth bed so that the baby could have the crib. The youth bed had a six-inch rail going halfway down the bed to keep her from rolling off in the middle of the night. The bottom half had no rail. The first morning that Leah awoke in her new bed, we heard her familiar wake-up cry: "Daddy! Daddy! Mommy! Mommy!" We went into her room, and there she was, on her knees, with her hands on the little rail, saying, "Pick me up!"—just as she had done in her old crib with the two-foot sides. We were taken aback by her helplessness. She could easily have climbed over the bar or scooted down a few feet to the part of the bed that had no railing at all. "Leah," I said with enthusiasm, "you can get out of your new bed all by yourself!"

"I can't," she said, sticking out her lower lip. "I'm stuck."

"Leah, look down here," I implored, patting the part of the bed without rails. "You can climb down right here!" She knelt frozen in place. Finally, we had to get up on the bed with her and show her how to do it. With our encouragement, she was able to follow close behind us, overcome her resistance to change, and get out of bed.

I once saw a more dramatic demonstration of paralysis in the face of change while watching the evening news. A local TV station carried a story about a little boy who had been born with severe immune deficiency, and from the moment of birth had to spend his life encased in a plastic bubble, sealed off from life-threatening germs. His devoted mother and father were by his side every day of his life, but they were separated from him by the plastic, and the only way they could touch him was by putting on long sterile gloves that were permanently inserted into the bubble.

Shortly after the boy's fifth birthday, he was given a successful bone-marrow transplant, and after elaborate testing, the doctors decided that his immune system was sufficiently developed to allow him to leave his sterile world. On the day he was scheduled to come out, the bubble was slit open, and his overjoyed mother and father held out their arms to him. This was the first time in their lives that they would be able to kiss and hug their son. But, to everyone's surprise, the boy cowered in the back of the bubble. His parents called to him, but he wouldn't budge. Finally his father had to crawl inside and carry him out. As the little boy looked around the room, he started to cry. Since he had lived all his life in an eight-by-ten-foot enclosure, the room must have looked enormous to him. His parents hugged him and kissed him to reassure him, but he wasn't used to any physical contact, and he arched backward to escape their embraces.

The closing segment of the story, filmed a few days later, showed that the child was growing more comfortable with life outside the bubble. But on the day of his emancipation it was clear that his fear of confronting the unfamiliar was stronger than his desire to explore the world.

That little boy lived for five years inside his bubble. The couples that come to me have been living for two, ten, twenty—as many as forty years inside a restrictive, growth-inhibiting relationship. With so many years invested in habituated behaviors, it's only natural that they should experience a great reluctance to change. After all, I am asking them not only to risk the anxiety of learning a new style of relating, but also to confront the pain and fear that have been bottled up inside them for decades—the reason for their dysfunctional behavior in the first place.

THE PROMISED LAND

TO GIVE YOU some insight into the difficulties of creating a conscious partnership, I want to recount my highly abridged version of the story of Moses and the Promised Land, which I view as a parable of the human psyche.[2] It goes like this:

Many centuries ago, the Israelites were a great tribe of people living in a country near the Mediterranean Sea. There came a drought to their land, and, in order to survive, the Israelites migrated south to Egypt, where the bins were full of grain. But in exchange for the grain they were forced to become slaves to the Egyptians and were subjected to cruel treatment and the dreary labor of making bricks without straw. After more than four hundred years of this meager existence, along came a man named Moses, who said to the Israelites, "Good grief. You're going through painful, repetitive behavior that is getting you nowhere. You've forgotten your heritage. You're not slaves of the house of Egypt, you are the children of the great God Yahweh! The God of all gods is your creator, and you are his special people."

Moses' words stirred a sense of recognition in the Israelites, and they became aware of their mental imprisonment. This made them restless and unhappy—not unlike many of the couples that come to me for counseling.

Lured by a vision of the Promised Land, the Israelites followed Moses. But the Israelites were not prepared for the hardships of the journey, and they had little faith in God's protection. When they came to the first obstacle, the Red Sea, they complained bitterly to Moses: "You got us out of our comfortable huts with a promise of a better way of life. Now our way is blocked by an enormous sea! Was it because there were no graves in Egypt that you brought us to the desert to die? What are we to do?"

Moses himself wasn't sure what to do, but he believed that if he had faith a way would appear. While he was pondering their fate, a huge dust cloud appeared on the horizon. To the Israelites' horror, they realized it was a cloud kicked up by thousands of rapidly approaching Egyptian soldiers coming to capture them and return them to their chains.

At this moment Moses lifted his hand and a strong east wind miraculously parted the Red Sea. Awed by this great miracle, the Israelites summoned their courage, took one last look back at Egypt—the only home they had known—and followed Moses fearfully into the watery chasm. There were walls of water to their right and to their left. When they were safely across the sea, Moses raised his hand once more, and the great sea walls collapsed, drowning all the Egyptians in a rushing torrent of water.

The Israelites had only moments to celebrate their safe passage. As they looked at the new land, they were dismayed to learn that they had arrived on the edge of a barren, trackless desert. Once again they cried out in anguish. "You disrupted our secure lives. You urged us to follow you on a long journey. We were almost captured by the Egyptians. We were nearly drowned in the Red Sea. And now we are lost in a barren land with no food or water!"

Despite their fears, the Israelites had no choice but to continue. They wandered for many months in the foreign land, guided by a pillar of cloud by day and by a pillar of fire by night. They encountered great hardships, but God was merciful and made their burden lighter by performing miracles. Finally the Israelites arrived at the end of the desert. Just over the ridge, said Moses, was the Promised Land. Scouts were sent ahead to survey the territory. But when the scouts returned, they brought more bad news: "The Promised Land really does flow with milk and honey, but it is already occupied! This is the home of the Canaanites, gigantic creatures seven feet tall!" The listening crowd cried out in terror and once again yearned for the safety and security of their life in Egypt.

At this point God spoke to them: "Because you have no faith, and because you keep remembering Egypt, you have to wander in the desert for forty years, until a new generation arises that does not remember the old ways. Only then can you go into the Promised Land." So for forty more years the Israelites camped out in the desert. Children were born, and old people died. Finally a new leader arose to take them into Israel to begin the hard work of wresting the land from the Canaanites.

What can we learn from this familiar story that will help us in our exploration of love relationships? One of the first truths we can learn is the fact that most of us go through our relationships as if we were asleep, engaging in routine interactions that give us little pleasure. Like the Israelites in their four hundred years of servitude to the Egyptians, we have forgotten who we are. In the words of Wordsworth, we come into the world "trailing clouds of glory," but the fire is soon extinguished, and we lose sight of the fact that we are whole, spiritual beings. We live impoverished, repetitious, unrewarding lives and blame our partners for our unhappiness.

The story also teaches us that we are prisoners of the fear of change. When I ask couples to risk new behaviors, they become angry with me. There is a part of them that would rather divorce, break up the family, and divide up all their possessions than acquire a new style of relating. Like the Israelites, they tremble in front of the Red Sea, even though the way lies open to them. Later, when they are in a difficult stretch of the journey, their emotional difficulties seem like hordes of pursuing Egyptians and seven-foot-tall monsters. But, unlike the case of the Israelites, the enemy is within; it's the denied and repressed parts of their being threatening to come to awareness.

The final truth in the story of Moses is that we expect life's rewards to come to us easily and without sacrifice. Just as the Israelites wanted the Promised Land to be the Garden of Eden, God's ready-made gift to Adam and Eve, we want the simple act of falling in love to cure all our ills. We want to live in a fairy tale where the beautiful princess meets the handsome prince and they live happily ever after. But it was only when the Israelites saw the Promised Land as an opportunity, as a chance to create a new reality, that they were allowed to enter. And it is only when we see love relationships as a vehicle for change and self-growth that we can begin to satisfy our unconscious yearnings.

What Lies Ahead

THIS CHAPTER MARKS a turning point in the book. Up until now, I've been describing the unconscious partnership, a relationship characterized by old-brain reactivity. In the rest of the book, I will explain how to transform your partnership into a more conscious, growth-producing relationship. Here's an overview of what lies ahead. Chapter 7 explores an old-fashioned idea, commitment, and explains why it is a necessary precondition for emotional growth. Chapter 8 shows you how to turn your relationship into a zone of safety—a safe and secure environment that rekindles the intimacy of romantic love. Chapter 9 gives you some techniques for gathering more information about you and your partner. Chapter 10 explores the paradoxical idea that the only way to satisfy your childhood needs is to commit yourself wholeheartedly to the satisfaction of your partner's needs. Chapter 11 talks about creating a deep sense of connection by eliminating negativity from your relationship. Chapter 12 is an interview with two couples who are well on the way to creating a conscious partnership. Part III contains a series of exercises that will help you translate all the insights you have gained in Parts I and II into practical, growth-producing behaviors. (It is important that you finish Parts I and II before you do the exercises. They will be more meaningful to you once you understand the theories behind them.)

COMMITMENT

A life allied with mine, for the rest of our lives—
that is the miracle of marriage.
—DENIS DE ROUGEMONT

WHEN A COUPLE walks into my office for their first counseling session, I know little or nothing about them. All I know with any certainty is that they have lost the vital connection between them and are mired somewhere in the power struggle. They might be anywhere along that tortuous path. They might be newlyweds reeling from the shock of discovering that they have married the wrong person. They might be a middle-aged couple trying to cope with the stress of having two careers, teenage children, and a relationship that has degenerated into a series of ongoing battles. They might be an older couple who have lost all feeling for each other and are contemplating a "friendly" divorce. But, whatever their circumstances, I can rightly assume that they have journeyed past the romantic stage of relationship and become embroiled in conflict. They have lost something; they want it back; and they don't know how to get it.

Years ago my approach, and the approach of many of my colleagues, was to wade into the details of their power struggle. In the first few sessions I would determine whether a couple's main problems centered on communication, sex, money, parenting, role expectations, alcohol or drug dependency, and so on. Over the course of the next few months, I would help them gain insight into these problems. An important part of the therapeutic process was teaching them to communicate their feelings more directly: "Tell Mary how you felt when she said that." Or "Turn to George and explain why you hung up the phone on him." At the end of each session, I would help them negotiate a contract that would specify a course of action. George, for example, would agree to give Mary one compliment a day, and Mary would agree to express her anger in words instead of withdrawing in silence. This was standard problem-oriented, conflict-resolving, contractual relationship counseling. Many therapists still employ these techniques.

The couples learned a lot about each other in the time that we spent together, and they became more skilled at communication. But, to my dismay, few of them were able to transcend the power struggle. Instead of arguing about the issues that brought them into therapy, they were now arguing about who had violated which contract first. At times it seemed as though my function as a therapist was merely to quantify and formalize their conflicts.

My work was being supervised in those early days, and I would share my frustration with my adviser. What was I doing wrong? Why were my couples making such slow progress? All I seemed to be doing was giving people something new to fight over. My adviser would smile knowingly and then chide me for having a vested interest in whether or not my clients were able to change. If they wanted to change, he assured me, they would. Perhaps I was confusing my agenda with theirs. My role, he reminded me, was to teach people communication skills, help them gain insight into their problems, and let them go on their way.

It was several years before I discovered that relationship therapy cannot dwell on surface issues like money and roles and sexual incompatibility. Underneath these superficial problems is a much larger issue. As one woman told me, "My husband and I had a bigger fight going on than other therapists could help us with. We couldn't put the problem into words, and they couldn't see it. But it was the fuel that ignited all our smaller conflicts."

This "larger problem" my client was referring to is common to most couples who seek relationship therapy. Many people experience a ruptured connection in childhood. By this I mean that their caregivers failed to satisfy their primal needs, especially their needs for safety and for a secure parent-child bond. Years later, when they have an intimate partner, a similar rupture can begin to split apart their present-day love relationship. They no longer feel a sense of connection with their partner, and oftentimes the partner has experienced the same ruptured connection, causing both parties to spend their time criticizing each other rather than being helpmates and friends. Better communication skills and behavioral contracts are not going to provide the longed-for bridge to connection.

I began to realize that I had to look at relationship therapy in a different way. While mulling it over, I recalled the words of Harry Stack Sullivan, a psychiatrist who wrote *The Interpersonal Theory of Psychiatry* in the 1950s. Sullivan said, "It does not matter so much what happens inside an individual. What matters is what happens between them." I discussed this idea with Helen, and she reminded me that Martin Buber, a Jewish mystical theologian, has a similar philosophy. In his famous book, *I-Thou*, written in the same decade as Stack's *Theory*, Buber made it clear that his interest was not so much on the "I" and the "Thou" as on the hyphen between the two words, which he called the "sacred between." According to Buber, "All life is meeting."

As I reflected on Sullivan and Buber, a light bulb went on in my head. When I worked with couples, I was going to need to shift my attention away from the nature of the conflict between the two individuals to the *quality of the relationship* between them. Only then could I help them create a safe and stable connection. Once they became secure in this new relationship, they could begin to heal the ruptured connection they had experienced decades ago with their caregivers.

Armed with this knowledge, I began to work with couples more intensively, spending less time with the surface phenomena and more time focusing on the ruptured connection between the two parties. As the couples began shifting their focus away from demanding that their existing relationship meet all of their needs to focusing on what their relationship needed from *them*, they began to make remarkable progress.

The Need for Commitment

VIEWING COUPLES FROM this new relationship paradigm, I quickly learned that one of the necessary first steps was to ask both partners to commit to the therapy process. One of the first rules was that they had to agree to come to me for at least twelve consecutive sessions. Barring genuine emergencies, they were to orchestrate their lives so that they came to each and every appointment. The reason I asked for a twelve-session commitment was that I knew from my own experience and from statistical surveys that a majority of couples quit therapy before their fifth appointment. Interestingly, this is about the time it takes for unconscious issues to begin to emerge, which often triggers anxiety. As we know, a tried and true method for reducing anxiety is avoidance. Some couples react to their anxiety by claiming that therapy is making matters worse, and they fire the therapist. Others claim that they "can't find time" to keep their appointments. A twelve-session commitment helps nip this avoidance behavior in the bud. However, this does not mean that twelve sessions are enough for all couples. Those who are the most deeply conflicted might have to work with me for a year or longer. But, at the very least, I had the assurance that the two partners would stay with me long enough to work through their initial resistance, weather their anxiety, and become fully involved in the therapy process.

When you are working on the exercise section of this book, you may also experience a reluctance to complete the process. Some exercises will be easy for you—even fun. But others will give you new information about yourself and challenge you to grow and change. As you do the more demanding exercises, the temptation will be to put the book aside or alter the instructions. It is precisely at these moments that you need to commit yourself wholeheartedly to the process. You will discover that if, before you begin, you make a strong commitment to finish all of the exercises and do them exactly as prescribed, it will be easier to overcome your resistance.

My second order of business with couples is to help them define their relationship vision. Before I hear all the things they don't like about their relationship, I want to know how they would prefer it to be. What would it be like if they lived in the relationship of their dreams? Defining the vision turns their energy away from past and present disappointments toward a more hopeful future. Achieving their vision is the goal of therapy.

It is surprisingly easy for couples to create this vision—even those who are in a great deal of turmoil. To get them started, I ask them to list a series of positive statements beginning with the word "we" that describe the kind of relationship they would like to have. They are to frame these statements in the present tense, as if the future were already here. Here are some examples: "We enjoy each other's company," "We are financially secure," "We spend time together doing things we both enjoy." In just one work session, they are able to define their separate visions, isolate the common elements, and combine these elements into a shared goal. Once the vision is defined, I ask them to read it daily as a form of meditation. Gradually, through the process of repetition, the vision becomes imbedded in their subconscious.

THE COMMITMENT AGREEMENT

AS SOON AS the work on the vision is completed, which is usually about the second or third session, I ask couples to make a second commitment, and that is to stay together for the initial twelve weeks of therapy. The reason for this is obvious: relationship therapy isn't possible if there is no relationship to work on. For three months they are not to separate, nor to end the relationship in a more catastrophic way, such as by suicide, murder, or insanity. (Although separation and divorce are by far the most common ways my clients contemplate terminating their relationships, a significant minority have had a feeling that they might go crazy, and there have been several couples who fantasized about more violent options.) I call the decision to close all four of these escape routes the "Commitment" agreement. When you turn to Part III, you will see that this decision is one of the first exercises you will be asked to perform.[1]

FUSER-ISOLATER DYNAMICS

THE TWO MEMBERS of a love relationship often react to the commitment to stay together in opposite ways. Typically, one partner feels relieved; the other feels threatened. The one who feels relieved is usually the "fuser" in the relationship, the one who grew up with an unsatisfied need for attachment. The one who feels threatened is the "isolater," the one who has an unsatisfied need for autonomy. The reason the fuser is relieved by the commitment is that the guarantee of a stable relationship—if only for three months—reduces the conscious or unconscious fear of abandonment. (For the fuser this fear is always there, but it is more acute in a troubled relationship.) The reason the decision to stay together makes the isolater feel apprehensive is that it closes an important escape hatch, triggering the isolater's archaic fear of absorption. Thus the Commitment Agreement tends to alleviate fear in one partner and exacerbate it in the other.

During the period of this agreement, I try to ease the anxiety of the clients who feel trapped. I remind them that the commitment is only for three months, and at the end of that time they are free to make other decisions. Because we are dealing with a finite amount of time, most people find they can cope. Furthermore, I explain that agreeing to stay together tends to make their partners less clingy or invasive. "One of the reasons your partner is so needy of your attention," I explain to the isolater, "is that you are not emotionally available. When you stay together and work on your relationship, your partner's fear of abandoment will begin to go away and your partner won't feel the same need to chase after you." Ironically, by making an agreement to stay within the relationship for three months, the isolater can end up with more psychic space than before.

A couple's response to the decision to stay together is a fascinating glimpse of more complex fuser-isolater dynamics. Most of the time, two partners in a love relationship push against an invisible boundary in an attempt to satisfy their dual needs for autonomy and attachment. Typically, each individual fixates on one of those needs: one person habitually advances in an effort to satisfy unmet needs for attachment; the other habitually retreats in an effort to satisfy unmet needs for autonomy. Some couples stay locked in this particular dance step for the duration of their relationship.

Others experience a startling reversal. For a variety of reasons, the person who typically advances begins to retreat. The partner who habitually retreats turns around in amazement: where's the pursuer? To everyone's surprise, the isolater suddenly discovers an unmet need for closeness. The pattern is reversed, like the flip-flop of magnetic poles, and now the isolater does the pursuing. It's as if all couples collude to maintain a set distance between them. If one person starts encroaching on the other's territory, the other has to back away. If one person starts vacating the territory, the other has to pursue. As with a pair of magnets with like charges facing each other, there's an invisible force field keeping couples a critical distance apart. There is not enough safety in their relationship for them to feel comfortable being more closely connected.

Noncatastrophic Exits

One couple I worked with had mastered this game of push and pull. Sylvia and Ricardo had so many exits of the type that I refer to as "non-catastrophic" that they were rarely together—an indication of their success at staying apart was that they hadn't made love in over three years. Non-catastrophic exits are often difficult to detect; nonetheless, they can drain a great deal of energy—and intimacy—from a relationship.

As an assignment, I asked Sylvia and Ricardo to spend just one day together doing something they both enjoyed. The very next day, which happened to be a Saturday, they agreed to go for a hike in the country and then go out to dinner.

That morning, just as they were about to leave the house, Sylvia suggested that they invite a mutual friend along on the hike. It had been a long time since they had seen this friend, she reasoned, and, besides, the friend always liked to get out of the city. Ricardo said that sounded like a bad idea. The whole purpose of the day was to spend time together. Why did she always want to louse things up? They argued heatedly for a good hour; then Ricardo gave in. Sylvia called the friend, who was happy to come along. As they waited for him to show up, Sylvia read the paper and straightened the house, while Ricardo disappeared into the den to work his way through a stack of bills.

The friend arrived and the three of them got in the car and drove out to the country. On the drive, the two men sat in the front seat of the car—ostensibly because they had longer legs and needed the legroom—while Sylvia sat in the backseat, reading a book. During the hike, either Sylvia or Ricardo talked with the friend, while the other partner tagged along behind.

When they got back to the city, the friend went home and the couple made plans to go out to dinner. They decided to go to a restaurant that featured live entertainment. At the restaurant, Ricardo suggested they choose a table right in front of the musicians so they could pay more attention to the music. They had dinner and tried to carry on a conversation, but gave up because the music was so loud they couldn't hear each other. They left the restaurant at precisely a quarter to nine so they could be home in time for a favorite TV show. As soon as they entered the house, they automatically poured themselves a couple of drinks and stationed themselves in front of the television. Sylvia went to bed at eleven o'clock (after ritually urging Ricardo not to drink too much), and Ricardo stayed up until one in the morning, happily nursing his Scotch and watching TV. With consummate skill, they had managed to spend the whole day together without a moment of intimacy. Although they didn't realize it, they were living an invisible divorce.

The Invisible Divorce

TO ONE DEGREE or another, most couples who are involved in a power struggle follow a similar pattern: they structure their lives in such a way that true intimacy is virtually impossible.

The way that they do this is often ingenious. By asking my clients a simple question, "What does your spouse do to avoid you?" I have come up with a list of over three hundred different answers. Here's a fragment of that list. According to my informants, their mates were avoiding them by: "reading romance novels," "disappearing into the garage," "camping out on the phone," "worshiping the car," "spending too much time with the kids," "being wedded to the computer," "volunteering for every committee at church," "spending too much time with the boat," "spending time at her mom's," "having an affair," "avoiding eye contact," "memorizing every word of *The New York Times*," "falling asleep on the couch," "being a sports junkie," "coming home late for dinner," "fantasizing while making love," "being sick and tired all the time," "not wanting to be touched," "four Scotches a night," "spending too many evenings at the Rotary," "lying," "refusing to make love," "having sex but not making love," "living on the tennis court," "bulimia," "jogging ten miles a day," "going on weekend fishing trips," "going shopping," "having her own apartment," "daydreaming," "refusing to talk," "smoking marijuana," "playing video games until two in the morning," "talking on the cell phone," "working on the house all the time," "masturbating," "playing his guitar," "keeping separate bank accounts," "picking fights," "reading magazines," "doing crossword puzzles," "refusing to get married," and "going to bars."

The fact that so many couples perforate their relationships with exits raises an obvious question: why do men and women spend so much time avoiding intimacy? There are two very good reasons: anger and fear. Why the anger? In the romantic stage of a relationship, people find it relatively easy to be intimate, because they are filled with the anticipation of wish fulfillment. Their partners seem to be Mommy and Daddy, doctor and therapist all rolled into one. Months or years later, when they come to the realization that their partners are committed to their own salvation, not theirs, they feel betrayed. A tacit agreement has been broken. In retaliation they erect an emotional barricade. In effect, they are saying, "I am angry at you for not meeting my needs." Then they begin systematically to seek pleasure and satisfaction outside the relationship. Like a cow in a pen stretching its neck over a fence to graze on green grass, they look elsewhere for gratification. The husband who stays late at the office even when he has finished the day's work, the wife who spends the entire evening reading to the children while her husband watches TV—both of these individuals are trying to find pleasure that is missing from their relationships.

The other reason couples avoid intimacy is fear, specifically the fear of emotional pain that might replicate what they experienced in childhood. On an unconscious level, many people react to their partners as if they were enemies. Any person—whether parent or partner or next-door neighbor—who is perceived by the old brain to be a source of need gratification and then appears to be withholding that gratification is cataloged by the old brain as a source of pain, and pain raises the specter of death. If your partner does not nurture you and attend to your fundamental needs, a part of you fears that you will die, and it believes that your partner is the one who is allowing this to happen. When a basic lack of nurturing is coupled with an onslaught of verbal and in some cases physical abuse, the partner becomes an even more potent enemy. The unconscious reason some people avoid their partners, therefore, is not that they're looking for greener pastures, but that they are fleeing death. The appropriate image in this case is not the bucolic scene of a cow foraging for food, but that of a terrified lamb running away from a lion.

In most cases the fear of the partner is unconscious. All that couples are aware of is a mild feeling of anxiety around each other and a desire to be with other people or to be involved in other activities. Occasionally the fear is closer to the surface. One client told me that the only time she felt truly safe around her husband was when the two of them were in my office. He had never physically abused her, but their relationship was so filled with conflict that a part of her felt that her life was in danger.

NARROWING YOUR EXITS

WHAT DO I mean by "exits" and why is it important to limit them? Basically, exits are a way to act out our feelings rather than put them into words. As an example, it's easier to stay late at work than to tell your partner that you feel unhappy every time you walk in the front door. You have an understandable reason for staying away—you don't want to feel depressed. Also, it would take a tremendous amount of courage to tell your partner how you really feel about being together. It is far simpler to stay late at work and avoid all the pain and the drama.

But in order to have a satisfying love relationship, both partners need to draw their energy back into the relationship. First of all, it is very difficult to identify what is wrong in a relationship if the participants keep themselves distant and distracted. Even more important, two intimate partners cannot reconnect with each other until they are physically and emotionally available.

To help couples overcome their resistance to narrowing their exits, I rely on the principle known as "graduated change."[2] You've probably discovered this principle in your own life. It is easier to tackle a difficult project if you divide it into small, manageable tasks. You can then rank the tasks in order of difficulty and attack the easy ones first. Graduated change makes the entire project seem more manageable.

When you come to Part III, you will find complete instructions for making a commitment to first narrowing, then closing your exits, but I want to emphasize here that this is an ongoing process and not a one-time event. Bascially, it involves talking with your partner about your feelings rather than acting them out. Here is an overview of how it works:

Imagine two people who are trapped in an unsatisfying relationship. To make up for the emptiness, they have filled their lives with substitute pleasures. Let's focus on the woman's exits. In addition to the responsibilities involved in having a career and raising two children, she has an active social life, a position on the community board, a passion for physical fitness, two music lessons a week, and an addiction to science fiction novels. These activities help reduce her underlying feeling of despair, but they drain vital energy away from her love relationship.

If this woman were to decide to cut back on some of her activities, she would first have to determine which of her numerous involvements could properly be termed an "exit." Like many people, she would probably find a degree of validity in virtually everything she did. When you do the commitment exercise in Part III, you may have this same initial confusion: what is an exit and what is an essential activity or a valid form of recreation? The way to find out is to ask yourself the following question: "Is one of the main reasons I'm doing this activity to avoid spending time with my partner?" Most people know whether or not this is the case. If the answer is "yes," that makes the activity an exit, and a subject for a conversation with your partner.

Let's suppose that this woman has asked herself this question and identified activities that she would be willing to curtail or eliminate. Next, she would rank them according to difficulty and choose the ones that would be easiest for her to give up. For example, she might decide it would be relatively easy to make two changes: jog three days a week instead of five, and read her novels on her lunch hour, not in the evenings, when she could be spending time with her husband. She might also decide that it would be difficult but not impossible for her to find someone to take over her position on the community board. Other changes would be even more difficult. If she were to go ahead and make the two easy changes, however, she would liberate several additional hours a week to devote to her relationship. This would be a good place to start. Other changes, if necessary, could come later.

At the same time that this woman would be eliminating her exits, her husband would be going through a similar process. He, too, would be examining his activities, identifying his exits, asking for a conversation about those exits, and beginning a systematic program of reduction. As a result of this exercise, they would be spending significantly more time together.

As we have said, and it bears repeating, the commitment to closing an exit is not a specific event that occurs at a particular moment. It is a process that may take considerable time, sometimes several months. One reason it takes so long is that it requires a lot of soul searching for people to identify their own exits and the reasons behind them. Then it takes courage to discuss the exits with their partners. But, paradoxically, once the conversation takes place, the exits become much easier to narrow and eventually close. Talking openly about them creates a deeper sense of connection between the two individuals and reduces their need to stay isolated.

The best way for couples to talk about closing their exits is to ask for a dialogue. (See the Imago Dialogue on pages 143–57.) They could start by saying: "One way I act out in our relationship (rather than put my feelings into words) is (thinking about suicide a lot; or fantasizing while we are making love) . . ." "The reason I do this is because (I feel I will never get your attention; or you are passive when we are making love) . . ." And then continue to talk until all the feelings are expressed. Then the other partner does the same until both have put all their unexpressed feelings into words and asked for appropriate changes in behavior. When they do this on a regular basis, the need to act out diminishes and is replaced with deeper feelings of connection.

The reaction to this heightened interaction varies from couple to couple. Some couples enjoy the additional contact.

Others find that commitment to narrowing down and closing off their exits leaves them fewer avenues of escape from painful situations. Although this is not a pleasant outcome, they learn from the exercise nonetheless. They begin to understand why they've been avoiding each other, and this is an important first step in therapy.

TIL DEATH DO US PART

WHEN I LEAD couples through these series of commitments—an agreement to: (1) come to a minimum of twelve therapy sessions, (2) define their relationship vision, (3) stay together for a specified period of time, and (4) gradually commit to closing their exits—I let them know that all of these separate agreements ideally lead to a larger commitment: a decision to join together in a journey that will last the rest of their lives. Although this decision cannot be made at the beginning of therapy, I want couples to know that, in order to obtain maximum psychological and spiritual growth, they need to stay together not for three months or three years or even three decades, but for all of their remaining years. Childhood issues do not present themselves to be resolved in one tidy package. They come to the surface slowly, usually the more superficial ones first. Sometimes a problem has to present itself a number of times before it is even identified as a significant issue. And sometimes a psychological need is so deeply buried that it is only triggered by a crisis or the demands of a particular stage of life. Ultimately it takes a lifetime together for a couple to identify and heal the majority of their childhood wounds.

In a culture where serial monogamy is a way of life, the idea of a permanent commitment to one partner has a quaint, old-fashioned ring to it. The prevalent question of the 1950s—"Can this relationship be saved?"—has now become "*Should* this relationship be saved?" And millions of people decide that the answer is no. In fact, ironically, many people now view divorce as an opportunity for personal growth. It's not within relationship that people grow and change, according to this increasingly popular view, it's when the relationship falls apart. People believe that separation opens their eyes to their self-defeating behaviors and gives them an opportunity to resolve those problems with a new partner. But unless they understand the unconscious desires that motivated their dysfunctional behavior in the first relationship, and learn how to satisfy those desires with the new partner, the second relationship is destined to run aground on the same submerged rocks.

Ironically, the more Helen and I have become involved in a psychological study of love relationships, the more we find ourselves siding with the more conservative proponents of love relationships. We have come to believe that couples who decide to make a lifelong commitment should make every effort to honor their vows to stay together "'til death do us part"—not for moral reasons, but for psychological ones: fidelity and commitment create the feeling of safety that allows couples to work on their unconscious issues and heal their childhood wounds—the unconscious purpose of all committed love relationships.

IN PART III, you will have an opportunity to deepen your commitment to each other and begin a process of growth and change. The suggested time period for completing all eighteen exercises is ten weeks. Dedicating two and a half months of your time to improving your relationship may be all that you need to begin realizing your relationship vision. If you need more time, take it. It is a worthy investment to give love a chance, no matter how long it takes.

CREATING A ZONE OF SAFETY

*Perfect love means to love the one through whom
one became unhappy.*
— SØREN KIERKEGAARD

ONCE A COUPLE has made a commitment to stay together
and work on their relationship, the next logical step is to help
them become allies, not enemies. It's fruitless to take two
people who are angry with each other and try to lead them
along a path of spiritual and psychological growth—they would
spend too much time trying to knock each other off the road. In
order to make the surest and fastest progress toward their relationship vision, they need to become friends and helpmates.

But how is this going to happen? How can couples put an
end to their power struggle when they haven't had the opportunity to resolve their fundamental differences? Love and compassion are supposed to come at the end of the therapeutic
process, not at the beginning.

I found a solution to this dilemma in my studies of the
behavioral sciences. I learned that I could influence the way a

couple feels about each other by helping them artificially reconstruct the conditions of romantic love. When two people treat each other the way they did in happier times, they begin to identify each other as a source of pleasure once again, and this makes them more willing to take part in intensive therapy.

INSIGHT AND BEHAVIORAL CHANGE

YEARS AGO I was resistant to the idea of such a direct approach to changing my clients' behavior. Coming from a psychoanalytic tradition, I was taught that the goal of a therapist was to help clients remove their emotional blocks. Once they had correctly linked feelings they had about their partners with needs and desires left over from childhood, they were automatically supposed to evolve a more rational, adult style of relating.

This assumption was based on the medical model that, once a physician cures a disease, the patient automatically returns to full health. Since most forms of psychotherapy come from psychoanalysis, which, in turn, has its roots in nineteenth-century medicine, the fact that they rest on a common biological assumption is not surprising. But years of experience with couples convinced Helen and me that a medical model is not a useful one for relationship therapy. When a physician cures a disease, the body recovers spontaneously because it relies on genetic programming. Each cell of the body, unless it is damaged or diseased, contains all the information it needs to function normally. But there is no genetic code that governs relationships. Long-term love relationships are a cultural creation imposed on biology. Because people lack a built-in set of social instructions, they can be trapped in unhappy relationships after months or even years of productive therapy. Their emotional blocks may be removed, and they may have insight into the cause of their difficulties, but they have a tendency to still cling to habituated behaviors.

Like many couples therapists, I came to the conclusion that I would have to play an active role in helping couples redesign their relationships. Insight into childhood wounds is a critical element in therapy, but it isn't enough. People also need to learn how to let go of counterproductive behaviors and replace them with more effective ones.

CARING BEHAVIORS

A BEHAVIORAL APPROACH proved especially useful in restoring a couple's sense of love and goodwill. In his book, *Helping Couples Change: A Social Learning Approach to Marital Therapy,* psychologist Richard Stuart presents an exercise for couples that helps them feel more loving toward each other simply by engaging in more loving behaviors. Called "Caring Days," the exercise instructs husbands and wives to write down a list of positive, specific ways their partners can please them. For example, a man might write down: "I would like you to massage my shoulders for fifteen minutes while we watch television." Or "I would like you to bring me breakfast in bed on Sunday morning." The partners are to grant each other a certain number of these caring behaviors a day, no matter how they feel about each other. Stuart discovered that the exercise generated "significant changes in the details of the couple's daily interaction during the first seven days of therapy, a very firm foundation upon which to build subsequent suggestions for change."[1]

To see whether or not this behavioral approach actually worked, I decided to try it out on Harriet and Dennis Johnson. I chose the Johnsons because they were as unhappy with each other as any couple in my practice. One of Harriet's main anxieties was that Dennis was going to leave her. In a desperate effort to hold his interest, she flirted conspicuously with other men. To her dismay, Dennis responded to her flirtatious behavior the same way he responded to just about everything else she did—with stoic reserve. During one session, he mentioned that he was even trying to adjust to the fact that Harriet might one day have an affair. His quiet heroics exasperated his wife, who was trying everything within her power to penetrate his defenses and get him to be more interested in her. Those rare times when she managed to get him riled up, he would behave in typical isolater fashion and flee the house. Most of their fights ended with Dennis's zooming off to safety in his Audi sedan.

To lay the groundwork for the exercise, I asked Dennis and Harriet to tell me how they had treated each other when they were first in love. As I listened to them, I had the strange feeling that they were talking about two different people. I couldn't imagine Dennis and Harriet going on long Sunday bike rides together, leaving work to meet each other at the movies, and calling each other on the phone two or three times a day.

"What would happen," I asked them when I recovered from my amazement, "if you were to go home today and start doing all those things again? What if you were to treat each other the same way you did when you were courting?" They looked at me with puzzled expressions.

"I think I would feel very uncomfortable," Dennis said after a moment's reflection. "I don't like the idea of acting differently from the way I feel. I would feel . . . dishonest. I don't have the same feelings toward Harriet that I used to, so why should I treat her as if I did?"

Harriet agreed. "It would feel like we were playacting," she said. "We may not be happy, but at least we try to be honest with each other."

When I explained that taking part in the experiment might help them over their impasse, they agreed to give it a try, despite their initial objections. I carefully explained the exercise to them. They were to go home, make their lists, and volunteer to give each other three to five of those behaviors a day. The behaviors were to be gifts. They were to view them as an opportunity to pleasure each other, not as a bartering tool. And, most important of all, they weren't to keep score. They were to focus only on the giving end of the equation. They left the office promising to give the exercise an honest effort.

At the beginning of their next appointment, Dennis reported on the results of the experiment. "I think you're really on to something, Harville," he said. "We did what you asked us to do, and today I feel a lot more hopeful about our relationship."

I asked him to tell me more.

"Well, the day after our appointment, I found myself driving around town in a black mood," Dennis volunteered. "I can't even remember what made me feel so down. Anyway, I decided that it was as good a time as any to do what you asked, so I stopped off at a variety store and bought Harriet some flowers. That was one of the requests on her list. So I gritted my teeth and picked out some daisies, because I remembered she always liked daisies. The clerk asked me if I wanted a note card and I said, 'Why not?' I remember saying to myself, 'We're paying Dr. Hendrix a lot of money to make things better, so I'd better do this all the way.' When I came home, I signed the card 'I love you.'" He paused for a moment. "The thing that surprised me, Harville, was that, as I handed Harriet the flowers, I really did care for her."

"And when I read the card," Harriet added, "tears came to my eyes. It's been so long since he's told me he loved me." They went on to describe all the other things that they had done to please each other. She had cooked him pot roast and potato pancakes, his favorite dinner. He had agreed to curl up together in bed as they fell asleep instead of turning his back to her. She had gotten out her yarn and needles and started knitting him a sweater vest. As they were recounting these events, there seemed to be remarkably little tension between them. When they left the office, I noticed that as Dennis helped Harriet on with her coat she smiled and said, "Thank you, honey." It was a little thing, but it was the kind of pleasurable give-and-take that had been so absent in their relationship.

I asked Dennis and Harriet to continue to give each other caring behaviors, and at each session they reported a gradual improvement in their relationship. They not only were treating each other more kindly, but were also more willing to explore the issues that underlay their discontent. They spent less of their time in my office complaining about each other and more time exploring the childhood issues that were the reasons for their unhappiness in the first place.

Because Stuart's exercise proved so helpful for Dennis and Harriet, I used it as a model for an expanded exercise that I labeled "Reromanticizing" because it effectively restored the conflict-free interactions of romantic love.[2] I introduced the Reromanticizing exercise to my other clients, and, almost without exception, when couples began artificially to increase the number of times a day that they *acted* lovingly toward each other, they began to feel safer and more loving. This intensified the emotional bond between them, and as a result they made more rapid progress in their therapy.

I will explain the details of the Reromanticizing exercise more fully in Part III. When you carefully follow the directions, you, too, will experience an immediate improvement in the climate of your relationship. The exercise is not designed to resolve your deep-seated conflicts, but it will re-establish feelings of safety and pleasure and set the stage for increased intimacy.

WHY DOES IT WORK?

WHY IS THIS simple exercise so effective? The obvious reason is that, through daily repetitions of positive behaviors, your old brain begins to perceive your partner as "someone who nurtures me." Painful memories are overlaid with positive transactions, and your partner is no longer categorized as a bringer of death but as a wellspring of life. This opens the way for intimacy, which is only possible in a context of pleasure and safety.

But there are other, subtler reasons the exercise works so well. One is that it helps people erode the infantile belief that their partners can read their minds. During romantic love, people operate out of the erroneous belief that their partners know exactly what it is that they want. When their partners fail to satisfy their secret desires, they assume that they are deliberately depriving them of pleasure. This makes them want to deprive their partners of pleasure. The Reromanticizing exercise prevents this downward spiral by requiring couples to tell each other exactly what pleases them, decreasing their reliance on mental telepathy.

Another consequence of the exercise is that it defeats the tit-for-tat mentality of the power struggle. When couples take part in the Reromanticizing exercise, they are instructed to pleasure each other on an independent schedule; they mete out a prescribed number of caring behaviors a day, regardless of the behavior of their partners. This replaces the natural tendency to hand out favors on a quid pro quo basis: You do this nice thing for me, and I'll do that nice thing for you. Most relationships are run like a commodities market, with loving behaviors the coin in trade. But this kind of "love" does not sit well with the old brain. If John rubs Martha's shoulders in the hope that she will let him spend the day going fishing, a built-in sensor in Martha's head goes: "Look out! Price tag attached. There is no reason to feel good about this gift, because I'll have to pay for it later." Unconsciously she rejects John's attentions, because she knows that they were designed for his benefit, not hers. The only kind of love that her old brain will accept is the kind with no strings attached: "I will rub your shoulders because I know that you would like it." The back rub has to come as a "gift."

This need to be "gifted" comes straight out of our childhood. When we were infants, love came without price tags. At least for the first few months of our lives, we didn't have to reciprocate when we were patted or rocked or held or fed. And now, in adulthood, a time-locked part of us still craves this form of love. We want to be loved and cared for without having to do anything in return. When our partners grant us caring behaviors independent of our actions, our need for unconditional love appears to be satisfied.

A third benefit of the exercise is that it helps people see that what pleases them is the product of their unique makeup and life experience and can be very different from what pleases their partners. This reinforces the fact that they are separate people. Often, partners in a relationship cater to their own needs and preferences, not to each other's. For example, a woman I once worked with went to a great deal of trouble to give her husband a surprise fortieth-birthday party. She invited all his friends, cooked his favorite foods, borrowed a stack of his favorite 1960s rock-and-roll records, and organized lively party games. During the party, her husband acted as if he were enjoying himself, but a few weeks later, in the middle of a counseling session, he got up the courage to tell his wife that he had been secretly miserable. "I've never liked having a fuss made about my birthday," he told her. "You know that. And especially not my fortieth birthday. What I really wanted to do was spend a quiet evening at home with you and the kids. Maybe have a homemade cake and a few presents. *You're* the one who likes big noisy parties!"

His wife had taken the Golden Rule, "Do unto others as you would have others do unto you," a little too literally. She had unwittingly given her husband a party that suited her tastes, not his. The Reromanticizing exercise circumvents this problem by training couples to "Do unto others as *they* would have you do unto *them.*" This turns their random caring behaviors into "target" behaviors, behaviors that are designed to satisfy their partners' unique desires.

When couples regularly give each other these target behaviors, they not only improve the superficial climate of their relationship, they also begin to heal old wounds. I have an example from my personal history. Helen and I faithfully perform the same exercises that I assign my clients, and the Reromanticizing exercise is one that we have done so many times it has become integrated into our relationship: it's something we do without thinking. One of the things that I ask Helen to do for me is to turn down the covers before we go to bed. This request comes from an experience I had over forty years ago. After my mother died, I was taken in by my sister, Maize Lee. She was only eighteen at the time and recently married, but she did a wonderful job of caring for me. One of the things that touched me most was that she would always find time to go into my room before bedtime, turn down my covers, and put out a glass of orange juice or milk for me to drink. Today, when Helen turns down the covers for me before I climb into bed, I remember Maize Lee and all that she did for me, and I feel very loved indeed. On a deep level, this simple action is re-creating the vital parent-child bond. I feel secure again, and the injury of my childhood is repaired in an adult relationship that has become a zone of love and safety.

THE SURPRISE LIST

AFTER INTRODUCING THE Reromanticizing exercise to scores of couples, I began to notice a curious phenomenon: the positive value of doing this exercise seemed to flatten out after a few months. The couples were faithfully following the instructions, but they were no longer experiencing the deep pleasure they had when they began doing the exercise. It occurred to me that I needed to build the concept of "random reinforcement" into the exercise. Random reinforcement, one of the principles of behavioral science, is the idea that a pleasurable action loses its effectiveness if it's repeated with predictable regularity. For example, if your partner brings you coffee in bed every morning, it no longer feels as special as it did when it was an occasional act, or "treat." Random rewards, on the other hand, create an air of uncertainty and expectancy that increases their impact on the receiver. This concept was discovered accidentally by a group of scientists who were training laboratory animals by rewarding them with treats. One day the apparatus that dispensed the treats malfunctioned, and the animals were not rewarded for their efforts. The next day the machine was repaired and the regular reward schedule was resumed. To the trainers' surprise, the animals were even more highly motivated to perform than before. The fact that the reward had become unpredictable improved their performance.

The phenomenon of random reinforcement can easily be observed in daily life. Most husbands and wives give each other presents on special occasions like birthdays and Christmas and anniversaries. These gifts are so customary that they are almost taken for granted. Although the presents may be enjoyed, they don't carry the same emotional impact as a present that is given as a total surprise. A behaviorist would say that the reason routine gifts aren't as exciting is that the "psychoneurological system has become desensitized to predictable, repetitive pleasure." The same principle applies to the Reromanticizing exercise. When couples become locked into a particular kind of caring behavior—for example, when they give each other back rubs every night before bed or a bouquet of flowers every Saturday—they begin to derive less pleasure from them. A curve ball needs to be thrown in now and then to pique their interest.

To add this element of suspense, I created the idea of the Surprise List exercise. These were caring behaviors above and beyond those requested by either partner. Each would generate a list by paying close attention to their partner's wishes and dreams. A woman who causally mentioned to her husband that she liked a dress she saw in a store window might be delighted to find that very dress—in the correct size—hanging in her closet. A man who expressed his interest in Gilbert and Sullivan might open the mail and find a love note from his partner and two tickets to a Gilbert and Sullivan opera. When couples added unanticipated pleasures like these to their regular caring behaviors, the beneficial effect of the exercise continued on a gentle rise.

THE FUN LIST

AS TIME WENT on, I made another addition to the Reromanticizing process. I asked couples to engage in several high-energy, fun activities a week. These were to be spontaneous, one-on-one activities like wrestling, tickling, massaging, showering together, jumping up and down, or dancing. Competitive sports like tennis qualified only if a couple could play the game without stirring up tension.

The reason I added more exuberant activities to the list was that most people tend to choose fairly passive activities as their caring behaviors; they have forgotten how to have fun together. As soon as I noted this trend, I surveyed all my clients and found that they spent, on average, about ten minutes a week playing and laughing together. Improving this bleak statistic became a priority for me. I knew that when couples have fun together they identify each other as a source of pleasure and safety, which intensifies their emotional bond. When the old brain registers a positive flow of energy, it knows that the person associated with the energy is connected to life and safety, and the two people begin to connect with each other on a deeper unconscious level.

The Fear of Pleasure

WITH THE ADDITION of the Surprise List and the Fun List, I now had a useful tool to help couples begin therapy on a positive note. But, like any exercise that leads to personal growth, this simple exercise was often met with resistance. A certain degree of resistance is to be expected. When a husband and wife have been treating each other like enemies for five years, it's going to feel strange to start writing love notes again. The exercise is going to feel artificial and contrived (which, of course, it is), and to the old brain anything that is not routine and habituated feels unnatural. The only way to lessen this automatic resistance is to repeat a new behavior often enough so that it begins to feel familiar and therefore safe.

A deeper source of resistance to the exercise, however, is a paradoxical one—the *fear* of pleasure. On a conscious level, we go to great lengths to seek happiness. Why, then, should we be afraid of it? To make sense of this reaction, we need to remember that the sensation of being fully alive is deeply pleasurable. When we were young children, our life energy was boundless and we experienced intense joy. But some of our pleasure was curtailed by our caregivers so that we could be safe and conform to social norms: "Girls don't yell and run." "Don't jump on the couch." "Be careful! Come down from that tree." "You're making too much noise." But our fun was also cut short because it threatened the repressed state of our caregivers. They had long given up diving into the lake, rolling down the hill, skipping down the sidewalk, and jumping up and down for joy. As these limits were imposed on us, sometimes in punitive ways, we began to make an unlikely association between pleasure and pain. If we experienced certain kinds of pleasure or perhaps a high degree of pleasure, we were ignored, reprimanded, or punished. On an unconscious level, this negative stimulus triggered the fear of death. Eventually we limited our own pleasure so that we could reduce our anxiety. We learned that to be fully alive was dangerous.

However, applying the strange logic of children, we didn't blame our parents or society for equating pleasure with pain; it simply appeared to be our lot in life. We told ourselves, "My parents limited my pleasure, so I must not have been worthy of it." It was somehow safer to believe that we were intrinsically undeserving than to believe that our parents were incapable of meeting our needs or had deliberately diminished our happiness. Gradually we developed a built-in prohibition against pleasure.

People who grew up experiencing a great deal of repression tend to have a particularly hard time with the Reromanticizing exercise. They have difficulty coming up with any requests for caring behaviors, or they sabotage their partners' efforts to carry them out. For example, one of my clients, a man with low self-esteem, wrote down on his list that he would like his partner to give him one compliment a day. This was easy for his partner to do because she thought he had a lot of admirable qualities. But when she tried to give him a daily compliment, he would immediately contradict her statement or qualify it to the point that it became meaningless. If she were to say something like "I liked the way you were talking to our son, Robbie, last night," he would nullify it with a self-criticism: "Yeah. Well, I should do that more often. I never spend enough time with him." Hearing anything good about himself was ego-dystonic, incompatible with his self-image. His determination to maintain this negative opinion was so strong that I had to train him to respond mechanically to his partner's kind remarks with a "thank you" and leave it at that.

There was one man in my practice whose resistance to the Reromanticizing exercise took a different form: he just couldn't seem to understand the instructions. "Dr. Hendrix," he told me after the second session devoted to an explanation of the exercise, "I just don't get the hang of this. Now, what is it that I'm supposed to do?" I went over the instructions once again, making sure they were clearly understood. I knew, however, that his lack of comprehension was a cover-up for his inability to ask for something pleasurable. To help him over his emotional roadblock, I told him that, even though it appeared that asking his wife to do nice things for him was solely for his benefit, it was also a way for his wife to learn how to become a more loving person—which happened to be true. When it was put in this less self-serving context, he quickly understood the exercise. He was able to call a truce with the demon inside of him that told him he was not worthy of love. He took out a pencil and in a matter of minutes came up with a list of twenty-six things he would like her to do for him.

Isolaters often have a difficult time with this exercise. They want to cooperate, but they just can't think of anything their partners can do for them; they don't seem to have any needs or desires. What they are really doing is hiding behind the psychic shield they erected as children to protect themselves from overbearing parents. They discovered early in life that one way to maintain a feeling of autonomy around their intrusive parents was to keep their thoughts and feelings to themselves. When they deprived their parents of this valuable information, their parents were less able to invade their space. After a while, many isolaters do the ultimate disappearing act and hide their feelings from themselves. In the end, it is safest not to know.

It is often the case, as I've mentioned before, that isolaters unwittingly re-create the struggle of their childhood by marrying fusers, people who have an unsatisfied need for intimacy. This way they perpetuate the conflict that consumed them as children—not as an idle replay of the past, or a neurotic addiction to pain, but as an unconscious act aimed at the resolution of fundamental human needs. When a fuser-isolater couple does this exercise, it results in a predictable dichotomy. The isolater painfully ekes out one or two requests, while the fuser furiously scribbles a long list of "I wants." To the casual observer it appears that the isolater is a self-sufficient individual with few needs and the fuser has limitless desires. The fact of the matter is that both individuals have the identical need to be loved and cared for. It's just that one of them happens to be more in touch with those feelings than the other.

Whatever a person's reason for resisting this exercise, my prescription is the same: "Keep doing the exercise exactly as described. Even if it causes you anxiety, keep it up. Do it harder and more aggressively than before. Eventually your anxiety will go away." Given enough time and enough repetition, your brain can adjust to a different reality. The person with low self-esteem can gradually carve out a more positive identity. The isolater has a chance to discover that sharing secret desires does not compromise his or her independence. The fear of new behaviors gives way to the pleasure they stimulate, and they begin to be associated with safety and life. The caring-behavior exercise becomes a comfortable, reliable tool for personal growth.

INSIGHT AND BEHAVIORAL CHANGE

THIS CARING-BEHAVIOR exercise, and several other exercises that you will read about in coming chapters, have convinced me that insight and behavioral change make powerful allies. It is not enough for partners to understand the unconscious motivations that they bring to their relationship; insight alone does not heal childhood wounds. Nor is it sufficient to introduce behavioral changes into a relationship without the couples understanding the reasons behind them. In either case, the couples experience only limited growth. Experience has taught me that the most effective form of therapy is one that combines both schools of thought. As you learn more about your unconscious motivations and transform these insights into supportive behaviors, you can create a more conscious and ultimately more rewarding relationship.

INCREASING YOUR KNOWLEDGE
OF YOURSELF AND YOUR PARTNER

And ye shall know the truth,
and the truth shall make you free.

—JOHN 8:32

ALTHOUGH WE ALL agree in principle that our partners have their own points of view and their own valid perceptions, at the emotional level we are reluctant to accept this simple truth. We like to believe that the way we see the world is the way the world is. When our partners disagree with us, it is tempting to think that they are ill-informed or have a distorted point of view. How else could they be so wrong?

Some people are particularly entrenched in their private view of the world. This was especially true for a client of mine named Gene. The director of a successful corporation, he was very bright and accustomed to dominating those around him with the sheer force of his intellect. He totally eclipsed his wife, a gentle and good-hearted woman named Judy, who would sit beside him with her chin drawn in and her shoulders hunched forward, looking like a chastened child.

One of my objectives during their initial therapy sessions was to bolster Judy up so that she would have enough courage to express her opinions in front of her imposing husband. (In psychology textbooks, this is called "implementing the therapeutic balance.") Normally, as soon as she would utter a few sentences, Gene would pounce on her and refute whatever she had to say. "That's a lie! That's absolutely not true," he would blurt out. Then he would launch into a defense of his position. His summation was invariably the same: "This is not just my opinion, Dr. Hendrix. It happens to be the literal truth." And I could see that he truly believed that his point of view was the only valid one, that he alone had a grip on reality.

It was pointless for me to try to convince him verbally of the narrowness of his vision; he would have turned our conversation into a forensic debate, and I had no doubt who would win. At the beginning of our eighth session together, however, I had a sudden inspiration. Judy had just ventured an opinion about a recent encounter between Gene and his father. Apparently she and Gene and her father-in-law had gone out to dinner together, and Gene's father had said something to Gene that had wounded his pride. Judy's perception was that Gene's father had been trying to give him some constructive criticism; Gene's perception was that his father had been cruel and spiteful. "You are wrong again, Judy," Gene intoned. "How could you be so blind?"

I interrupted their conversation and told them that I wanted them to put their difference of opinion aside for a moment and spend ten minutes listening to a classical music tape that I happened to have in the office, a recording of Franck's Violin Sonata in A. I slipped the tape into the cassette player and invited them to listen to the music and pay attention to any images that came to their minds. They both were a little puzzled by my request, and I sensed an impatience in Gene: how was listening to music going to help them resolve their difficulties? But by now Gene had enough confidence in me to allow me to run the therapy sessions; he figured there must be some reason for my unusual suggestion.

The three of us sat back and listened to the music. I stopped the tape after the second movement and, knowing full well that I was walking into a minefield, casually asked Judy and Gene what they thought of the music.

Gene spoke first. "What a lovely piece," he said. "It was so lyrical. I especially enjoyed the violin part in the first movement." He hummed several bars, and I was impressed by his ability to remember the notes and to hum them on key. Among his numerous attributes, he apparently had perfect pitch. "Such a beautiful melody," he continued. "For some reason, the image that came to my mind was of the ocean. There were qualities to the music that reminded me of a Debussy sonata. Even though Franck is less impressionistic, there is the same sensuous texture. It must be the French heritage."

I turned to Judy and asked for her opinion.

"That's funny," she said, in a voice that was so low I had to strain to hear her, "I had a different feeling about the music." She burrowed deeper into the leather armchair, showing no desire to elaborate. How could she measure up to her husband's learned critique?

"Tell me what you saw in it, Judy," I urged. "I'd like to know what you were thinking, too."

"Well," she said, clearing her throat, "I guess the music seemed kind of stormy to me. Especially the piano part. All those chords, I got the image of storm clouds and wind—and a darkening sky."

"Honey, what makes you think it was so dramatic?" Gene asked, in the patronizing tone of voice he reserved for his wife. "I almost fell asleep, it was so soothing. Listen to it more closely, Judy, and you'll see what I mean. It has to be one of the most lyrical pieces of music ever written. Don't you agree, Dr. Hendrix?" (Like many people, he spent a great deal of time trying to get his therapist to see his side of the story.)

"Yes, I do, Gene," I obliged him. "I sensed a gentleness to the music, a romantic quality that at times was very soothing." Then I turned to Judy and said, "But I also agree with you, Judy. There were parts that seemed to have a real sense of passion and drama. I guess I'm agreeing with both of you." Gene started drumming his fingers on the arm of his chair.

"I have an idea," I said. "Why don't the two of you listen to the tape again, but this time I want you to see if you can find evidence that supports your partner's point of view. Gene, I want you to look for the dramatic tension; Judy, see if you can find the lighter, poetic touches."

I rewound the tape, and they listened to the piece for the second time. Once again I asked for their opinions. This time both Gene and Judy heard qualities in the sonata that had previously eluded them. Gene made an interesting observation. The first time he had listened to the sonata, he said, he had been instinctively drawn to the violin. When he forced himself to pay more attention to the piano, he could see why he and Judy had had such different initial reactions. "There is a lot of tension to the music," he conceded, "especially in those piano arpeggios in the beginning of the second movement. That was a beautiful passage that slipped by me the first time through. My mind must have been on something else. I can see how someone might think the music was stormy." Judy, meanwhile, had been able to understand Gene's first impression. The music hadn't seemed so overwhelming to her the second time around. "There are some lovely, quiet parts," she said. "In fact, the whole first movement is really quite subdued."

By listening to the music from each other's point of view, they had learned that the sonata was a richer piece of music than either of them had first perceived. There were serene passages and dramatic passages; it was complex, multifaceted.

"I wonder what would happen if we could talk to the performers and get their impressions," wondered Gene, "and then talk to a music historian? I bet each person could add a great deal to the music. The sonata would acquire more and more depth."

I couldn't have been more pleased with the way this discussion was going; my gamble had paid off. "That's exactly what I hoped you would see," I said to him. "That's the whole point of this exercise. If the two of you would look at everything in the same open-minded way, you would realize two things: first, that each of you has a valid point of view; second, that reality is larger and more complex than either of you will ever know. All you can do is form impressions of the world—take more and more snapshots, each time aiming for a closer approximation of the truth. But one thing is certain. If you respect each other's point of view and see it as a way to enrich your own, you will be able to take clearer, more accurate pictures."

Given their new spirit of cooperation, I guided Gene and Judy back through a discussion of Gene's encounter with his father. Gene was able to entertain the idea that there had been some goodwill behind his father's criticism. Perhaps he had been screening out his father's good intentions, just the way he had screened out the piano part to the Franck sonata. Judy, in turn, gained a greater appreciation for the long-term tension between father and son. When she mentally reviewed the dinner conversation in the context of the troubled history between Gene and his father, she could understand why her husband had been so upset by what had at first seemed to her to be a casual, well-intentioned remark. All of a sudden they had binocular, not monocular, vision.

HIDDEN SOURCES OF KNOWLEDGE

WHEN YOU ACCEPT the limited nature of your own perceptions and become more receptive to the truth of your partner's perceptions, a whole world opens up to you. Instead of seeing your partner's differing views as a source of conflict, you realize that they are a source of knowledge: "What are you seeing that I am not seeing?" "What have you learned that I have yet to learn?" Relationships give you the opportunity to be continually schooled in your own reality and in the reality of another person. Every one of your interactions contains a grain of truth, a sliver of insight, a glimpse into your hiddenness and your wholeness. As you add to your growing fund of knowledge, you are creating reality love, a love based on the emerging truth of yourself and your partner, not on romantic illusion.

In chapter 6 we discussed a number of specific areas in which you can increase your knowledge. You have the opportunity to become more aware of the hidden agenda you bring to your relationship, of your disowned character traits, of your partner's inner world, and of the healing potential of your relationship. As you can see from this brief look at Judy and Gene's relationship, acquiring this information depends to a large degree on your willingness to value and learn from each other's perceptions. Once both of you demonstrate a desire to expand your individual conceptions of the world, the details of everyday life become a gold mine of information.

An especially good area to mine for this hidden information is your spoken and unspoken criticisms of your partner: "You never come home on time." "I can never lean on you." "Why don't you think of me for a change?" "You are so selfish." At the time you are making these statements, you believe them to be accurate descriptions of your partner. But the truth of the matter is that they are often descriptions of parts of yourself.

Take a look at this example to see how much information can be gleaned from one chronic, emotional complaint. Let's suppose that a woman routinely criticizes her partner for being disorganized. "You are always disorganized! I can never depend on you!" When her partner demands some specific examples, she retorts, "You are terrible about planning for vacations. You always forget the essentials when we go camping. You never remember the kids' birthdays. And you always leave the kitchen a jumbled mess when you cook!" Not surprisingly, the man's automatic response to this barrage of accusations is a blanket denial followed by a countercriticism: "That's not true. You're exaggerating. *You're* more disorganized than I am!"

How can this heated argument be turned into useful information? First, the man would learn something about himself if he assumed that his partner's criticism contained an element of truth; most people are experts at spotting their mates' Achilles' heel. Unfortunately, most people also tend to deliver this valuable information in an accusatory manner, immediately arousing the partners' defenses. If this man were able to override his defensive response, he would be able to see that there are indeed many areas of his life in which he is not well organized; the pain of hearing a criticism is largely due to its accuracy. If he could accept the truth in his partner's remarks, he would become more aware of a significant disowned trait. That would eliminate his need to project this trait back onto his wife, and it would also give him the data he needed in order to grow and change.

This observation about the hidden information contained in a criticism can be expressed as a general principle:

Principle 1: Most of your partner's criticisms of you have some basis in reality.

What else could the couple learn from the above interchange? If the woman had an open mind, she might be able to gain some valuable information about her own childhood wounds. She could do this by following a simple procedure. First, she could write her criticism of her partner on a piece of paper: "You are always so disorganized!" Then she could answer the following questions:

How do I feel when my partner acts this way?

What thoughts do I have when my partner acts this way?

What deeper feelings might underlie these thoughts and feelings?

Did I ever have these thoughts and feelings when I was a child?

By going through this simple analytical process, she could determine whether or not her partner's behavior brought back any strong memories from her childhood. Let's suppose the exercise helps the woman discover that her parents were always disorganized and had little time or energy to pay attention to her needs. Not surprisingly, when her partner acts in a similar manner, she is filled with the same fears she had as a child. Buried in her criticism of her partner, therefore, is a plaintive cry from childhood: "Why can't someone take care of me?"

This leads us to a second general principle:

Principle 2: Many of your repetitious, emotional criticisms of your partner are disguised statements of your own unmet needs.

There is another piece of information that can be derived from criticism, one that usually requires a great deal of soul-searching. It is possible that the woman's criticism of her partner is a valid statement about herself. In other words, all the while she is berating her mate for his lack of organization, she may be as disorganized as he is. To find out if this is true, she could ask herself a general question: "In what way is my criticism of my partner also true of me?" She should keep in mind that the way in which she is disorganized may be quite different from her partner's M.O. She may keep an immaculate kitchen, for example, and be a whiz at planning vacations—the areas where he has difficulties—but have a hard time prioritizing her tasks at work or managing the family budget. With this new insight, she would be able to determine whether or not she was attempting to disown a negative part of herself by externalizing it, projecting it onto her partner, and then criticizing him for it. If she found that to be true, she would have the information she needs to allow herself to separate her own negative traits from her partner's: "I am disorganized in this specific way; my partner is disorganized in that specific way." In psychological terms, she would be "owning" and "withdrawing" her projections. Jesus said it more poetically: "Cast out the log in your own eye so that you can see the mote in your brother's eye."

This leads us to a third observation about criticism:

Principle 3: Some of your repetitive, emotional criticisms of your partner may be an accurate description of a disowned part of yourself.

Often, when a recurring criticism is not a description of a disowned part of the self, it is a description of another unconscious aspect—the lost self. If this woman were to scrutinize her behavior and find herself to be supremely well organized in all aspects of her life, her criticism of her husband might be an unconscious wish to be *less* organized—to be more relaxed, flexible, and spontaneous. When she criticizes her husband for behaving in a carefree manner, she may be secretly resenting his freedom. When partners criticize each other for being too energetic, too sexy, too playful, too dedicated to their work, they may be identifying an undeveloped or repressed area of their own psyches. Now we have our fourth and final principle:

Principle 4: Some of your criticisms of your partner may help you identify your own lost self.

In the next chapter, in an exercise called the Behavior Change Request Dialogue, I will show you how to take the knowledge that you can glean from your mutual criticisms and convert it into an effective, growth-producing process.

Understanding Your Partner's Inner World

AS WE HAVE seen, examining your criticisms of your partner turns out to be an excellent way to gather information about yourself. How can you increase your knowledge of your *partner's* inner world? The answer is through improved channels of communication. Throughout the course of your relationship, your partner has given you thousands of hours of testimony about his or her thoughts and feelings and wishes, but you have in turn registered only a fraction of this information. In order to deepen your understanding of your partner's subjective reality, you need to train yourself to listen and communicate more effectively.

To do this, it helps to know something about semantics, the science of describing what words mean. Even though you and your partner speak the same language, each of you dwells in an idiosyncratic world of private meanings. Growing up in different families with different life experiences has given you separate lexicons. As a trivial example, let's explore what the simple words "Let's play tennis" might mean in two different families. In family A, the full, unspoken definition of this phrase is: "Let's grab any old racket that happens to be lying around, walk to the local park, and lob the ball back and forth across the net until someone wants to quit. Rules are secondary; it's the exercise that counts." In family B, however, "Let's play tennis" has quite a different meaning. It means: "Let's reserve an indoor court at the private club, get out our two-hundred-dollar rackets, and then play tough, competitive tennis until one player is clearly the winner." Mark, raised in family A, is going to be taken aback by the aggressiveness and determination that his wife, Susan, raised in family B, brings to the game.

A less trivial example would be the associations that Mark and Susan might bring to the phrase "Let's talk about it."

Assume that in Susan's family "Let's talk about it" means "All the adults sit around the table and calmly and rationally discuss their various points of view until they come up with an agreed-upon plan of action." In Mark's family the same words mean "This is a topic that we will talk about briefly and then shelve until further notice." Underlying Mark's family's more casual approach is the philosophy that even the most difficult problems work themselves out over time. When Susan proposes to Mark that they "talk about" the fact that their son is getting poor marks at school, and Mark says a few sentences and then switches on the TV, she feels irate. Mark, in turn, is going to be stunned when Susan storms out the door and does not return for several hours. What did he do wrong? What he did wrong was assume that he and his wife shared the same unspoken language.

DENIAL

BESIDES THE PROBLEM of idiosyncratic language, there are other roadblocks to communication. Perhaps the most common mechanism is denial: you simply refuse to believe what your partner has to say. A recent example comes to mind. Joseph and Amira came to one of my weekend workshops. Joseph is a forty-year-old journalist, Amira a twenty-five-year-old television actress. They are both attractive, accomplished people. On Saturday evening, about midway through the seminar, the key source of their conflict began to emerge. During a discussion period, Joseph volunteered that he desperately wanted to start a family. "I'm going to be old enough to be a grandfather before I'm a father," he lamented. But Amira wanted to wait. Her career was just getting off the ground, and she didn't want to take time off to have a baby until her mid-thirties. She protested that she had told Joseph before they got married that she wasn't interested in starting a family until much later. "I was very clear about it in my own head, and I told him over and over again. But he didn't listen to me. I should have worn a T-shirt with big block letters: *I'm not ready to have children.*" Joseph acknowledged that Amira had indeed made her position clear to him, but he had convinced himself that she didn't mean what she said. "I was sure that she was only kidding herself. How could acting a bit part on a soap opera be more important than being a mother?" Satisfying his urgent need to have children was so important to him that he had discounted his wife's priorities.

We all have a number of these subterranean "hot spots" in our relationships, places where our expectations of our partners collide with reality. When our partners behave in ways that deviate from our idealized view of them, we have an arsenal of weapons to help us maintain our illusions. We can condemn them: "You are a bad (ungrateful, insensitive, boorish, stupid, spiteful, uninformed, crass, unenlightened, etc.) person for feeling that way." We can "educate" them: "You don't really feel that way. What you really feel is . . ." We can threaten them: "Unless you change your mind, I'm going to . . ." We can ignore them: "Uh-huh. Very interesting. As I was saying . . ." And we can analyze them: "The reason you have such unacceptable thoughts and feelings is that years ago your mother . . ." In all of these responses, we are trying to diminish our partners' sense of self and replace it with our own, self-serving illusion. Unfortunately, this is exactly what happened to our partners in childhood. In dozens of ways, their caretakers told them: "Only some of your feelings are valid. Only a portion of your behaviors are permitted." Instead of helping our partners repair this emotional damage, we add further injury.

THE IMAGO DIALOGUE

TO MOVE BEYOND this tragic state of affairs, we have to learn a new way of talking, which, as you will soon see, is also a new way of knowing. Working with Helen and my Imago colleagues, I gradually developed an exercise called the "Imago Dialogue." Imago Dialogue involves three different steps—mirroring, validation, and empathy.

The Imago Dialogue plays a number of roles in the creation of a conscious partnership. First of all, it focuses your attention on the actual words your partner is saying. If you are like most people, you do not pay full attention when your partner is talking. When you should be listening, you are instead responding to the impact of what you are hearing: "My partner just said that he wants a separate vacation. What does that mean? Does he want to spend less time around me? Is he going to meet someone else?" In a sense, you are listening to yourself react. When you focus on your inner reaction instead of on the words your partner is saying, your partner senses that disconnect. Second, when you listen carefully and then ask your partner what those words mean to him or her, you discover that you do indeed live with another person, someone whose inner experience is quite different from yours. This awareness is called "differentiation," and it is a necessary precondition for a safe, intimate relationship. While there are many similarities in nature—leaves on the same tree, for example, are very similar to one another—no two leaves are the same. Difference is a fact of nature. When you assume that your partner is identical to you, you are negating your partner's existence. In a healthy relationship, you realize that you live with another person who is not an extension of you. Your parner is a unique individual who has an equally valid point of view. Failure to recognize each other's separate existence is the major source of conflict between partners.

Finally, the regular use of the Imago Dialogue creates a deep emotional connection between you and your partner. This is especially true when you are in conflict. Using this structured way of talking creates emotional safety, which is necessary for a lasting connection. When you feel safe, your defenses relax. You become aware of parts of yourself that have been hidden from view since childhood, and you sense enough trust in the relationship to express them: "I really am musical." "I am basically a peaceful person." When you put these experiences into words, they are rewoven into the fabric of your being and you experience "becoming whole." Ultimately, this experience extends beyond your personal boundaries and helps restore your connection to the universe. When talking together reaches this profound level, it becomes a spiritual experience. When you connect at the local level of a personal relationship, you connect at the cosmic level with the transcendent.

The Three Steps of the Imago Dialogue

LET'S TAKE A closer look at the three steps of the Imago Dialogue. The first is called "Mirroring." When one of you has something important to say, you begin by stating that thought or feeling in a short sentence beginning with "I." For example, "I don't enjoy cooking dinner for you when you don't seem to appreciate all the effort involved." Your partner restates the sentence in his or her own words and then asks if the message was received correctly: "Let me see if I got it. You find it hard to put the effort into cooking dinner every night when I don't show my appreciation for all that you've done. Did I get you?" You repeat this process until your partner clearly understands what you mean to say.

Mirroring, like many of the tools we use in Imago Relationship Therapy, had its origin in my relationship with Helen.

One day, before we were married, Helen and I were engaged in an intense discussion. Although we were not angry, we were determined to get our points across. Suddenly, Helen paused the conversation and said: "Stop. We're not listening to each other. I have an idea. Why don't we take turns talking and listening. You can talk while I listen. Then I'll say back to you what I heard. Then we can switch. I'll talk and you listen." I agreed, and we ended up having a very good conversation. In fact, we felt unusually close to each other.

I was not a stranger to the value of listening. As a therapist, I made it a practice to listen carefully to all of my clients. I also encouraged couples to listen closely to one another. But I had always viewed mirroring as a way to help them understand each other's words and solve specific problems. Until that experience with Helen, I hadn't realized that mirroring has a deeper healing effect: it can strengthen the feelings of connection between couples, giving it a value in and of itself.

After a few years, I added another step to the mirroring portion of the exercise. Once the receiving partner had understood what the sending partner had said, I coached the receiver to add these words: "Is there more?" This gave the sender a chance to expand on the topic. "It takes me at least an hour to cook dinner, and I do my best to make it attractive and delicious. I feel sad when you eat without comment." The sender continues adding more information until he or she has no more to say.

In my ongoing work with couples, I have found that this "tell me more" part of the mirroring exercise is one of the keys to its success. When you ask your partner to continue talking, it sends the message that you care about your partner's inner experience. This deepens the sense of connection between you. You benefit in another way as well, because you gain enough additional information about your partner that you can more fully comprehend his or her point of view. Meanwhile, your partner discovers that being encouraged to keep on talking can bring up thoughts and feelings that he or she hasn't been able to put into words before. Saying them out loud at long last helps your partner integrate them into his or her sense of self and become more whole.

Although mirroring is a relatively straightforward process, it is very different from the way that couples normally talk to each other, a phenomenon which might be called a "parallel monologue." Breaking the old habits can require a great deal of practice. Here's an example of the common problems that people have with mirroring (it's also a good example of a parallel monologue). The conversation took place at an Imago Workshop when I asked a couple to volunteer to come to the front of the group and talk about a sensitive issue, just as they would at home. Greg and Sheila, a young couple who had been living together for only a few months, volunteered. Greg started the conversation.

> GREG: Sheila, I'm really bothered by your smoking, and I'd like you to be more considerate when you smoke around me.

Because I had yet to introduce Sheila and Greg to the mirroring exercise, Sheila followed her natural instincts and responded with an automatic defense.

> SHEILA: You knew that I smoked when you asked me to live with you. You accepted that fact in the beginning. Why are you always so critical of me? You should accept me as I am. You know that I'm trying to cut down.

Greg, operating on automatic pilot, returned her remarks with an intensified criticism. The conversation was turning into a tennis match.

> GREG: I acknowledge your efforts to smoke less. But I find it interesting that, when we come here and the sign in the

dining room says "No Smoking," you follow it. Yet I feel invaded at home with the smell of tobacco smoke all over the place.

SHEILA: Well, this is not my home. And I feel I have a right to smoke in my own home!

Sheila delivered this last message with some force, and there was a smattering of applause from the crowd. The score was love-fifteen. It was time for me to referee.

HENDRIX: OK. Let's start this all over again and see if we can turn it into an exercise in connection, not confrontation. Greg, would you repeat your opening statement?

GREG: I'm really glad that we're making a home together, but, with regard to your smoking, when we joined together I didn't realize how difficult it was going to be for me.

HENDRIX: OK. Now I would like you to simplify that statement so it will be easier to understand.

GREG: Let's see. . . . Your smoking bothers me. I didn't think it would at first, but it does.

HENDRIX: Good. Now, Sheila, I want you to paraphrase Greg, trying to mirror his feelings and thoughts without criticizing him or defending yourself. Then I want you to ask Greg if you have heard him correctly.

SHEILA: I'm truly sorry that my smoking interferes—

HENDRIX: No, I'm not asking you to apologize. Just reflect back to Greg what he was saying, and show your understanding and acceptance of his feelings.

SHEILA: Could he possibly repeat himself?

GREG: Your smoking bothers me. I didn't think it would at first, but it does.

HENDRIX: Now, try to feed that back to him with receptive warmth.

SHEILA: I think I'd rather stop smoking! *(Group laughter.)*

HENDRIX: Take a deep breath and be aware that he is experiencing some discomfort at one of your behaviors. Rather than hearing it as a criticism of your behavior, hear it with concern for his well-being. Whether it's justified or not, he is feeling uncomfortable, and you care about him. I know this is hard to do in front of a lot of people, and I know that this is an issue you feel strongly about.

SHEILA: What could be done—

HENDRIX: No, don't try to solve it. You just want to paraphrase his message and the emotional content behind it, so that he knows that you understand what he is feeling.

SHEILA: *(Takes a deep breath.)* OK. I think I get it now. I understand that it really bothers you that I smoke. You didn't realize how much it would bother you until we actually started living together. Now you are very troubled by it. Is that what you are saying?

HENDRIX: Excellent. I could hear Greg's concern reflected in your voice. Did that check out with you, Greg? Is she hearing what you have to say?

GREG: Yes! *(I could see his facial muscles relax)* That's just how I feel. What a relief! This is the first time she's ever really bothered to listen to me.

As Greg's reaction shows, there is a tremendous satisfaction in simply being heard, in knowing that your message has been received exactly as you sent it. This is a rare phenomenon in most relationships. After demonstrating this exercise for workshop groups, I send the couples back to their rooms so they can practice sending and receiving simple statements. Invariably they return to the group reporting that it was a novel, exhilarating experience. It is such an unexpected luxury to have your partner's full attention.

VALIDATION

ONCE COUPLES HAVE become adept at mirroring each other, I encourage them to go on to the next step of the Imago Dialogue: validation. In this part of the exercise, they learn how to affirm the internal logic of each other's remarks. In essence, they are telling each other, "What you're saying makes sense to me. I can see how you are thinking, and why you would think that way."

I had my first and most indelible experience with the power of validation when I was a young man. It was 1960, and I had been sent to Louisville, Kentucky, to be a chaplain in a mental hospital where I was assigned to a ward for schizophrenic patients. I was given very little training in the beginning. Basically I was told, "Go in there and relate the best you can." As time went on, I would be given more supervision, but in the first few weeks it was sink or swim. One of the first patients I tried to get to know was a gaunt man in his fifties whom I will call Leonard. One thing I remember about Leonard is that he was a nonstop smoker. I always saw him through a veil of smoke. But the reason he has stayed in my mind all these years is that he was convinced he was Jesus.

"Hello, Leonard," I said to him when we were first introduced. "My name is Harville."

"I'm Jesus," he replied calmly, drawing on his cigarette, "not Leonard."

I was taken aback, but I covered up my reaction. "Oh," I said, "I'm a theological student, so I have a different concept of Jesus. But I'm pleased to meet you."

As the days went on, I found myself drawn to Leonard, primarily because I was so fascinated by his unshakable conviction that he was Jesus. I didn't try to convince him otherwise because I could see that that would have been pointless. I just studied his internal logic. Eventually, Leonard began to feel safe enough with me that he started to share some of the voices inside his head. When I found out exactly what the voices were saying to him and that those voices were as real to him as the words coming out of my mouth, Leonard's view of himself as Jesus began to make complete sense to me. I hasten to add that *I* didn't think he was Jesus, but I could see why *he* thought that he was. It made all the sense in his world.

The day came when I decided to address Leonard as Jesus. This didn't seem blasphemous to me. Indeed, it seemed a form of respect. Why add yet more conflict to his life when his head was already a battleground? If *he* thought he was Jesus, I was going to go along with it. I walked up to him that morning and said, "Hello, Jesus." To my surprise, he said, "I'm not Jesus. I'm Leonard." I sputtered for a moment and said, "But you've been telling me for weeks that you're Jesus!"

"Yes," he said, "but my voices are now telling me that I don't have to be Jesus with you."

Validation had moved him one step closer to sanity.

ADDING VALIDATION TO MIRRORING

WHEN I FIRST worked with couples, the communication exercise stopped with mirroring. I didn't require them to go on and validate the internal logic of each other's messages. As I gained more experience, I began to see that validation is a vital step in the process. I remember the first time I asked a couple to add validation to mirroring. The two people, I'll call them Rita and Doug, were in their forties. Rita was a schoolteacher, and Doug was an insurance salesman. Their central problem was their inability to connect emotionally. When Rita tried to talk with her husband about something important, Doug would answer halfheartedly and then emotionally withdraw. Over time, I learned that one reason he withdrew was that he often felt critical of her, and he was trying to keep from being her constant critic. In his own way, he was trying to improve the relationship. But, understandably, his unwillingness to respond to Rita infuriated her. To get the sense of connection she was longing for, she would raise her voice and exaggerate her statements until he would finally respond. As I write this, I can almost see Doug react to one of Rita's outbursts. He would start breathing very shallowly. His face would flush. Then he would cross his arms and lean his body away from her. If Rita persisted long enough, Doug would finally react. Unfortunately, his response, once it came, was cold and accusatory and served only to throw gasoline on her fire.

To help them break out of this destructive pattern, I taught them the mirroring exercise. It helped a great deal because Rita had to slow down her torrent of words, and Doug had to stay in contact. But the exercise did not produce the kind of results I was used to seeing. Their communication improved dramatically, but there was little enhanced sense of connection. At a loss, I remember turning to Rita one day and asking her, "What do you want from Doug that you're not getting?" Her response was immediate. "I want him to tell me that I make sense. That I'm not crazy!" A light went on in my head. Rita wanted more than to be heard. She wanted her thought processes to be validated. She wanted her husband to tell her that her worldview made sense. I turned to Doug and asked him if he would be willing to add another step to the mirroring exercise. As soon as he had paraphrased Rita correctly, would he tell her that what she was saying made sense to him? Doug thought for a long moment and then said, "But what if she *doesn't* make sense to me?" I told him that he didn't have to agree with Rita or give up his own point of view in order to validate hers, he just needed to suspend his view of the world for a moment and make an honest effort to see hers. Doug thought it over and said he would try.

Rita made a statement—I no longer remember what it was—and Doug paraphrased it back to her. Instead of waiting for me to structure the next part of the exercise, however, Rita blurted out, "Well, do you agree, Doug?"

For once, Doug was equally quick on the draw. "No," he said belligerently, "I do *not* agree."

Rita persisted, "But do I make *sense* to you? Does what I say make sense? Do you think I'm crazy?"

"No, I don't think you are crazy," Doug said, "but I certainly don't agree with you."

Rita got out of her chair and grabbed Doug's forearms. "So, what I say makes *sense* to you?"

"Yes," Doug acknowledged, "when I see it from your point of view, yes, you do make sense. I just see things differently."

I'll never forget how Rita responded. She sunk to her knees in front of Doug and began crying. "That's all that I wanted to hear!" she said. "I haven't heard that before, from you or from anybody! I'm not crazy! I make sense!"

Finally, someone was affirming her truth.

Even today, I am impressed by how aggressively each of us defends our separate reality. It must be connected to our fear of the loss of self. If I see it your way, I will have to surrender my way. If I feel your experience, I will have to invalidate mine. If what you say is true, then what I say *must* be false. There can be only one center of the universe and that center is me! But if I muster the courage to suspend my own point of view for a moment and then manage to see a fraction of your reality, something miraculous happens. First of all, you feel safer around me. Because I am no longer challenging your worldview, you can start to lower your defenses. As you do this, you become more willing to acknowledge a portion of my reality. Because I have abandoned my centrist position, you are more willing to let go of yours. To our mutual surprise, a drawbridge begins to descend on its rusty hinges, and you and I connect.

EMPATHY

THE THIRD STEP in Imago Dialogue is empathy. It makes sense that empathy would follow on the heels of validation. If you listen carefully to your partner, understand the totality of what he or she is saying, and then affirm the logic behind your partner's words, you are ready to acknowledge and respond to the feelings behind those thoughts. Your first task is to try to imagine what those feeings might be. If your partner's feelings are conveyed beyond his or her words, by facial expression or tone of voice, you will have little trouble intuiting them. If your partner's feelings are not so obvious, you will have to imagine what they might be. In either case, you need to check with your partner to see if you perceived their feelings accurately. "Given the fact that you said I neglected you, I'm wondering if you feel hurt by my neglect. Is that how you feel?" Checking to confirm the accuracy respects your partner's reality and enhances your emotional "presence," an essential ingredient of healing. Asking for confirmation also deepens your partner's experience of empathy; he will think: "My partner is being very respectful of my feelings. She cares how I really feel."

For some people, validation of their thought processes is more important to them than validation of their feelings. But for others, empathy is the key to their healing. Once someone affirms their raw emotions, they begin to feel loved and whole. I hate to say it because it perpetuates our gender stereotypes, but, in my experience, women tend to value empathy more than men. At least at first. If you stop and think about it, this makes sense. In our culture, indeed in most cultures, women are allowed to express their feelings more freely than men. Although this is beginning to change, many men still believe it is unmanly to disclose their emotions, especially their tender feelings or feelings of fear and weakness. So if we men feel uncomfortable showing our feelings to others in the first place, you can hardly expect us to want our partners to empathize with us should we happen to let a feeling slip out. We'd just as soon that they overlook the momentary lapse and focus on our steely logic instead.

Many women, on the other hand, have had the opposite experience. The culture has allowed them to keep more of their emotional wholeness, but they've had to live with men who are relatively devoid of feeling. Their partners not only fail to empathize with them, they'd just as soon ignore the fact that they have feelings altogether. "Why can't you be more rational? Why can't you be more like me?"

When couples master the three-step process of mirroring, validation, and empathy, these gender differences begin to diminish. A man who is emotionally repressed starts to value empathy as much as his female partner. The reason this occurs is that seeing and acknowledging his partner's feelings makes him more comfortable with his own. Meanwhile, a woman who is emotionally volatile can become less so. Because she no longer needs to amplify her feelings in order to have her stoic partner acknowledge them, she can express them with less force. This is especially true for anger. It is always surprising to me to see how quickly anger will dissipate once it's been received and fully acknowledged.

As you might imagine, the ease with which you can empathize with your partner depends a great deal on the situation. It's very easy to be sympathetic when the two of you share the same experience and react similarly to that event. Let's suppose you and I have just been through a major earthquake. We survived the quake without any injuries, and we are relieved to see that the house still stands on its foundation. But there were several frightening minutes when we both thought we were going to die. "I was so terrified!" your partner exclaims. You respond immediately, "I can see that you were! I was, too!" Because you've had the same response to the same situation, there is no stretching involved. What you feel, I feel. We had the same reaction.

Empathy is a more challenging response. It is the ability to understand what another person is experiencing even though you have not had that identical experience. Let's assume that your partner was in the earthquake but you were gone on business 500 miles away. Your partner reaches you on the phone, describes the horrific event, and then cries out to you, "I was so terrified!" Although you didn't experience the earthquake yourself, it's not too much of a stretch to imagine that you might have been terrified as well. "I can imagine you were," you reply with only a moment's hesitation.

Problems tend to arise when two people react quite differently to similar events. For example, your partner might be terrified of flying but you can fall asleep during takeoff or landing. You're going to have a harder time empathizing with your partner's fear because you've never experienced it in this situation. "Just breathe deeply," you tell your partner. "Think about something else, and the feelings will go away." And, quite frankly, you wish that they *would* disappear. They seem so irrational. You want to *deflect* your partner's feelings, not empathize with them.

The most difficult situation of all, however, may be those times when your partner has strong, negative emotions, and you, poor soul, seem to have triggered them: "I am so angry at you that you told Janice she could go to the movies when you know I already told her she has to stay home and clean her room! You always do this!" Or "I felt so humiliated when I saw you flirting with Paul in front of all of our friends. You know how jealous that makes me!" Your instinctual response is to defend yourself and then counterattack. Being empathetic is the farthest thing from your mind. To do so requires tremendous discipline, practice, and emotional maturity.

SENDER RESPONSIBILITY

WHEN I FIRST developed the Imago Dialogue and began to teach it to couples, I did not focus much on the responsibilities of the person sending the message. I thought that the sender should have full license to express their thoughts and feelings without inhibition, and I encouraged the receiver to mirror back whatever they heard, without reacting. Over time, as I trained more Imago therapists and workshop presenters, I learned that most of their couples found it difficult not to overreact.

My colleagues began experimenting with coaching the sender as well as the receiver. They developed a concept called "sender responsibility." This meant that the person sending the message had to follow certain rules that were designed to make the message easier for the receiver to "hear." The first rule was to use "I" language when expressing a frustration. Instead of blurting out, "You made me feel so ashamed when you treated our neighbor that way," you say, "I felt ashamed when you treated our neighbor that way." The second rule is that you should avoid making critical remarks about your partner's character and focus instead on your partner's behavior. Instead of saying, "You are always late. You have no sense of responsibility," you say, "When you are late, I feel frustrated and scared." In addition, you moderate the intensity of your emotions so that your partner feels safe enough to relax and listen. After all, your goal is not to wound your partner but to deepen the connection between you.

We learned that being a responsible sender is just as important as being a good listener. When you manage both ends of the transaction so that you can talk to each other without rupturing your sense of connection, you will have mastered one of the most effective tools for creating a safe and lasting union.

BUT! ISN'T DIALOGUING WITH YOUR PARTNER TEDIOUS?

AS HELPFUL AS the Imago Dialogue may be, people have an almost universal reaction to it: "Do we really have to go through all those steps in order to communicate something meaningful?" The answer to this specific question is no. If all you're seeking is effective communication, then mirroring alone may be sufficient. But if you want to move beyond communication to *communion,* then you need to include all three steps. That said, I don't want to diminish how time-consuming and artificial the Imago Dialogue can seem. There are times when you will rebel at the structure and want to revert to old habits. I am reminded of a seventeen-year-old son of a friend of mine who is a superb baseball player. He is so good, in fact, that he's been singled out by a ball club for special instruction even before leaving high school. To the boy's dismay, however, his new coach wants him to change virtually everything about the way that he pitches and hits the ball. He's been given a series of exercises to help him build up certain muscles and stretch out others, and he is required to hit a hundred balls a day using an alien-feeling stance and grip. At times, he has been close to tears because he feels as though he's had to abandon everything he knows about baseball.

So it is with the Imago Dialogue. It requires you to abandon some deeply ingrained habits and adopt a formulaic way of relating. Much of the time, it's going to feel forced. But as you begin to experience some of its benefits, you will become less resistant. Eventually—and it may take years—you will have transformed your relationship to the point that you will be able to abandon the exercise altogether. When that day arrives, you will be communing, not just conversing.

THE IMAGO WORKUP

ONCE COUPLES HAVE been taught the Imago Dialogue, I introduce them to an information gathering tool called "the Imago Workup." This is a guided imagery technique that helps each partner become better acquainted with their own childhood wounds. When the exercise is completed, I have them share their observations, using the Imago Dialogue. This is an effective way for couples to begin to see each other as they really are, as wounded beings on a quest for spiritual wholeness.

Before the exercise begins, I ask the couples to close their eyes and relax. I often put on some soothing music to help them shut out distractions. When they are sufficiently relaxed, I ask them to try to remember their childhood home, the earliest one they can recall. When the vision begins to take shape, I tell them to see themselves as very young children wandering through the house searching for their caretakers. The first person they meet is their mother, or whichever female caretaker was most influential in their early years. I tell them that they are suddenly endowed with magical powers and can see these women's positive and negative character traits with crystal clarity. They are to note these characteristics and then imagine themselves telling their mothers what they always wanted from them and never got.

In a similar manner, I have them encounter their fathers, or primary male caretakers, and then any other people who had a profound influence on them in their formative years. When they have gathered all the information they can about these key people, I slowly bring them back to reality and have them open their eyes and write the information down on a piece of paper.

I am often surprised by how much information people can gain from this simple exercise. For example, a young man did the exercise and realized for the first time how lonely and isolated he felt as a child. He had blocked out this crucial piece of information because it hadn't made any sense to him. How could he feel lonely in a family with four children, a minister for a father, and a devoted homemaker for a mother? In his fantasy, however, he had searched and searched around the house for his father, never to find him. When he encountered his mother, his spontaneous question to her was "Why are you always so busy? Can't you see that I need you?" Having these insights helped him understand his chronic depression. "Until this moment," he said, "my sadness has always been a mystery to me."

Once people have completed the guided-imagery exercise, they have the information they need to construct their imagos, the inner images of the opposite sex that guided them in mate selection. All they need to do is group together the positive and negative traits of all the key people from their childhood, highlighting the traits that affected them the most. These are the traits that they were looking for in a mate.

When this work is completed, I ask couples to share what they have learned. I ask them to listen to each other with full attention, making no effort to interpret each other's remarks, enlarge upon them, compare them with their own, or analyze them. The only allowable comments are mirroring comments that indicate the degree of their understanding. By doing this exercise, people begin to see behind their partners' neurotic, puzzling, or compulsive behavior to the wounds they are trying to heal. This creates a more compassionate, supportive emotional climate.

THE PARENT-CHILD DIALOGUE

IN THE YEARS since the original version of this book was written, a number of other Imago workshop presenters have contributed to the workshop and to Imago therapy. Maya Kollman, a master trainer, suggested a new exercise called the

Parent-Child Dialogue. In this exercise, which in our workshops occurs after the exercise called the "Imago Work-up," couples deepen their awareness of their childhood wounds and increase their empathy for each other. Sitting face to face, one partner takes on the role of the caretaker and the other partner imagines him or herself as a small child and talks to the caretaker from a child's point of view. The person playing the caretaker asks a series of questions, beginning with: "Tell me what it was like living with me?" The "child" responds. After mirroring the "child" with empathy, the caregiver then asks: "What was the worst thing for you about all that?" Once again, the "child" talks about what was most difficult. Mirroring the "child's" response with warmth and empathy, the caregiver now asks, "What do you need from me that would heal all that?" Typically, the "child" says something like: "I need you to be there for me and listen when I talk." The partner who is playing the caregiver role closes the exercise by saying: "I want you to have all of that, whenever you need it. Thanks for telling me about your pain and what you need from me." Then they switch roles and repeat the exercise.

This exercise is powerful for both partners. The partner playing the role of the child recalls his or her childhood wounds more deeply than in other exercises. The partner in the caregiving role gains a greater understanding of the other partner's early vulnerability. The most exciting thing about this particular exercise is that the empathic response of the listening partner is so different from the type of wounding response one might have gotten from one's actual caretaker, that it begins to heal the partner's wound. If the real-life caregiver had responded this way in the past, the emotional injury would not have occurred in the first place.

What fascinates me most about the Parent-Child Dialogue is that when the partner who has regressed into childhood memories talks about his or her pain from the past, the listening partner often recognizes that he or she has frustrated the speaking partner in similar ways, unwittingly reopening childhood wounds. However, the structure of the exercise prevents any reaction. Then, in the closing statement, when the regressed child says what he or she needs from the parent, the listening partner gains new insight into what needs to be done to help the other person heal. The Parent-Child Dialogue is an indirect way of learning how to be each other's healers.

DEFINING YOUR CURRICULUM

One of the deep secrets of life is that all that is
really worth doing is what we do for others.
— LEWIS CARROLL

SO FAR IN this book, I've described the initial steps in the creation of a conscious partnership. I've talked about making a
commitment to narrow your exits so that more of your energy
is available for your relationship. I've talked about increasing
the pleasurable interactions between the two of you to set the
stage for greater intimacy. And I've discussed several ways to
increase your knowledge of yourself and your partner. Now is
the time to talk about the healing of deeper childhood wounds.
In this chapter I will describe a way you can turn your chronic
frustrations about your partner into avenues for growth. In the
next chapter I will talk about ways to remove the underlying
cause of most explosive conflicts.

When a couple has spent several weeks practicing the
Reromanticizing exercise described in chapter 8, they experience a revival of positive feelings, and they begin to bond with

each other much the way they did during the early stages of romantic love. Just as they grow accustomed to this more intimate, nurturing environment, however, a disheartening event occurs: conflicts begin to emerge, the very ones that brought them into therapy in the first place. Once again they are plagued with the same troublesome issues, the same basic incompatibilities. It seems as though the Reromanticizing exercise has resurrected romantic love only to let it disintegrate once again into a power struggle.

The reason the good feelings don't last is that, through increased pleasurable interactions, the two individuals have unconsciously identified each other once again as the "one who has it all," the ideal mate who is magically going to restore their wholeness. After the anger and withdrawal of the power struggle, they are once again turning to each other for salvation. And once again they make the unpleasant discovery that neither of them has the necessary skills or the motivation to meet the other's deeper needs. In fact, on their own, many people make the same sobering discovery I made in my first marriage: what they want most from their partners, their partners are least able to give.

What can be done to resolve this central dilemma? The question bedeviled me in my early years as a marital therapist. Given these two facts—(1) that we enter our love relationships bearing emotional scars from childhood, and (2) that we unwittingly choose mates who resemble our caretakers, the very people who contributed to our wounding in the first place—it seems that intimate love relationsihps are destined to repeat, not repair, our early misfortunes.

Years ago when I lectured to groups, this pessimistic view came through loud and clear. During one talk I was explaining the self-defeating nature of mate selection, and a woman raised her hand to say, "Dr. Hendrix, maybe the way to avoid reinjuring old wounds is to marry people you *don't* feel attracted to. That way you won't wind up with people who have the same faults as your parents." Everyone laughed, but at the time I could offer no better solution. Relationships determined by signs of the zodiac, go-betweens, or computerized dating services appeared to have a better chance of succeeding than relationships based on an unconscious selection process. Our tendency to select partners who share the positive and negative traits of our caretakers seemed to doom conventional love relationships from the start. My only advice to couples was to become more aware of their hidden reasons for marrying each other and to embrace the cold, hard facts of reality. Awareness, insight, understanding, and acceptance—that was the only solace I had to offer.

At the time I was getting the same counsel from my own therapist. "You have to accept the fact that your mother didn't have any energy for you, Harville," he would tell me. "And your wife can't give you what you want, either. She can't make up for those early years. You just have to let go of those longings." In other words, "You didn't get it then, and you're not going to get it now. Grow up and get on with life." I tried to accept what he was telling me, but I was aware that in the core of my being I was unwilling to let go of my unfinished business. A part of me felt that I had an inalienable right to a secure and loving upbringing. As I scrutinized my clients, I could see that they were clinging just as tenaciously to their needs. They might repress them; they might deny them; they might project them onto others. But they couldn't let go of their childhood needs once and for all. There had to be a different and better way, so I continued looking.

WHY SELF-LOVE DOESN'T WORK

EVENTUALLY I SOUGHT out a different therapist, one with a more optimistic view about the possibility of resolving childhood needs. He believed that it was possible for people to make up for what they didn't get in childhood through self-love. One of his techniques to help me overcome my craving for nurturing was to have me imagine the scene in the kitchen with my mother that I talked about earlier. He would guide me through a deep relaxation exercise, then say to me, "Harville, imagine yourself as a little baby wanting your mother's attention. She is standing at the stove with her back to you. Imagine how you want to be hugged. Call out to her. See her come over to you and pick you up with a big smile on her face. She is now holding you close. Put your arms across your chest. See that little boy! He's right there in front of you and wants to be hugged. Hold him and hug him and fill him with love. Now pull the little boy into your chest. Pull that happy little boy inside of you."

It was his belief that, if I succeeded in creating a vivid picture of myself being loved by my mother, I would gradually fill up my need for maternal love. His approach seemed to work for a while; after each session I would feel less alone, more loved. But the feeling gradually disappeared, and I would once again be filled with emptiness.

The reason this approach doesn't work is that it is sabotaged by the old brain. When we were infants, unable to meet our physical and emotional needs, pain and pleasure came magically from the outside world. When the bottle or the breast appeared, our hunger was satisfied. When we were cuddled, we felt soothed. When we were left alone in our cribs to cry, we felt angry and afraid. As we grew older, our old brain remained frozen in this passive worldview: good feelings and bad feelings were created by the actions of other people; we couldn't take care of ourselves; others had to do it for us. The part of me that hurt couldn't accept love from within myself because I had no way to receive self-love. Nor does anyone else. Salvation is not an "inside" job; it is the outcome of being nourished by others. But at that time, I did not know this fundamental truth.

The Limits of Friendship

I GRADUALLY RESIGNED myself to the fact that healing love has to come from outside oneself. But did it have to come from an intimate partner? Couldn't it come from a close friend? At the time when I was musing over this possibility, I was leading several counseling groups and had an opportunity to observe the healing potential of friendships. Close bonds often develop between members of therapy groups, and I encouraged this love and support. In a typical session I might pair Mary, who grew up with a neurotic, unaffectionate mother, with Susan, a strong, earth-mother figure. I asked Susan to hold Mary on her lap and stroke her and let her cry. Mary would feel soothed by the exercise, but she wouldn't be healed. "I enjoyed the hugging," she said, "but Susan's not the right person. It's not Susan I need hugs from. It's someone else."

After numerous experiments like this, I concluded that the love we are seeking has to come not just from another person within the context of a safe, intimate relationship, but from an *imago match*—someone so similar to our parents that our unconscious mind has them fused. This appears to be the only way to erase the pains of childhood. We may enjoy the hugs and attentions of other people, but the effects are transitory. It's like the difference between sugar and Nutrasweet. Our taste buds may be deceived by the taste of artificial sweeteners, but our bodies derive no nourishment from them. In just such a way, we hunger for love from our original caretakers *or from people who are so similar to them that on an unconscious level we have them merged.*

But this brought me back full circle to the original dilemma: *How can our partners heal us if they have some of the same negative traits as our caretakers?* Aren't they the least likely candidates to soothe our emotional injuries? If the daughter of a distant, self-absorbed father unconsciously selects a workaholic for a husband, how can her relationship satisfy her need for closeness and intimacy? If the son of a depressed, sexually repressed mother chooses to marry a depressed, frigid wife, how can he recapture his sensuality and joy? If a girl whose father died when she was young moves in with a man who refuses to marry her, how can she feel loved and secure?

An answer began to take shape in my mind. It was the only logical conclusion. If people were going to be healed, I conjectured, *their partners would have to change.* The workaholic husband would have to willingly redirect some of his energy back to his wife. The depressed, frigid wife would have to recover her energy and sensuality. The reluctant lover would have to lower his barriers to intimacy. Then and only then would they be able to give their partners the consistent nurturing they had been looking for all their lives.

It was at this point that I began to see the unconscious selection process in a new light: while it was often true that what one partner needed the most was what the other partner was least able to give, it also happened to be the precise area where that partner needed to grow! For example, if Mary grew up with caretakers who were sparing in their physical affection, she most likely has chosen a husband, George, who is uncomfortable with bodily contact; the unmet childhood need in Mary is invariably matched by George's inability to meet that need. But if George were to overcome his resistance to being affectionate in an effort to satisfy Mary's needs, not only would Mary get the physical reassurance she craved, but George would slowly regain contact with his own sensuality. *In other words, in his efforts to heal his partner he would be recovering an essential part of himself!* The unconscious selection process has brought together two people who can either hurt each other or heal each other, depending upon their willingness to grow and change.

Turning the Theory into Practice

I BEGAN TO focus my attention on turning the healing potential of love relationships into a workable reality. The unanswered question was: how could people be encouraged to overcome their limitations so they could meet their partners' needs? Wouldn't most people be reluctant to change for their partners' sake alone? Wouldn't they want something for themselves? Of course they would! What could be more rewarding, I thought, than for them to be able to get back parts of themselves that they had repressed in childhood? I decided that this would become the "bait" that would encourage people to become a healing resource for their partners.

I began to develop an exercise called "The Behavior Change Request Dialogue" that would help make this happen. It had some of the same features as the Reromanticizing exercise. One partner would be asked to come up with a list of requests, which the other partner would be free to honor or not. In this exercise, however, the requests would be for changes in behavior, not for simple, pleasurable interactions; in fact, virtually every one of the requests would zero in on a point of contention. For instance, people would be asking their partners to become more assertive or more accepting or less manipulative. In essence, they would be asking them to overcome their most prominent negative traits.

As in the Reromanticizing exercise, these general requests would have to be converted into specific, measurable, time-limited activities. Otherwise the partner wouldn't have enough information to be able to change, and there would be too much room for misinterpretation and evasive maneuvers. Also, like the Reromanticizing exercise, the Behavior Change Request Dialogue would have to rely on the principle of the "gift," not the contract. Otherwise the unconscious mind would reject the change in behaviors. This was very important. If one person made a small change and then waited for the partner to match those efforts—"I'll work on becoming less domineering if you will work on becoming more nurturing"—the whole process would quickly degenerate into a power struggle. The old animosities would flare up, and there would be no possibility of healing.

People would have to learn how to overcome their limitations and develop their capacity to love, not because they expected love in return but simply because their partners deserved to be loved. The unconscious mind accepts only unconditional gifts. It is not interested in "deals."

With the general framework of the new exercise in place, I began to fill in the details. How would people determine exactly what behaviors to request of their partners? Two individuals may be quick to complain and criticize each other, but they are rarely able to state in positive, specific terms exactly what they need from each other. How could they come up with this information when it was not readily available to their consciousness? Wouldn't it take months or even years of intensive therapy?

There was an easier solution, I realized, and that was for them to examine their criticisms of their partners. As I explained in the previous chapter, couples can get an accurate picture of what they did not get in childhood by analyzing their chronic complaints about their partners. The details aren't there—who did what when—but the raw material is sitting right on the surface, ready to be mined. The months or years that the couple have spent together have worn away their softer, more superficial annoyances and exposed the stony outcrop of their fundamental needs. "You never . . . !" "You always . . . !" "When are you ever going to . . . !" At the heart of these accusations is a disguised plea for the very things they didn't get in childhood—affection, affirmation, protection, independence, attachment. To come up with the list of requests for this exercise, therefore, the couples would simply need to isolate the desires hidden in their chronic frustrations. They needed to let go of the frustration and go straight to the wish embedded within. Then they could convert these general desires into specific behaviors that would help satisfy their needs. Other Imago therapists have labeled these "SMART" requests—small, measurable, achievable, relevant, and time-limited. This list of positive, specific requests would become the ongoing curriculum of the couple's relationship.

DEFINING THE CURRICULUM

HERE'S AN EXAMPLE from a recent couples workshop to show how the Behavior Change Request Dialogue works. To begin the demonstration, I asked a volunteer to state a significant gripe about his or her partner. Melanie, an attractive woman wearing a bright print dress, raised her hand. She shared what at first appeared to be a superficial frustration about her husband, Stewart. "Stewart has a terrible memory," she said. "It seems to be getting worse. I'm always nagging at him about his memory. I wish he would take a memory course."

Stewart, a mustached, scholarly looking man, was sitting next to her and, as if on cue, promptly began to defend himself in a weary tone of voice. "Melanie," he said, "I'm a lawyer. I have to remember thousands of pages of legal briefs. I have an excellent memory."

Before Melanie had a chance to restate her criticism, I asked her what bothered her most about Stewart's inability to remember. When did it make her the most upset?

She thought for a moment. "I guess when he forgets to do something that I've asked him to do. Like last week, when he forgot that we had a date to go out to lunch. Another thing that upset me was when we were at a party a few days ago, and he forgot to introduce me to his friends. I stood there feeling like a complete idiot."

I then prompted her by giving her the beginning of a sentence: "And when he did that, I felt..." I was trying to help her pinpoint the deeper feelings, such as sadness, anger, or fear, that might underlie her frustrations. Basically, I was helping her identify the desire that was hidden in her criticism, a process I had described earlier in the workshop. But first, it was important that she identify her most frequent feeling, and then identify the fear behind that feeling. "Well," she said, "when he does those things, I feel unloved. I feel he doesn't care for me. I feel rejected." Then I gave her another sentence stem and asked her to fill in the blank so that she could make the connection of this chronic feeling to her childhood. "And when I feel that, it reminds me of..." Melanie filled in the blank with, "It reminds me of my father who was never there for me. He was always so preoccupied with other things and he often forgot to attend my sporting events." I gave her a third sentence stem: "And what scares me about that is..." She replied, "I am afraid he doesn't love me. That I am not important to him."[1]

I turned to Stewart and asked him to restate Melanie's frustration and mirror everything she had said so far—to give what I call a "summary mirror." With a little coaching, Stewart finally said, "If I got it all, your frustration is that I have a poor memory. And I forget what you ask me to do and also ignore you at parties, and this reminds you of your dad's constant preoccupation, which made you feel unloved and you were afraid that he did not love you. Did I get it all?" With tears in her eyes and astonishment that he remembered everything so well, Melanie said, "Yes."

I asked Stewart if he would validate Melanie's experience and express empathy by imagining the feelings she had as a child. While this was difficult for him and he needed some prompting, he finally said, "I get it. Given the fact that your father was often preoccupied and forgot about your school events, it makes sense that when I forget things you ask me to do that it would remind you of your father's forgetfulness, and it also makes sense that you would be hurt and feel that you were not loved. I get that now."

And then he showed his empathy—spontaneously: "And I can imagine that you feel angry when I forget things. Is that the feeling?" She confirmed his validation with some sobbing, saying that this was the first time ever that she had felt heard, had felt important to him.

Next I asked Melanie to state what she wanted that would remove her frustration and the fear and hurt behind it. I asked her to put it in global terms using words like "always" and "never." In the unconscious mind, our wishes have no boundaries. We want "everything, all the time!" I have learned that it is important for people to state this global wish. Even though they realize they will not get it, it helps them focus on the childhood wish embedded in the frustration. After she came that far, I knew I would ask her to break it up into manageable, bite-sized behaviors.

"WHAT I WANT most," Melanie started saying, "is to know that I am important to you all the time, that you are always thinking of me, and that I am more important than your work, always." At first, Stewart's face softened with this request. But then he looked overwhelmed.

"Now, Melanie," I continued, "I want you to write down a list of specific behaviors that would help you feel more cared for, important, and loved. Will you give Stewart some concrete information about how he could become a more positive force in your life?"

She said she would.

Next I gave Melanie and Stewart and the rest of the group some detailed instructions. I explained that their partners would ask for behaviors that could be difficult for them to enact, because they had not been allowed in childhood. Understandably, they would feel some resistance. Some might feel that it was impossible to respond. But, I continued, if you stretch and give your partner what they need from you, it will activate that part of you that was shut down in childhood, and you will develop hidden parts of yourself. Your partner's needs are an invitation and opportunity for you to grow.

I then sent the workshop participants back to their rooms, having asked them to identify a chronic complaint, isolate the desire that was at the heart of the complaint, connect it with a childhood experience, and come up with a list of concrete, doable behaviors that would help satisfy the unmet desire. They should then look at each other's lists and rank the behaviors according to how hard they would be to act upon. I told them that sharing this information did not obligate them to meet each other's needs, but that the purpose of the exercise was to educate each other and to develop their capacity for empathy. If their partners then made the decision to stretch into new behaviors, they would now possess some specific guidelines. Any suggestion of obligation or expectation on my part would reduce the exercise to a bargain, bringing with it the likelihood that the whole experience would end in resentment and failure.

When the group reconvened, Melanie volunteered to share her list. She had followed the SMART behaviors guideline and made her requests small, measurable, achieveable, relevant, and time-limited. Here are a few of them:

"For the next four weeks, I would like you to set aside one night a week so that we could go out for the evening. And during that evening, I want you to tell me three times that you love me."

"I would like you to introduce me to your friends when I meet you at the office for lunch next Thursday; and for the next three months, each time I come to your office, I would like you to introduce me to another friend."

"I would like you to give me a special present on my next birthday that you have bought and wrapped yourself, and during my birthday, I want you to look me in the eye three times, for one minute each, and say: 'You are the most important person in my life.'"

"For the next three weeks, I would like you to call me on the phone once a day just to chat."

"For the next two months, when we go out to dinner, I would like you to remember to pull my chair out for me, and then lean over and kiss me."

"For the next two months, I would like you to reduce your hours at the office so that you don't have to work on Saturdays and Sundays."

"For the next four weeks, I would like you to call me if you're going to be more than fifteen minutes late coming home for dinner."

"For the next three months, I would like you to give up your separate bedroom so that we can sleep together every night."

According to my instructions, Stewart had reviewed Melanie's requests, ranked them according to difficulty, and chosen a request that he could honor with relative ease. In fact, he announced to the group that he would begin the exercise that very evening by remembering to pull Melanie's chair out at dinner. There was a marked contrast between his earlier, antagonistic response to Melanie's complaint about his poor memory and his cheerful response to these specific requests. Because he understood that these behaviors addressed one of Melanie's unmet childhood needs, because he was allowed to rank them according to difficulty, and because he was free to choose whether to do any of them or not, he found it relatively easy to comply.

A sign that Melanie's list contained some growth potential for Stewart, however, was the fact that there were some requests that he found very difficult to do. For example, he thought it would be very hard for him to give up his own bedroom. "I really cherish my time alone," he said. "It would be difficult for me to give that up. I'm not willing to do that now." It came as no surprise to me that that was the thing Melanie wanted most: *one partner's greatest desire is often matched by the other partner's greatest resistance.* "I don't feel like we're really married unless we sleep in the same bed," she said. "I cried myself to sleep for a week after you moved into your own room. I really hate it!" I reminded Melanie that letting her husband know how much she wanted him to share a bedroom with her was an important piece of information for him, but he was not obligated to cooperate. The only legitimate power she had in the relationship was to inform Stewart of her needs and to change her own behavior to meet Stewart's needs.

COMPLEX CHANGE SET IN MOTION

WHEN WE WERE through working with Melanie's list, Stewart volunteered to share his list. He, too, had identified a chronic complaint, isolated his desire, connected it with a childhood need, and composed a list of target activities. His main criticism of Melanie was that she was too judgmental. It seemed to him that she was always criticizing him. This was painful to him, he acknowledged, because he had judgmental parents. "Which," he added with a smile and a sideways glance at me, "given all the information I've gotten at this workshop, is probably one of the reasons I was attracted to her."

One of Stewart's specific requests was that Melanie praise him once a day for the next two months. Melanie acknowledged that some days it would be hard for her to do that. "I don't think I'm being hypercritical," she said with sincerity, "I think the problem is that Stewart does a lot of irresponsible things. The basic problem is not my attitude—it's his behavior!" The main reason it was going to be difficult for her to praise Stewart, I realized, was that she was denying the validity of her husband's complaint. She saw herself as a realistic judge of his character, not as a perpetual critic. Stewart had homed in on a disowned negative trait.

One of the benefits of the Behavior Change Request Dialogue however, is that Melanie didn't have to agree with Stewart's assessment of her in order for the healing process to work. All she had to do was comply with his simple request for one compliment a day. When she did this, she would become more aware of her husband's positive qualities, and eventually she would learn how immersed she had been in the role of judge and critic. Ultimately, both Stewart and Melanie would gain from the exercise. Stewart would be able to bask in some of the approval that he deserved, and Melanie would be able to accept and transform a denied negative trait. In the process of healing her husband, she would be becoming a more whole and loving person herself.

When couples faithfully perform this exercise for several months, they discover another hidden benefit of the exercise: *the love that they are sending out to each other is touching and healing their own wounds*—wounds they didn't even know they had. Stewart and Melanie continued to work with me in private therapy sessions for over a year. About six months after the workshop, Stewart was finally able to overcome his resistance to sharing a bedroom with Melanie. He didn't like the idea, but he saw how important it was to her and decided to give it a one-month trial.

The first week, he had trouble sleeping and resented that he had agreed to the change. In his own bedroom he had been free to open the window and get more fresh air whenever he wanted to, and turn on the light and read when he couldn't sleep. Now he felt trapped.

By the second week, he was able to sleep, but he still felt as though he were compromising himself. By the third week, he found that there was some compensation to sharing a bed. First of all, Melanie was a lot happier. And, second, they were having sex more often: it was much easier to make love when they didn't have to make appointments. By the last week of the experiment, he decided that he could live with the new arrangement. "I've gotten used to having her sleep beside me now," he admitted. "I guess I'm not the hermit I thought I was."

Melanie and Stewart's relationship continued to improve, and during a session several months later, Melanie said that things had gotten so good between them that she no longer needed the reassurance of having Stewart sleep with her. "I know you love your own room," she said. "I'd rather have you stay with me, but I don't think I need it any more." Through the Behavior Change Request Dialogue, he had been able to give her enough reassurance that he cared about her and valued her so that she was able to let go of that particular request. But, to her surprise, Stewart would have no part of it. "I'd be lonely in my own room," he said. "I wouldn't know what to do with myself."

What was going on here? Somehow, in the act of responding to Melanie's need for more intimacy, Stewart was discovering a hidden need of his own. In the conversations I had with Stewart, I learned that his mother and father had not been comfortable with physical or verbal expressions of love. Stewart maintained that this didn't bother him. "I knew that they loved me," he said. "They just showed it in other ways." In other words, his way of adapting to their lack of affection was to decide that he didn't need any. "I remember visiting other kids' homes," he told me, "and their parents were more affectionate to me than my own. One woman would even hug and kiss me. I was really uncomfortable around her. I was much more used to my parents' style of parenting."

When he and Melanie were first married, he was drawn to her because of her affectionate nature, but eventually her need for intimacy seemed excessive to him, and he began to withdraw, just as he had pulled away from the adults who had been physically demonstrative to him when he was a child. But now, with more insight into the nature of his problems and with a desire to be more intentional in his relationship, he had been able to overcome his resistance and respond to Melanie's needs. In the process he had discovered his own repressed need for affection and was able to satisfy a hidden need of his own.

I have witnessed this phenomenon of two-way healing so many times in my work with couples that I can now say with confidence that most husbands and wives have identical needs, but what is openly acknowledged in one is denied in the other. When the partners with the denied need are able to overcome their resistance and satisfy the other partners' overt need, a part of the unconscious mind interprets the caring behavior as self-directed. Love of the self is achieved through the love of the other.

To understand why the psyche works in this peculiar way, we need to recall our earlier discussion about the brain. The old brain doesn't know that the outside world exists. Instead, it responds to the symbols generated by the cerebral cortex. Lacking a direct connection to the external world, the old brain assumes that all behavior is inner-directed. When you are able to become more generous and loving to your spouse, therefore, your old brain assumes that this activity is intended for you.

Rewards and Resistance

TO SUMMARIZE, Melanie and Stewart reaped three important benefits from doing the Behavior Change Request Dialogue:

1. The partner who requested the change in behavior was able to resolve some childhood needs.
2. The partner who made the changes recovered aspects of the lost self.
3. The partner who made the changes satisfied repressed needs that were identical to the partner's.

The result of all this growth was a dramatic increase in positive feelings between them. Both Melanie and Stewart felt better about themselves because they had been able to satisfy each other's fundamental needs. Meanwhile, they felt better about their partners because their partners were helping them satisfy *their* needs. This made them more willing to stretch beyond their resistance into more positive, nurturing behaviors. Through this simple process of defining their needs, understanding how they are connected with the past, and then converting them into small, positive requests, they had turned their relationship into a self-sustaining vehicle for personal growth.

Resistance

THIS BENEFICIAL CHANGE always involves some resistance. One of Freud's insights was that underneath every wish is a fear of having that wish come true. When your partner starts treating you the way you long to be treated, you experience a strange combination of pleasure and fear. You like what your partner is doing, but a part of you feels that you don't deserve it. In fact, a part of you believes that in accepting the positive behavior you are violating a powerful taboo. I touched on this common reaction before when I talked about the taboo against pleasure, but in the case of the Behavior Change Request Dialogue your resistance will be even stronger.

An example will help clarify the nature of this resistance. Let's suppose that you grew up with parents who were quick to point out your faults. Out of a misguided attempt to help you be more successful, they highlighted every one of your failings. They assumed that making your faults known to you would motivate you to correct them. All they managed to do, however, was erode your self-confidence. When you managed to triumph over their negative influence and act with a degree of self-assertion, you were told to "Stop being so cocky!" You were stung by their reaction, but you were a young child and had little choice but to cooperate. Anything else was dangerous to your survival. Over time, you began to identify with their negative view of you: "I am cocky!" Outside of your aware-ness, these negative feelings toward yourself deepened into self-hatred. When you looked for a mate, you unwittingly chose someone who perpetuated your parents' critical nature, and once again you were under attack—but this time from both the inside and the outside.

Let's suppose that for some reason your partner begins to treat you more kindly. At first you thrive on this turn of events. But gradually an inner voice makes itself heard: "You can't be respected," says the voice. "That's not allowed. If you continue along this path, you will not survive. Your existence is in the hands of others, and they won't let you be whole!" To silence this voice, you find ways to undermine your partner's behavior. Maybe you deliberately pick a fight or become suspicious of his or her motives. Ironically, you are looking for a way to deny yourself the very love and affirmation you so desperately want. Why do you do this? On an unconscious level, accepting love from your partner feels too dangerous because it contra-dicts a parent's view that you are unworthy of love. Going against a parent's edicts can trigger the fear of abandonment and death. To your old brain, it's far safer to turn away your partner's love than to trigger a parent's rage.

The defense against receiving love is more common than most people would believe. The fear can range from an inabil-ity to accept compliments to an inability to form an intimate partnership. The way to overcome this fear is to keep on with the process. I urge my clients to continue using the Behavior Change Request Dialogue until their anxiety becomes more manageable. Given enough time, they learn that the taboos that have been impeding their growth are ghosts of the past and have no real power in their present-day lives.

I was working with one man who was doing an excellent job of stretching into new behaviors. In response to his wife's requests to be more available to her and their children, he was slowly rearranging his priorities at work. He had stopped bringing work home on weekends, and he was home by six o'clock in the evening most days a week. But when his wife asked him to become a more active parent, he ran headlong into his resistance. He came into my office one day and exploded: "Harville, if I have to change one more thing, I'm going to cease to exist! I'm no longer going to be me! It's going to be the death of my personality!"

To change in the way that his partner wanted him to change meant that the "me" that he was familiar with had to go away. The rushed, successful executive was going to have to become more of a relaxed, nurturing parent. On an unconscious level, this change was equated with death. I assured him that, if he were to continue to change his behavior, he would feel anxious from time to time, but he wasn't going to die. He was not going to disappear, because he was not his behaviors, his values, or his beliefs. He was much bigger than all those things combined. In fact, if he were to change some of his more limiting behaviors and his beliefs, he would become more fully the person he was—the whole, loving, spiritual being he had been as a child. He would be able to develop the tender, nurturing side of his personality, which had been shoved aside in his efforts to excel in the business world. His family would benefit, and at the same time he would become a more complete human being.

So that he could triumph over his fear of death, I advised him to keep on with the activities that stimulated his fear. "At first you'll think you're really going to die," I told him. "A voice from deep inside you is going to say, 'Stop! This is too much! I'm going to die! I'm going to die!' But if you continue to change, eventually your old brain will recycle, and the voice will quiet down. 'I'm going to die. I'm going to die. . . . I'm going to die? But I'm *not* dying!' Ultimately the fear of death will no longer be an inhibiting factor in your campaign for self-growth."

AGAPE

WHEN THE BEHAVIOR Change Request Dialogue (which is explained in detail on pages 280–84 in Part III) is integrated into your relationship, the healing power of love relationships is not just an unconscious expectation, it is a daily fact of life. A love relationship can fulfill your hidden drive to be healed and whole and to be deeply connected with another human being. But it can't happen the way you want it to happen—easily, automatically, without defining what it is that you want, without asking, and without reciprocating. You have to moderate your old-brain reactivity with a more intentional, conscious style of interaction. You have to stop expecting the outside world to take care of you and begin to accept responsibility for your own healing. And the way you do this, paradoxically, is by focusing your energy on healing your partner. It is when you direct your energy away from yourself and toward your partner that deep-level psychological and spiritual healing begins to take place.

When making a request, rather than reacting, becomes your standard method for dealing with criticism and conflict, you will have reached a new stage in your journey toward a conscious partnership. You will have moved beyond the power struggle and the stage of awakening to the stage of transformation. Your relationship will now be based on mutual caring and love, the kind of love that can best be described by the Greek word "agape."[2] Agape is a self-transcending love that redirects eros, the life force, away from yourself and toward your partner. As one transaction follows another, the pain of the past is slowly erased, and both of you will experience the reality of your essential wholeness.

CREATING A SACRED SPACE

Before you speak, ask yourself: Is it necessary?
Is it true? Does it improve on the silence?
— SHIRDI SAI BABA

THROUGHOUT THIS BOOK, I have been talking about the vital role that safety plays in creating lasting love. Two people cannot be passionate friends unless they feel safe in each other's company. Couples need to feel physically safe, to be sure, but they also need to feel emotionally safe. Without safety, they cannot say what's on their minds, express their full range of feelings, or be who they really are. They cannot lay down their armor and connect, even if they truly want to. We are all built that way. Danger activates our defenses.

During my early work, I designed four exercises, discussed in earlier chapters, to help couples create a climate of safety. To refresh your memory, the exercises are: 1) closing down the exits that prevent intimacy, 2) returning to the caring behaviors of romantic love, 3) using the Imago Dialogue to deepen understanding and compassion, and 4) defusing anger and frustration by transforming criticisms into respectful requests. These exercises help couples develop trust and goodwill and experience more joy in their daily lives.

In addition to developing these basic exercises, Helen and I have also spent many years searching for ways to help couples manage their intense feelings of anger and rage, those outbursts that are typically fueled by childhood pain and disappointment. When people spew this archaic anger at their partners, the relationship can become a war zone. But, on the other hand, when they *repress* their anger, they can also jeopardize the relationship. When people deny this critical part of their being, they dampen their enthusiasm for life and their capacity to love. To make the relationship a safe haven, couples need to find a way to *manage* their anger that brings them closer together and sustains a feeling of connection.

MY STORY

I KNOW, FIRST HAND, the destructive power of repressed feelings. I endured subclinical depression for the first thirty-three years of my life, and my emotional numbness was one of the main reasons for the failure of my first marriage. I was depressed because I was not in touch with my sorrow and anger over the death of my parents. When I look back, it is astonishing to me that I could lose both of my parents by the age of six and not experience any emotional pain. My father died when I was eighteen months old, and I have no memory of that event. My mother died from a sudden stroke five years later. I am told that I showed little reaction. I didn't even cry. In fact, I remember my adult siblings taking me aside and praising me for being such a "brave boy." Operating on naive childhood logic, I converted their compliment into a blanket assumption: "I am loved when I deny my pain."

I learned the lesson well. In young adulthood, I was able to look back on my early life and tell myself I was fortunate that both my parents had died: it gave me the opportunity to leave the farm and live in town with my sisters, where I got a better education. This myth had its uses. I went through my childhood numb to the pain of abandonment. I pictured myself as a "lucky" person, not a poor orphan boy, and I wasted little time bemoaning my fate. I took on challenges well beyond my years and succeeded at most of them. I was on my way.

But, decades later, my repressed sorrow wreaked havoc in my first marriage. Cut off from my pain, I was not fully alive. To survive, I had anesthetized an essential part of my being. Unconsciously, I looked to my wife for what I was missing. I hungered for emotional and physical contact, but she was unable to give me enough—partly because of deficiencies in her own childhood and partly because she experienced me as withholding, cold, demanding, and needy. It was a vicious cycle. The more I wanted, the more she withheld.

One of the most telling moments in our relationship took place the day after her father died. We were alone in our bedroom, and her grief over his death was just hitting her. She cried and cried. I circled my arms around her, but my body was stiff and unyielding. There was no warmth in my embrace. Inside, I felt deeply conflicted. Intellectually, I knew that it was reasonable for her to cry over her father's death, and I wanted to comfort her. But a larger part of me was cold and unsympathetic. That part was thinking, "What's the problem? I lost both of my parents when I was a little boy, and *I* didn't cry. Why is she so emotional?" Lessons learned early in life persist.

A few years later, when I was thirty-three, I saw a therapist for the first time— not because I thought I needed any help but because personal therapy was a recommended part of my training. In one of the first sessions, the therapist asked me to tell him about my parents. I told him that they had both died when

I was very young, but that a lot of good luck had come my way as a result. Because they both died, I got to live with my sisters, get out of South Georgia, get a better education, and so on.

"Tell me about your mother's death," he said to me, cutting short my highly edited autobiography.

I started to tell him how she died, but for some reason my throat felt constricted.

"Tell me about her funeral," he said.

Once again I tried to talk. Once again, my throat seized up. Then, to my great astonishment, I burst into tears. I began to sob. There was no stopping me. I was an adult man, and there I was sobbing like a six-year-old boy. After a few minutes, my therapist looked at me kindly and said, "Harville, you are just beginning to grieve over your mother's death."

After that momentous day, I began to feel my own pain and anger—not just from the past, but from the present as well. I became less anxious. I had more compassion for other people. If my needs or wishes were disregarded, I experienced the normal feelings of sadness or anger—but not rage or depression. Because I was being reunited with my full range of feelings, I was beginning to feel fully alive. I was more in touch with who I was and where I had been, and I became open to the rhythm of my own heart.

An Exercise that Failed

IN THE ORIGINAL edition of this book, published in 1988, I included an exercise to help couples release their repressed sorrow and anger. I called it "The Full Container Exercise." It was based on the psychodynamic model of psychology that views the self as a container that is filled with pent-up emotions. According to this school of thought, purging those emotions helps people relieve their anxiety and depression and go on to live more satisfying lives.

I agreed with this theory, so I adapted a new technique for couples. First, I would ask them to sit down in chairs that faced each other. I designated one partner the "sender," and the other the "receiver." Then I would ask the sender to identify a chronic frustration that was interfering with their relationship: "You're always late." "You don't really listen to me." "You don't help with the housework." "You're on my case all the time." "You don't value what I have to say." Next, I asked the sender to think about how that frustration might be linked with painful childhood experiences. Once the connection was made, I encouraged the sender to express that frustration, amplifying the annoyance until it turned into outright anger. To protect the psyche of the receiver, I would ask him or her to create an imaginary shield to deflect the anger and to keep from feeling under attack. "The anger is not just about you," I would advise the receiver. "Its roots are deep in your partner's child-hood." Once the catharsis was complete, I would help the couple deal with the original frustration by using the Stretching exercise described in chapter 10.

Years ago, I viewed the Full Container exercise as one of the flagship techniques in Imago Therapy. But as time went on, I saw that it produced mixed results. The final portion of the exercise, the Stretching exercise, always worked. But, sometimes, the first part, the emotional catharsis, had the *opposite* effect of the one I intended. Couples would become more conflicted than they were before. Eventually, I discovered literature from other therapists that confirmed my experience. I stopped using the Full Container exercise in workshops and private sessions, and I have removed it from this revised edition of *Getting the Love You Want*. Having two people in a love relationship vent their anger at each other—even within the confines of a structured exercise and under the watchful eye of a therapist—could cause more harm than good. This was a clear example of reality not supporting the theory.

Why Anger Breeds Anger

WHAT WAS WRONG with the exercise? First of all, some partners on the receiving end of the anger still felt threatened by the outburst, no matter how much they tried to deflect the torrent. Their old brains couldn't comprehend that their partner's anger was part of a clinical exercise. When the receiving partners felt threatened, they had a hard time feeling empathic. They might mirror their partner's experience and mouth the right words— "I'm sorry you're in so much pain," but their primal instinct was to batten down the hatches or abandon ship.

There was another, more puzzling problem with the exercise. After the exercise, the partner who had vented the anger could feel angrier than usual in coming days. The exercise that had been designed to *release* stored up anger seemed equally capable of *generating* it.

I began to understand why when Helen had started reading books about neuroscience. She was fascinated by this field, partly because it shed new light on relationship dynamics. She learned that the adult brain is far more adaptable than we first thought. I was intrigued and began reading the literature myself. I discovered that scientists have known for decades that a young person's brain is greatly influenced by experience. If nerve connections are not stimulated, they are "pruned" away. When a child has new experiences, however, new pathways are formed. This plasticity gives the child a highly efficient, adaptable brain, ready for all that life has to offer.

Once upon a time, scientists believed that the adult brain was hardwired, thus immune to experience. The only way the brain changed beyond adolescence, according to early thinking, was to lose neurons with advancing age. This bleak view of the adult brain has now been revised, thanks to sophisticated imaging devices that can show physical changes in brain activity. These images have made it very clear that what adults do, think, and even feel alters the physical structure of their brains. Although the adult brain is not as adaptable as a child's brain, it remains a highly responsive organ.

A number of studies have shown that the more time adults engage in a particular activity, the more nerve cells are marshaled to the task. The brain acts like a military commander summoning new troops as they are needed. In one such study, Harvard medical researchers instructed a group of volunteers to practice a simple piano exercise for two hours a day for a week. After each practice session, the neuroscientists took images of the volunteers' brains so they could measure the size of the area devoted to finger activity. By the fifth day, they observed a significant increase in the size and activity of that area. Apparently, one of the reasons that "practice makes perfect" is that repeating an activity commandeers more neurons to the job.

Remarkably, researchers discovered that the same brain expansion takes place when people merely *imagine* doing a specific activity. As an extension of the piano experiment, the Harvard team asked another group of volunteers to imagine that they were playing a simple piece of music. They had no pianos in front of them. In fact, they were asked to keep their hands and fingers perfectly still. When the volunteers' brains were scanned at the end of a week, the scientists were amazed to see that the virtual piano players had the same expanded neural pathways as the people who actually played the piano. They had discovered that mental training and imagery can literally rewire the brain.

For the purposes of my work with couples, I was keenly interested in the fact that changing your thoughts can change your brain. In a type of therapy called Behavior Change Therapy, or BCT, people are trained in how to use their rational minds to challenge the thoughts and beliefs that can trigger depression. As an example, a person might generate this irrational train of thought: "I've made a number of calls to family and friends, and only one person has called back. Nobody loves me anymore." Taken to its illogical extreme, it becomes "Because no one loves me, I'm going to be abandoned and die." The emotional part of the brain reacts to this depressing thought as though it were real, and the person feels rejected, lonely, and scared.

When people see the absurdity of this type of catastrophic thinking, they can begin to think more rationally: "So, people are not returning my calls. That doesn't mean they don't love me. They may be busy or out of town." Avoiding the dooms-day thinking can prevent the depressive feelings.

Research now shows that BCT can relieve depression just as well as antidepressant medications. Brain scans help explain why. When people use their rational minds to defeat depression, the part of the brain that is linked with rumination and obsessive thinking calms down. On a computerized image, that area appears darker, indicating that less oxygen is being consumed. This calm state extends beyond the mental exercise. People trained in BCT can go through life with a less reactive brain, no longer triggering depressive or anxious thoughts. Once again, thinking alone has been shown to alter the physiology of the brain. Mind over gray matter.

THE HOLDING EXERCISE

TAKEN TOGETHER, THESE new findings about the change-able adult brain, combined with my own observations about couples and similar observations of other Imago Therapists, have changed Imago Therapy. First of all, my colleagues and I no longer encourage couples to direct their archaic rage at each other. The new research shows that dwelling on anger has the potential to enhance the anger, not defuse it. I used to think that venting anger was like blowing the foam off a glass of beer: A few puffs, and you're done with it. Instead, it's like blowing on a fire—the more you blow, the hotter the flame. On a physiological level, expressing anger on a regular basis enlarges the part of the brain devoted to negative emotions. What you do is what you get. With so much cerebral real estate devoted to anger, an angry response can become a conditioned response.

Another fact about the brain is that the unconscious mind experiences all anger as dangerous to the self. It cannot determine whether the anger is directed at itself or at someone else. Indeed, new studies in the neurosciences of a phenomenon called "mirror neurons" tell us that in face-to-face situations, when neurons fire in someone else's brain, identical neurons fire in our own brain. When others are angry, we become angry. In other words, what you see is what you feel.

So, now, we encourage couples to share emotions—other than anger—that they experienced in childhood, such as grief, fear, and sadness. These less volatile emotions underlie the anger, and we have found that expressing them to a receptive partner helps relieve the hostility without reinforcing it. When couples share their childhood wounds with one another, they deepen their understanding of each other's past. They also experience renewed empathy for each other's suffering. Ultimately, they begin to see one another as "wounded" people, not "bad" people. Through this more accurate lens, they can see that most of their conflicts originate from childhood pain, not from any present-day malicious intentions.

One of the exercises we use to facilitate the sharing of childhood experiences is called the Holding exercise. Unlike the Full Container exercise, this one helps relieve repressed feelings without generating more negative emotions. I got the idea for the specific form of the exercise while going for a walk. I found myself looking into the window of a bookstore—a habit of mine—and in the window I saw a parenting book with the word "holding" in the title. The cover drawing showed a woman holding a child on her lap with the child's face on the left side of her chest, over her heart. Many mothers instinctively hold their babies in this position. It appears to be a great source of comfort for infants, perhaps because hearing the mother's heart and being held close to her body is reminiscent of being inside the womb. As I studied the drawing, I began to imagine couples holding each other in this fashion and talking about early childhood experiences. My gut feeling was that this primal holding position would elicit a flood of emotions.

When I went home to share this idea with Helen, she reminded me of her earlier work with a model of therapy in which the therapist holds and comforts a client—essentially "reparenting" them. Using her insights, we developed a similar holding exercise. But instead of having the therapist hold the client, we asked the partners to hold each other, so that the bonding experience would take place between the partners rather than with us. We asked one partner to sit in a comfortable position and hold the other partner with his or her head across the heart. From this position, they would recount painful childhood experiences while the holding partner gently and warmly mirrored their comments.

We decided to experiment with the Holding exercise at the next couple's workshop. An older couple, John and Vivian, volunteered to be the first guinea pigs. I instructed John to sit against a wall and then hold Vivian in his arms as though she was a young child, and I positioned her head next to his heart. Next, I asked John to ask his partner to recall memories from her childhood. To facilitate the flow of memories, I suggested that he make encouraging sounds and mirror back to her what she was saying. When she was through expressing a thought or feeling, he might ask, "Is there more?"

After momentary embarrassment, John and Vivian began to follow my instructions. Vivian spoke in a very quiet voice, keeping most of what she had to say between the two of them. John bent over her, listening intently. Their murmured expressions went on for several minutes. Then, suddenly, Vivian began to sob. John held her more tightly and began to rock her. Tears filled his eyes as well.

The experience was very powerful for the couple. John's compassion for Vivian's pain was evident to everyone in the room. Later in the session, I had them switch roles, with Vivian holding her partner, and John was able to experience what it was like to feel safe and nurtured as he told his own story. When the two of them talked about their experience in front of the group, they said they had learned a lot about each other's inner worlds and felt deep empathy for one another. Like many couples, they discovered that they had endured many of the same insults in childhood, but had adapted to them in different ways. The unconscious agenda that each had brought into the marriage was beginning to be revealed, and their wounds were healing in the process.

When couples take part in the Holding exercise, they get the response they have been longing for all their lives. Their old brains perceive their partners as surrogate parents. Only this time around, those parents have become attuned parents: accepting, nurturing, calm, attentive, and nonjudgmental. Pain from the past can be healed in the present when you receive attention and empathy from a loving partner.

REMOVING ALL NEGATIVITY

ONCE WE REMOVED the Full Container exercise from Imago Therapy and added the Holding exercise, couples began to make more rapid progress. Their conflicts became more subdued and their mutual admiration grew. But there was yet more ground to gain.

We discovered that couples had an even more joyful relationship when they abolished all forms of negativity. This involved getting rid of blatant forms such as anger, shame, and criticism, but also eliminating more subtle forms as well, including such well-known ploys as "helpful" criticism, inattention, condescension, "the silent treatment," and using a bored or weary tone of voice. Ideally, this ban would extend all the way to eliminating even negative thoughts. Because we all have internal radar that makes us astute at picking up nonverbal cues from our partners, we can detect the subtle changes in posture and expression that accompany their negative thoughts, which means that a complete transformation cannot be made until that aspect of negativity is addressed.

Keep in mind that the goal is not to repress the *feelings* behind our negative thoughts and behaviors—that would only add to our store of pent-up emotions—but rather to bring them out into the open and see them for what they really are: a warning sign that some aspect of the relationship needs work. And as you have learned in earlier chapters, the best way to start solving a relationship problem is to look at your own contribution: "Here I am, having critical thoughts about my partner again. What does this say about me? What am I doing or *not* doing right now that is feeding my negative attitude?"

The task may seem daunting, but the rewards are great. As negativity recedes, goodwill rushes in to fill the void. Without conscious effort, you find yourself focusing on your partner's admirable qualities, much as you did during courtship. Only this time, you will have the insights and tools you need to sustain your regard. Meanwhile, your partner will also be seeing *you* in a much more positive light, and you will both thrive in its warm glow. Eventually, a sacred space will well up between you, one that both of you want to nurture and protect. With conflict removed, connection will deepen and passion will flow.

WHAT IS NEGATIVITY?

I WANT TO stop for a moment and clarify what I mean by negativity. Negativity is any thought, word, or deed that tells your partner: "You're not okay when you think what you think or act the way that you act." In essence, you are rejecting your partner's "otherness." We sometimes feel the need to negate our partners when they do or say something that makes us uncomfortable. Usually, they are just being themselves. But from our point of view, they are threatening an image that we have of them, or they are failing to meet an unspoken need of our own.

Typically, negativity makes its first appearance in a love relationship as denial: "I can't believe you did that!" "You never said anything like that before!" "You can't really mean that." "You're not that kind of person." The fact that your partner is a separate individual with wishes and needs different from yours is starting to dawn on you, and you feel threatened. Your denial is a desperate ploy to hold on to your illusions: "Say it ain't so!"

When your partner continues to depart from your projected image, the tendency is to bring out the big guns, one by one. Your arsenal includes shame, blame, criticism, invasiveness, avoidance, and, finally, blanket condemnation. First you shame. "How do you think that feels?!" "You ought to be ashamed by the way you treated my friend." In essence, you are trying to make your partner feel guilty for being who he or she is.

Then you blame. "You were late, and that made me really upset. That's why I haven't been talking to you." "If you hadn't been so angry, we would have been able to settle the matter in very little time." When you blame, you put all the burden of your frustrations on your partner.

Next, you begin to criticize your partner's character traits in addition to his or her unacceptable behaviors: "You are so insensitive." "You are untrustworthy." "You always think about yourself first." You are attempting to paint your partner not only as the source of all your frustration but to make them into a "bad" person as well.

A more subtle ploy is to invade your partner's psyche and act as if you had x-ray vision: "That is *not* what you really think." "The reason you're so crabby is that you are obsessing too much about work." "If you'll just listen to me, I'll tell you what you need to do."

The final weapon is absolutism: "You *never* listen to me!" "You *always* leave the hard work for me." "That's just the way you are." "*Every time* I make a simple suggestion, you have a big fit."

It's no wonder that our partners feel depressed, stay late at work, drink too much, don't want to make love, or stay up late by themselves. Being with us is not a safe place to be. They experience being chopped up into little pieces, dissected, and rejected. This is a form of emotional annihilation. At the base level, it expresses contempt. No one can be healed or grow in such a toxic environment. To get the love we want, we need to eliminate negativity in all its forms.

There's another good reason to stop negativity: the negativity that we express toward our partners comes back like a boomerang and affects us as well. That's because the old brain does not know whether the negativity is being directed outward or inward. This theory has been backed up by studies showing that when one person yells at another, the person being yelled at produces more of the stress hormone cortisol. That's to be expected. But, perhaps more interestingly, the same increase in cortisol is seen in the angry person as well. One could say that any negativity that we direct toward others is a form of self-abuse.

COLD TURKEY

REMOVING ALL NEGATIVITY from our love relationship was the final turning point for Helen and me. When we succeeded, we finally achieved the relationship we had wanted all of our adult lives—one that was safe, intimate, and passionate. For us, eliminating negativity was a two-stage process. The first stage was a gradual working through of the power struggle. One would think that two therapists would be able to avoid the power struggle altogether, but this was not so. Like many readers of this book, Helen and I had difficult childhoods. We are also intense, highly motivated people, each burdened with a heavy dose of perfectionism. On top of that, we have strong opinions about nearly everything, and we both tend to think that we are "right." It took us a long time to realize that each of us could be "right" all the time, or we could be in a relationship! During the worst of times, our conflicts were on a par with many of the couples I counseled.

Over a period of many years, we overcame most of our problems by using the exercises in this book. We practiced the Imago Dialogue and used it with some success within our own relationship and with our children. We still marvel at its power to defuse conflict and forge understanding. We became more thoughtful lovers and made frequent expressions of love and gratitude through words, notes, gifts, and thoughtful gestures. Over time, we learned how to work together harmoniously as business partners. There were moments when we felt deep love and empathy for each other. But it was not enough. We still felt a lingering tension lurking in the relationship.

The underlying problem, we eventually discovered, is that we were allowing negativity to rupture the connection between us. It didn't take much. A critical comment. Impatience. A raised tone of voice. Sometimes, we would degenerate into loud arguments. Whenever we descended into negativity, our pain was acute. Negativity never got us what we wanted. It always made matters worse. When we cooled off, we realized that it would take us hours or even days of repair work to feel connected again. Eventually, it became clear as day that being negative with each other was irrational, abusive, and counter-productive. We agreed that the only solution was to eliminate all forms of negativity once and for all. We decided to go cold turkey.

To enforce our decision, we instituted a rule: whoever initiated a negative comment or behavior would have to counter it with three positive statements about the other person: "I appreciate the fact that you were an attentive listener to me last night, even though you were very tired." "You gave me such great feedback on the letter I was writing to the board members." "I loved it when you took the time to go for a walk with me, even though you were busy." Each positive statement had to be unique and specific, and we couldn't repeat anything we had said before. A hidden benefit of this rule was that we discovered many wonderful things about each other that we had been overlooking when we were upset.

Our statements of appreciation increased the flow of love between us. Every time Helen told me something she genuinely admired about me, I was deeply moved—each and every time. She had the same response when I praised her. Our admiration gradually evolved into a state of "chronic adoration."

Finally, we were giving each other the respect we both wanted on a continual basis. What's more, we found it easier and easier to do. Our relationship had become such a sacred place for us that we had no desire to violate it. To slip back into old behaviors became unthinkable.

Helen and I felt so blessed by what we had achieved that we held two recommitment ceremonies, the first of which was at our annual conference with our colleagues in the Imago community. We wrote new vows of commitment that were in keeping with all we had learned and recited them before the group.

Afterwards, our colleagues lifted us high in the air and paraded us around the room while everyone sang and danced. Two months later, we held a New Year's Eve ceremony in the majestic Riverside Church in New York City, where we are members. Our pastor led us through our vows in front of 250 family members and friends, after which we retired to a grand hall on the Hudson River where we ate and danced and were roasted and toasted until midnight. When the fireworks exploded, we felt like they were just for us. We included all the celebrants of the New Year as witnesses to our love and our future.

SAM AND AMELIA

IT WASN'T LONG before Helen and I were integrating all we had learned about negativity into our therapy sessions and workshops. Since then, we have been pleased to discover how rapidly some couples can weed out negativity, even those who have at times been in grave distress. Helen and I witnessed a particularly amazing and rapid transformation at a recent week-long Imago workshop. Sam and Amelia's story is a poignant illustration of the healing power of "owning" and then subsequently withdrawing the negativity that you bring to a love relationship.

Sam and Amelia stood out from the other couples from the very first day. During group sessions all the couples sat side-by-side in a semicircle. Most of them talked easily with each other during the breaks. Several couples who were there to enrich, not salvage, their relationships would give each other affectionate looks and touches on a regular basis. But not Sam and Amelia. They talked to each other only when taking part in an exercise. They kept their chairs more than a foot apart, preventing even casual contact. Whenever I looked at them, I saw that Amelia's face and body were heavy with grief. Sam had a blank look on his face, and he seemed withered and wan. The two of them came to the dining room at different times or sat down at separate tables. They seemed to be a couple barreling toward divorce.

On the third day of the workshop, however, after Helen had spent some time counseling them individually, Amelia had a profound breakthrough. She and Sam were working on an exercise designed to help them identify their exits—the tactics they used to distance themselves from one another. At one point, Amelia put down her notebook, walked over to Helen and asked her a question. "Is criticism an exit?" she asked in a quiet voice. "Is it possible to exit a relationship by constantly criticizing your partner?" Helen replied that criticism was a tried and true exit and that intimacy was not possible when either or both partners were under attack. Amelia nodded and went back to her chair.

When the exercise was completed, it was time for a break. We asked the couples to spend thirty minutes of their break time talking with each other about their exits. To keep the experience positive, we asked them to share the information using the Imago Dialogue.

The group reassembled in the early afternoon, and Helen asked if anyone wanted to talk about what they had learned. Amelia was the first to raise her hand. "I feel utterly devastated," she whispered, her voice low and tremulous. The other couples leaned closer so they could hear. "I'm at a total loss. I've just realized that I criticize Sam all the time. I've been in therapy before, several times, and we've been to two marital therapists, but I've never seen this about myself. I feel so horrible about what I've done to this relationship. And I have no idea where to go with it. I don't know what to do. If I take away the criticism, there's nothing left. I'd have nothing to say to him. I feel like I've just stepped off a ledge and I don't know how long I'm going to fall or where I'm going to land." We were all transfixed. People rarely make such a candid confession in front of others.

Helen and I asked Amelia and Sam if they were willing to come up to the front and continue their story. They both nodded. We took two chairs and turned them so they were facing each other. As Amelia and Sam sat down in the chairs, Amelia drew in a ragged breath. Sam reached out and took her hands, and they looked into each other's eyes. All exits were closed.

I knelt down so that I was at their eye level. "Would you be willing to talk about what it feels like to be in your relationship?"

Amelia began. "My criticisms aren't subtle," she said. "They are overt. Right in your face. If Sam does anything that threatens me, I won't let him get away with it. If he does something I don't like, like flirting with a woman at a party, I give him the third degree on the way home. I tell him exactly what I saw him do. And he will say, 'No I didn't do that.' I'll tell him, 'For an hour, this is exactly what you did. You looked at her this way. You said this. You touched her there.' The blaming has been so intense, and I was a hundred percent sure I was right. I thought that if I could just beat him into believing how bad he was, he would change. I did that for twenty years. More, maybe."

"Did it work?" I asked.

"No. Never!" she laughed at the absurdity.

Sam took his turn. "We almost didn't come to this workshop because we were going to get a divorce anyway. During most of the first day, I was mentally planning where I was going to live. I wasn't even thinking about resolving anything. I couldn't listen to what you and Helen were saying. There was nothing I had to learn. Nothing I had to resolve. I just kept thinking, 'What am I doing here with this person? I have to get away.'"

I asked Sam how he defended himself against Amelia's criticism. Amelia jumped in and answered for him.

"Sam didn't counter-blame," she said. "He'd just retreat. He'd disappear emotionally or go to another room. And I chased him so I could blame him some more."

Amelia continued with the same remarkable candor. "During these last two days, I have had no place to go but to accept the fact that I am a blamer. To deny it, I would have felt even more pain than I was in already. It was the bottom. I was so overwhelmed by my insight into myself, I couldn't listen to anyone. I couldn't talk. I realized, 'This is what I do. I blame all the time. I try to control everything. I want to keep Sam in a little box so that I can know what he's doing. I want to keep him in box so that I can try to survive over here.' But all of a sudden, this afternoon, I realized I couldn't control him or blame him anymore. I have to stop. I have no choice. Now that my eyes are opened, I have to stop the constant criticism. It's insane. Criticism doesn't work. It gives you the opposite of what you want. It makes you feel very bad."

Later that day and the next, Amelia and Sam sought out Helen for more private counseling and support. During breaks, the two of them would sit off by themselves, talking intently, looking dazed and earnest. Their body language was the opposite of what it had been when they arrived at the retreat. They leaned toward each other, looked into each other's eyes, and touched each other constantly. The connection between them was palpable.

On Friday, the final day of the workshop, Amelia asked if she and Sam could talk to the group once again. Something remarkable had happened to them the night before that they wanted to share. They came up to the front of the semicircle holding hands.

Sam began, "We haven't slept in the same bed for years. We didn't want to be that close to each other. So, last night, I was lying in my bed unable to sleep, and Amelia was over in her bed. I could hear her sighing."

Amelia said, "I was wide awake, and I was having negative thoughts about Sam. I tried to stop them, but I couldn't. Suddenly, I knew that if I stayed in my own bed and remained in my critical state of mind that it was going to be the end of our marriage. There would be no hope for us if I didn't act on what I was learning. I knew I should go over and talk with him. But I was frightened—if I broke out of our mold, everything would be different. I had no idea what was going to happen. Then I heard Harville and Helen say in my mind, 'Just keep on pedaling. Keep on working the exercises.' So I got up and lay down next to Sam, and said that I wanted to have a dialogue with him. He agreed. I began telling him what I was thinking and feeling. He was present. He listened to me. He supported what I was saying. He mirrored me back. He validated me. He was absolutely incredible. The next thing I knew, all my fear had turned into peace and calm, and I felt this amazing love for him. I've treated him so badly, yet he still was willing to listen to me and understand me."

"It was easy for me to do," Sam said. "I just followed the steps of the dialogue exercise. Because I knew how to respond to her, what would work, I felt much more self-confident. I could handle her. I didn't need to retreat or run away. I could just hold her in my mind and see her as a wounded child."

"This was my very first glimpse of real power in this relationship," said Amelia. "The real way to be safe. Before, I thought that safety depended on being on guard. I found that being honest and vulnerable in front of him—instead of being critical and controlling—was the only way to connect. For the first time in decades, we both feel safe enough to reach out to each other. We found the bridge to connection."

In just one week's time, Sam and Amelia had gathered most of the insights and skills they needed to transform their relationship. They have a great deal of work ahead of them, and they've wisely decided to continue the work with a therapist. But in my mind, they've made the most important transformation already. They've realized on a gut level that their reliance on the complementary defenses of criticism and avoidance was destroying their love for each other. Once Amelia found the courage to acknowledge the extent of her negativity, Sam was able to open his arms, forgive her, and comfort her. For the first time, Amelia felt safe enough to lay down her weapons.

CORE SCENE REVISION

CORE SCENE REVISION is another exercise that I rely on to help couples eliminate negativity. It is designed for couples who go beyond criticism and avoidance and engage in yelling matches and long, drawn out fights. I call these recurring battles "Core Scenes" because they replay the central childhood traumas of both individuals. Basically, the childhood adaptations of one partner are pitted against the childhood adaptations of the other, making the encounter doubly wounding. Typically, core scenes end in an impasse, with both individuals in deep emotional pain. These futile, hurtful exchanges must end before love can begin.

One couple, Jack and Deborah, had recurring fights that would last until the early hours of the morning. They named them "three-o'clockers" because, typically, that's when the fights would end. These were not explosive fights, but wearing, exhausting, and repetitive confrontations that ended without resolution. Following a three-o'clocker, the two of them would be tired and depressed for days.

During one therapy session, I asked them to recount several of their recent fights to see if they could identify what the fights had in common. Jack was quick to see their repetitive nature, and once they had reduced their fights to their lowest common denominators, they both laughed. But then Jack said with a note of sadness, "This isn't something that I feel very proud of. Why do we fall into the same trap over and over again? I'm sick of it."

According to their description, their core scene goes something like this:

Act I: It is five o'clock in the evening. Jack comes home from work and is confronted by Deborah, who wants him to do a chore. It could be anything—help plan a vacation, do some yardwork, sort through the mail. Jack says he would be happy to do it—later. After he has had a chance to take his evening run.

Act II: Jack goes jogging. He comes home. As he enters the door, Deborah approaches him again and asks if he will now do X. Jack says, "Sure. After I take a shower."

Act III: Jack takes a shower. Deborah tracks him down and insists that now is the time to do X. Jack says, "Just let me have a drink."

Act IV (the climax of the drama): Jack has several drinks. He begins to relax and enjoy himself. Deborah enters the room, irate. "Why don't you either do it now or tell me you aren't going to do it?" Deborah yells. "You are driving me crazy!" "But I *do* want to do it," counters Jack. "Just give me time. I'm tired. I want to relax. Back off."

Jack works on a crossword puzzle or watches TV and ignores his wife. She gets hysterical. "I hate you!" she cries out. "You never do what you say. You never listen to me! I feel like I'm living with a robot! I have no feelings for you!" Jack tries to block out her anger by concentrating more intently on what he is doing. Then, finding no peace, he gets up and leaves the house.

Act V: Jack comes home hours later. He's had several more drinks. Deborah launches into her attack once more. The fight continues, with Deborah delivering devastating criticisms and Jack trying either to placate her or ignore her. Eventually they both get tired of the melodrama and turn away from each other in despair.

Let's analyze this drama for a moment. If one were to search for Jack and Deborah in the psychology textbooks, Jack would be described as "passive-aggressive." He is angry at Deborah for organizing his life and intruding on his space, but is afraid to express it directly. Instead he stalls, jogs, showers, drinks, works on the crossword puzzle—in other words, takes full advantage of the numerous exits he has built into the relationship. Deborah would be labeled as "aggressive-aggressive." "She's a bulldog," says Jack, not without admiration. She is up front with her demands and her anger. The irreducible element in their core scene is that the more Deborah attacks, the more Jack retreats, and the more Jack retreats, the more Deborah feels abandoned. Deborah's anger at Jack's passivity is, in reality, disguised panic. She is terrified of being left alone, and Jack's inertness makes her feel as if she were dealing with a nonentity, a ghost partner.

I explained to Deborah and Jack that, in order to end the impasse, it might help to rewrite their play—not metaphorically, but literally. I suggested that they go home, take out paper and pencils, and rewrite the drama to give it a happier ending. It might help to read their new script several times so that the new options would be just as instructive to them as their habituated ones. I assured them that any change at all would be beneficial. Indeed, just being able to recognize a given fight as a core scene would be a positive step. Then, even if they managed to change just one of the acts, they would be creating the possibility of a new resolution.

Here are a couple of ways Jack and Deborah's core scene might be revised: Deborah could become less aggressive, essentially honoring Jack's request to "back off." After asking him once to do a particular chore and getting no response, she could stop making the request. Jack's need to withdraw might become less intense. He might gain the psychic space he needs to be able to do the chore before taking a shower or doing the crosswords.

Or the script might be rewritten so that Jack states his position more openly. "No. I don't want to do that job. It's not all that important to me. I'd rather do Y." Deborah would be startled by his assertiveness, but if he persisted in affirming his own priorities, she would eventually become relieved. After all, what she really wants is a partner who is an independent, confident human being, not an automaton.

This practice of defining a core scene and then writing alternative versions can be an effective tool. When couples are able to objectify their arguments, identify the key elements in the drama, and then create different options, they are using the rational new brain to defeat the old brain's fight or flight response. They are creating new neural pathways that channel their feelings into a more calm and positive direction.

Positive Flooding

IN RECENT YEARS, I've added another key exercise to Imago Therapy. Its purpose, as in all the exercises I've described in this chapter, is to help couples leave their negativity behind them and look towards a future free of emotional toxins. This final exercise is the grand finale, the ultimate expression of love and regard between couples. I call it "Positive Flooding."

In its basic form, two people in a love relationship write down all the things they appreciate about one another. The list can include what they love about each other's bodies and character traits, appreciation for favors or activities they've done in the past, and overall statements of love and adoration. Then the partners take turns "flooding" each other with these specific expressions of love.

In the second part of the exercise, each person gets out a piece of paper and makes a list of all the qualities her or she would like to have praised. "Tell me that you appreciate how hard I work to support us." "Tell me that you like how intently I listen to you." "Tell me that you like my long, shapely legs." Then the partners exchange lists and take turns flooding each other with their specific requests. It's like making a list of all the things you want for Christmas, only in this case, you get to receive them all.

Helen and I practice the flooding exercise regularly. Even though we designed the exercise and have watched it performed over and over again, we still feel moved by the intensity of the love and affirmation we receive from each other. It makes us feel deeply, thoroughly loved.

In the workshop version, all of the couples perform the exercise simultaneously. One person in each couple sits in a chair while the other partner circles around the chair. For the first minute, I ask the speakers to describe what they like about their partners' physical features—a graceful curve to the lips, silky skin, a handsome nose, and so on. For the next minute, I ask them to speak a little louder and talk about their partners' admirable character traits—trustworthiness, honesty, kindness, bravery, intelligence, etc. The third time around, I ask them to speak louder still and proclaim their gratitude for favors their partners have done for them—nursing them through a cold, putting chains on the tires in the middle of a snowstorm, going willingly to a family reunion, being a source of comfort when a family member had died. At the culmination of the exercise, the admiring partners proclaim their overall feelings of love and appreciation—"I can't believe I am married to such a marvelous person." "I love you, I love you, I love you." "You are the woman of my dreams!" "You are my best friend and lover!" The energy is contagious. There are shouts of laughter, bear hugs, and tears of joy.

Many of us have never heard someone say to us in a strong voice, "I love you." "You are wonderful." Instead, we've heard people yell, "Be quiet!" "Go away." "Mind your own business." "You are crazy!" This exercise opens the flood gates and inundates people with joy.

PORTRAIT OF TWO RELATIONSHIPS

What makes a happy marriage? It is a question which all men
and women ask one another. . . . The answer is to be found, I think,
in the mutual discovery, by two who marry, of the deepest need
of the other's personality, and the satisfaction of that need.

— PEARL BUCK

I STARTED OUT life as a minister, not a therapist. I was introduced to the ministry at a tender age. As a young boy, I was a
member of the First Baptist Church in Statesboro, Georgia,
and was involved in a youth group called the Baptist Training
Union. Once a year our church sponsored what we called
"Youth Sunday," a special day devoted to the young people in
the community. The year I turned fifteen, I happened to be
chosen to deliver the traditional youth address. I remember
standing behind the pulpit dressed in a suit and tie, a cold sweat
slicking my shirt to my back. I looked out over a church filled
with young people and their parents and somehow managed to
open my mouth and talk. Despite my anxiety, I must have
given a reasonably good sermon, because several people came
up to me afterward and said, "You should be a preacher."

Apparently the minister of our church, George Lovell, thought so, too, because several weeks later he called me to his office. "Harville," he said, "there's a little Baptist church about twenty miles out of town. They just lost their minister. They called me and asked if I knew anyone who could preach for them the next couple of Sundays. Would you like to do that?" Flushed with success from my youth address, I said that I would.

For the next few days, I studied the Bible with a new sense of responsibility and pored over a book Lovell had given me called *Great Sermons,* a collection of sermons from famous religious leaders. On Sunday, my sister and brother-in-law drove me to church because I was too young to drive. If I recall, the message that I delivered that morning from the depths of my experience went something like this: "Man is a sinner. We have a loving God. In order to be saved, we have to meet God. And you do that through commitment, confession, Baptism, prayer, and trying to lead an exemplary life." I believe I also warned about what Baptists call "backsliding," the tendency of even devout Christians to fall away from a faithful life.

I preached at the little church for the next couple of Sundays, and word got back to George Lovell that I was doing a good job. From that point on, he began to think of me as his "preacher boy," and for the next few years, when other small communities needed a stand-in minister he would send me.

One Sunday he sent me out to a little church in Guyton, Georgia, called the Pine Street Baptist Church. I preached for four consecutive weeks. After the fourth sermon, the church leaders held a meeting and decided to ask me to be their permanent preacher. I was only seventeen at the time—a gangly young man with a cracking voice—but they wanted me anyway. (In the Baptist church, you don't have to have extensive theological training to be ordained; you just need to be called by God and by a congregation. If your home church honors the request of the petitioning congregation, then you can become a minister.)

As I look back on that period of my life, I realize that being called to preach at the Pine Street Baptist Church was one of the real gifts of my life. The Pine Street congregation was a very loving congregation, and they ministered to my hidden depression and loneliness. Their love for me enhanced my self-confidence, and in a few years I managed to increase the active church community from thirty to a little over two hundred people. I preached there every Sunday for two and a half years. Between the ages of seventeen and nineteen and a half, I baptized over fifty people and buried eighteen.

In the summers I began to be called upon by various churches to lead youth revivals, and as a result of all this experience, my sermonic style got better and better. During one revival I looked around me and realized that there were over a thousand people straining to hear my every word. At the end of the session, sixty young people came down the aisle and gave their lives to Christ. Twelve of them decided to join the ministry. My reputation as a youth evangelist began to grow outside Georgia.

I wanted to continue as a minister, but to do that I felt the need for a college education. Eventually I saved enough of my weekly fifty-dollar paycheck from the Pine Street Church to buy a car and pay my tuition at Mercer University, a Baptist college about a hundred miles away. I studied hard during the week and drove back to the Pine Street Church each weekend to deliver the sermon.

In my third year of college, I took an excellent course in philosophy, and a whole new world of logical thinking opened up to me. As I became absorbed in the realm of abstract ideas, nothing seemed simple any more, and when I went out to preach, my sermons were filled with probing questions.

I soon discovered that you don't win souls to Jesus by engaging in a linguistic analysis of the Bible. The summer after completing that fateful philosophy class, I was invited to lead a revival at a church in a fairly good-sized town, a church where I had worked wonders the year before. The first night, all the seats in the arena were filled with people eager to hear the new preacher boy. To their surprise, my opening speech was about the concept of "eternal life" and whether the word "eternal" referred to the quality of life or its duration. When I got up to speak the second night, I looked up and noticed that there were some empty seats in the balcony. By the third night, there were empty seats riddling the main floor. At the end of the weeklong revival, only a faithful few had stayed to listen. When it was all over, the minister took me aside to have a heart-to-heart talk. He brought up the fact that the previous year I had convinced 120 people to devote their lives to Christ; this year only eight people had ventured down the aisle. "You've started college, Harville, haven't you?" he said, the disappointment evident in his voice. I nodded. "Well, college has ruined you," he concluded.

My brief career as an evangelist rapidly drew to a close, but my intellectual curiosity about philosophy and religion flourished. In my remaining year of college, I added a third interest—psychology. To me, theology, philosophy, and psychology were three portholes into one central reality, the reality of man's existence, and each one offered a slightly different perspective. If I looked through all three portholes at once, I believed that I saw more of the total picture. When I enrolled in graduate school at the University of Chicago, it was in the new interdisciplinary field of psychology and religion.

From that point on, the events of my life led me deeper and deeper into the study of just one of these disciplines, psychology. When I finally arrived at my destination, I looked up and discovered that I had landed in the rather specialized field of couples therapy. From my beginnings as a preacher boy in South Georgia, I had wound up as a marital therapist in upper

Manhattan. But the formative years that I spent preaching and baptizing and bringing souls to Christ were not left behind me. To this day they continue to be very much a part of the way I view the world. To me, man's spiritual wholeness is inextricably linked with his psychological wholeness, and the work that I am now doing as a therapist feels just as much a part of God's work as my summer revivals. When I help a man and a woman heal the rift between them and become passionate friends, I believe that I am bringing them closer to God.

What leads me to believe that couple's therapy is a spiritual path? How can talking to people about mundane things such as "behavior changes" and "caring behaviors" and "childhood wounding" have anything to with helping them experience the divine? I had better define my terms. When I use the word "spiritual" I'm not giving the word its most common usage. I'm not talking about going to church or following the doctrines of a particular religion or attaining a rarefied state of mind through meditation, fasting, or prayer. What I'm talking about is a native spirituality, a spirituality that is as much a part of our being as our sexuality, a spirituality that is a gift to us the moment we are conceived, a spirituality that we lose sight of in childhood but that can be experienced once again in adulthood if we learn how to heal old wounds. When we regain awareness of our essential inner unity, we make an amazing discovery: we are no longer cut off from the rest of the world. Because we are in touch with the miracle of our own being, we are free to experience the beauty and complexity of the world. The universe has meaning and purpose, and we experience ourselves as part of a larger whole.

It is my conviction that one of the surest routes to this exalted state of being is the humble path of becoming committed partners. When we gather the courage to search for the truth of our being and the truth of our partners' being, we begin a journey of psychological and spiritual healing.

INTEGRATION

THE PREVIOUS CHAPTERS detail various ways in which this healing process takes place. Now let's stand back and get an overview of the entire process. The first step is to become more conscious of our old wounds. We look into the past for evidence of how we were denied adequate nurturing and how we repressed essential parts of our being. We do this through therapy, prayer, and reflection, and by becoming more astute observers of everyday events. As we gather new insights, we share them with our partners, because we no longer assume they can read our minds. When our partners share their thoughts and feelings with us, we listen with understanding and compassion, knowing that this sharing is a sacred trust. Gradually we start to "reimage" our partners, to see them as they really are—wounded children seeking salvation.

Once we have this more accurate image, we begin to redesign our relationships to heal our wounds. To do this, we first build an atmosphere of safety and trust. By closing our exits, renewing our commitment to each other, and deliberately pleasuring each other, we create a safe and nurturing environment. We add to this feeling of safety and validation by learning to communicate openly and effectively. As we overcome our resistance to this new way of relating, we begin to see our partners with even more clarity. We learn that they have fears and weaknesses and desires that they have never shared with us. We listen to their criticisms of us and realize that these illuminate our own darkness. We tell ourselves: "My partner has something to say about me. There is probably a measure of truth in this comment." Gradually we come to accept the fullness, the dark and the light of our own being.

The next step in the healing process is perhaps the most difficult: we make a decision to act on the information we are acquiring about ourselves and our partners and become our partners' healers. We go against our instinct to focus on our own needs and make a conscious choice to focus on theirs. To do this, we must conquer our fear of change. As we respond to our partners' needs, we are surprised to discover that, in healing our partners, we are slowly reclaiming parts of our own lost selves. We are integrating parts of our being that were cut off in childhood. We find ourselves regaining our capacity to think and to feel, to be sexually and spiritually alive, and to express ourselves in creative ways.

As we reflect on all that we are learning, we see that the painful moments in life are in reality opportunities for growth. Instead of blocking the pain, we ask ourselves: "What truth is trying to emerge at this moment? What primal feelings are hiding beneath these feelings of sadness, anxiety, and frustration?" We learn that the underlying feelings are pain and rage and the fear of death, and that these feelings are common to us all. Finally, we find a safe and growth-producing way to express these powerful emotions and no longer allow them to jeopardize our relationships.

One by one, the elements of our partnership that were once unconscious—the fears, the anger, the childhood needs, the archaic pain—are brought to the surface, first to find acceptance, then, ultimately, to be resolved. As our wounds heal and as more hidden parts of ourselves come into our awareness, we have a new sense of our inherent unity and wholeness.[1]

CREATING AN INTIMATE love relationship is a spiritual path, but it is not necessarily an exalted path. For the most part, it is a very practical, day-by-day sort of struggle. To give this process greater reality, I want to share with you the story of two couples.

There are obvious differences between these two couples. The first couple, Anne and Greg Martin, are in their forties. They have been married for only five years. Both of them have been married before and have children from their previous relationships. Both of them have full-time careers. The Martins learned about Imago Relationship Therapy early in their relationship and managed to resolve their major conflicts in just three years. Kenneth and Grace Brentano are in their mid-sixties and have been married for thirty-five years. They have four grown children. Kenneth provides most of their income, and Grace is primarily a homemaker. Kenneth and Grace struggled for thirty years before achieving a satisfying relationship. Much of this they did on their own before becoming acquainted with my ideas.

What these couples have in common, however, is more significant than their differences. Both the Martins and the Brentanos have managed to create an intimate love relationship that satisfies each individual's need for healing and wholeness—a relationship that makes each individual feel safe and vital and loved.

ANNE AND GREG

ANNE AND GREG met in Santa Fe, New Mexico, in 1981. Anne, who lived in Dallas, was spending the weekend in Santa Fe with two friends. She had been divorced for three years and had dated several men casually, and was just getting to the stage where she wanted to remarry. "I wasn't interested in casual relationships anymore," she says. "I was looking for something permanent." That weekend, however, Anne was not thinking about meeting men; she was mainly interested in having a good time with her friends Josie and Shelley. On Friday night the three women went out to a lounge. During dinner Josie mentioned that she wasn't very good at meeting men. Anne jokingly agreed to be Josie's coach. "You don't have to do anything seductive," she told Josie. "If you see an interesting man, just look his way when he looks at you and smile. And if anybody asks you to dance, get up and dance. Then the guy will know that you're willing to dance and will have more courage to come over."

Anne was having a fun time giving Josie pointers on how to meet a man, when she glanced up and happened to see a lone man walk into the room. He was tall and slender, and he was wearing a corduroy jacket. Anne remembers thinking that he looked "rugged yet neat." She also thought he had a presence about him, an aura of self-confidence and intelligence. Anne forgot all about her coaching job. "Now, *that* one's mine," she said to Josie.

Greg has an equally vivid memory of the encounter. He was in town for the weekend, celebrating his imminent divorce from his third wife. In fact, he had filed the divorce papers the day before. He was interested in having a good time but, with three failed marriages behind him, he had no interest whatsoever in establishing a permanent connection. He walked into the lounge and glanced around. He noticed Anne, a tall, animated blonde in her mid-thirties, and was immediately attracted to her. After a while he asked her to dance.

"We started talking right away," says Anne. "A lot of guys don't know how to talk to women, but we were going a mile a minute. I liked that about him." Another thing she liked about Greg was the fact that he wasn't daunted by her academic background. (She has a Ph.D. and is an associate professor of counseling at a Southern university.) Several of the men she had dated had been intimidated by her intelligence. To appear less threatening, she had learned to refer to herself as a "teacher." "But I knew right away that I wouldn't have to keep back anything from Greg," she says. "He told me he had a Ph.D. himself—in engineering—and that he admired bright women."

Greg and Anne talked and danced all evening, and Greg walked her back to her motel. The next morning they met for breakfast and went for a walk. The attraction was strong on both sides, but not overpowering. That weekend might have been the beginning and end of their relationship if Anne hadn't impulsively sent Greg a card the next week. When Greg opened the card, he telephoned Anne and asked if he could come to Dallas that weekend to see her. Anne had other plans, but rearranged her schedule so that she could spend time with him.

"That was it," says Anne. "We were off and running. It was almost as if a drug took over." When Anne reflects on those early days, she is amazed that she plunged so abruptly into the relationship. Greg had a lot of strikes against him. He had not one, not two, but *three* previous marriages, and he had four children from two of those relationships. Anne had written her doctoral dissertation on the difficulties of being a stepparent, so she knew exactly what she was getting into. On top of all this, she and Greg lived 250 miles apart and had well-established careers in their respective cities. "A sane person would have looked at those facts and run in the opposite direction," she says, "but the attraction between us was too strong."

WHAT WAS THE source of this attraction? To find out, we need to know something about their separate childhoods. Anne was an only child. Throughout her early years, her father was in the service, so she saw him only when he was on leave. Her mother joined the navy when Anne was six months old, leaving Anne in the care of her grandfather and stepgrandmother. By the time her mother came back a year later, Anne had become very attached to her grandparents and once again had to sever close bonds.

This early pattern of abandonment was reinforced when Anne was seven years old and her mother and father divorced. Her father left town, and Anne didn't see him again until she was thirteen and managed to locate him by writing to the Red Cross.

Anne has clear memories of her early years with her mother. Her mother was a flighty, social woman who frequently placed her needs above Anne's. There were many times when her mother stayed out all night and didn't come home until late the next day. Anne would wake up, discover that she was alone, and stalwartly go about getting herself ready for school.

When Anne's mother did happen to be around, she was not very nurturing, according to Anne. "I don't remember being held or touched or stroked," she said. But her mother was the source of some vital approval. "She really thought I was neat and was very confident in my ability. She didn't say ugly things to me or criticize me."

Partly because of the need to care for herself and partly because her mother praised her self-reliance, Anne became a responsible, independent child. She turned to her school and to church for the nurturing she missed at home. She denied the pain that came from the lack of security and warmth in her upbringing, because it was too overwhelming. To the outside observer, Anne appeared to be a self-confident, assertive young woman.

HER HUSBAND, GREG, the oldest of five children, grew up on a farm in Arkansas. What he remembers most about his childhood is that there was not much affection between his mother and father. "There was a lot of yelling," he says, "mainly on my mother's side. She was a real vocal person. She had a lot of anger. But she was also very loving."

Money was always an issue in Greg's family: "My mother would bitch about money, and my father would ignore her." He describes his father as a kind, intelligent man, though without a lot of drive. "He worked hard, but he wouldn't accomplish much," says Greg. "He always seemed to be living in the future. He would say things like 'If it rains in August, we'll get seventy bushels of corn, and everything will be all right.' Or 'If it rains, the soybeans will make it.' He was always saying, 'Next year things will be better.' He sustained himself with a vision that things were going to be OK." One of the things that bothered him about his dad was that he had dreams that he never realized. "He always talked about wanting a plane," says Greg. "It was really important to him. But he never did anything about it. If I wanted a plane, I would make it happen. I would do whatever was necessary to realize that goal. My dad just let life slip by him."

Greg's parents were never abusive to him or his brothers and sisters, but, in his words, "it wasn't a hugging family." Greg played on his own a lot, spending a lot of time roaming around the farm creating vivid fantasies in his head. By and large, Greg remembers his childhood as being a happy period. "I was cheerful. Not much bothered me. But I was usually alone. Kind of aloof. I had friends, but I didn't let them get close. I didn't feel lonely, just apart. I had a sense that I was different from everybody else. Not worse. Not better. Just different."

Greg didn't break out of his isolation until late in life, well into his second marriage, and, surprisingly, it wasn't his second wife who managed to get close to him; it was a male friend. Greg explains how this came about. "This casual friend of mine kept wanting to get closer," he says. "I didn't like the guy at first, but he kept moving in, moving in. He kept asking me to do things with him. When that didn't work, he arranged for a foursome with our wives. I kept saying no, but he persisted. Finally I remember saying to myself, 'I'd better get to know this S.O.B., because he's not going to go away.' He forced his way into my friendship. Kind of plowed his way in. He became my first intimate friend. It kind of broke the ice. But even though I finally learned what it was like to be close to someone, I didn't seek it out. I felt pretty self-sufficient as I was."

Greg's first marriage was to his high school sweetheart. "That one was easy," he recalls. "My first wife was more like a buddy or a friend. There never was a real strong love." The marriage lasted eleven years. Greg felt that they lived on different intellectual planes and that they had little in common, but to him the fact that they were different kinds of people didn't justify ending the marriage. "We had two kids," he says, "and it

wasn't considered proper in either of our families to divorce."
Eventually Greg got involved with another woman. "I think I
was using it as an excuse to end the marriage," he says. "In
everybody's eyes, an affair was a good enough reason to call it
quits. You have an affair, you get divorced."

The worst mistake in his life, says Greg, was marrying the
woman with whom he had been having the affair. "She wasn't
a very kind person. She was smart, and I felt a strong physical
attraction for her, but she wasn't the kind of person I wanted to
marry. We had a lot of problems. We had sexual problems,
communication problems, and she was always suspicious of
me. She kept accusing me of having other affairs." Their stormy
relationship lasted five years. During this time they had a child,
and Greg adopted her son by another relationship. (Now he
was the father of four children: two by his first marriage, two
by this one.) When his second wife threatened divorce for the
third or fourth time, Greg told her, "I've had it. I'm leaving and
not coming back. Go ahead with the divorce."

Greg was single for four years and then married his third
wife, a woman from a wealthy family in Alabama. She was five
years older than he and, in contrast to his second wife, a "high-
class" woman. He says that he married his third wife largely
because he wanted a mother for his ten-year-old daughter, the
only one of his children who was living with him. "I thought
she could give my daughter a lot of things that I could not, or
would not, provide for her." Greg and his third wife were good
friends, and he had a lot of respect for her. There was nothing
particularly bad about the relationship, according to Greg, but
"there wasn't anything really wonderful about it, either. The
highs weren't very high. The lows weren't very low. And there
was no communication. There was no intimacy. No sharing.
She was intimate with me, but my intimacy would only go so
far. So that was the end of number three."

Greg's casual approach to divorce and marriage might alarm
some people, but in an age where divorce is easy and genuinely

helpful information on marriage is scarce, he was choosing one of the few options available to him. All he knew was that none of his three intimate love relationships worked for him. There was something missing in all of them—and in his life—that made staying married intolerable.

ANNE'S FIRST MARRIAGE was similar to Greg's in that it was fairly serene, traditional, and uneventful. Her husband, Albert, was a high school math teacher in a private school. The first ten years of their marriage were smooth and serene: "Albert was busy with his teaching job, and I was busy raising our two little girls." Because of Anne's unusual childhood, she didn't have a good role model for married life. "I think I got my image of marriage from the television," says Anne, "and from books and watching other people. I didn't have any of the details. No skills. So my first one was all on the surface. But it didn't feel superficial; we were doing the best that we could."

Things went along fairly smoothly until Albert went through an emotional crisis in the tenth year of their marriage. It seemed to them that this was totally unrelated to anything that was happening in their lives. His suffering became so acute that he went to his doctor for help. The doctor told him he was suffering from anxiety and prescribed some sedatives to help him sleep. Albert dutifully listened to what the doctor had to say, and went to a pharmacy to fill the prescription, but when he got home his first words to Anne were "What does 'anxiety' mean?" She couldn't explain it to him. "That's how naïve we were," says Anne.

Albert went through the bottle of pills and still felt no better. Eventually he discovered a workable solution, which was to withdraw. He spent a lot of time by himself; when he and Anne were together, he wasn't emotionally available, because he was too busy trying to maintain his own internal equilibrium. Anne was deeply troubled by his withdrawal. Outside of her awareness, it brought back memories of her early abandonment. She struggled to break through to Albert, but nothing seemed to work. In desperation, she began to pull away from him. "I went back into my old childhood pattern of taking care of myself, that old coping mechanism of mine of being totally independent."

In addition to the lack of intimacy between them, Anne and Albert began to have other difficulties. "He wanted me to be a good faculty wife," Anne says. "I was friendly and outgoing and very involved, and the people at the school liked me. But there was a part of me that was not happy in this role." She, in turn, was unhappy with Albert's role as a teacher. "I wanted him to go back to school and get a degree in administration. I hoped that he would move into an administrative position at the school, which would spare him some of the pressures of teaching." When Anne reflects on the situation today, she realizes that she had hidden motives for wanting him to change careers. "Consciously I was thinking about what the degree would do for him, but underneath it all I think I was projecting my own unfulfilled ambitions onto him. I was the one who wanted to go back to school. I was taking my own frustrated career drive and putting it onto Albert," she says.

Albert eventually went back to school and got a Ph.D. When their children were old enough, Anne entered a master's program in counseling. She began to acquire a lot of information that helped her understand her own childhood, but she didn't learn much that she could apply to her relationship. Furthermore, she observed, "Most of the therapists I knew had relationships that were about the same as or worse than my own. They were getting divorced, having affairs. Why turn to them for advice?"

Meanwhile, the conflict between Albert and Anne intensified. As soon as Albert finished his degree, he decided to go back to teaching. This was devastating to Anne. "I thought all that schooling was going to be a springboard to launch him into a different career. I turned to Albert one day and said, 'What are the next twenty years of our life going to be like?' He said, 'This is it.' And I said, 'No, I don't think I want to do this.' What I was seeing in those twenty years was more of the same. I felt a void in my life. There was something very important that was missing."

By this stage of their relationship, there was little love between them. "We didn't fight much," says Anne, "but we were kind of at odds with each other. I wanted him to be different. He wanted me to be different. I was becoming more independent, and he wanted the sweet and supportive wife that he thought he had married. We were both growing individually, but we weren't integrating it back into our relationship. We didn't know where to get any help, and as I look back at it, I don't think we really wanted any. We were dead. Numb. We wanted something from each other that we weren't getting, but we didn't know what that was. We were both out of touch with our needs. On a scale of one to ten, I would say that our understanding of what was really going on in our relationship was about a three."

Anne and Albert got divorced in February of 1978. Their two children were ten and thirteen. "My older daughter took it very stoically, like her dad," says Anne. "But my younger daughter was very verbal and very clear about her pain. She acted out her anger." Anne and the two girls moved to Berkeley, California, where Anne entered a doctoral program in counseling and guidance. As part of her training, she underwent extensive therapy. Slowly, gaps in her self-knowledge started to fill in. She began to see that a lot of her discontent in her first marriage was due to the fact that underneath her confident exterior she was an anxious, fearful person. "For the first time I realized that I was still aching from my earlier abandonment," she says. "I had all this pain and didn't know it. I was removed from it, yet it was affecting everything in my life." At one point her therapist asked her if she had ever experienced an anxiety attack. She said, "Well, no." Later on she realized that she had been fighting off a constant state of anxiety all her life. "It was a constant barrage. If I'd had an anxiety attack, it would have been like a pebble in the ocean. But I wasn't aware of my anxiety. It was second nature to me. That's the way the world was."

Anne eventually moved to Texas, where she became an associate professor of counseling and guidance at a large university. During this time she learned about my views of relationship therapy. For the first time Anne had a more comprehensive understanding of the psychology of love relationships. "And, more important," she says, "I had a model of how to make it better. Once someone explains something to me and gives me a model, I can do it. Up until that time, I was really leery about remarrying. I kept asking myself, 'What makes you think that the next one is going to be any different?'"

THIS WAS ABOUT the time that Anne met Greg. Let's take another look at their initial encounter to see if we can now decipher any of the unconscious sources of attraction. When Anne describes her first impression of Greg, she describes him as an intelligent, resourceful man who possessed that enviable quality of inner contentment. Now that she has a lot more self-knowledge, she can see that he was also sending her clues that he was emotionally unavailable. Like the father who was always gone in the navy and later abandoned her, and like the mother who didn't come home at night, Greg, with his extreme self-reliance and history of three divorces, was not going to let her get too close. His isolation triggered Anne's primary drive, which was to make a person who was distant and unavailable become close and dependable. Meeting Greg crystallized all of her unfinished business.

Why was Greg attracted to Anne? A warm, loving, aggressive, volatile woman, Anne evoked strong memories of his mother. "I sensed that she could be just as loving as my mother," he said, "and just as aggravating. But one thing for sure, I knew she would stir things up. I may say I want peace, but the truth of the matter is, I want life to be challenging." And what he was also wanting, although he didn't know it, was to become involved with a woman who could break through his emotional barriers just as that persistent friend had done years ago. When he met Anne, he sensed that she had the willpower and the determination to do it.

Anne and Greg got married on New Year's Day, 1982, only four months after they met. For the first few weeks of their marriage, intimacy came easily. "I trusted Annie, more than I've trusted any other person," says Greg. But after a while he began to feel that Anne was using intimacy as a weapon. "I felt she was asking me questions to invade my space. She always wanted to know what I was thinking and feeling." Gradually, he began to shut down. Being self-contained was a safe and familiar experience for him; being emotionally vulnerable was not. When Greg withdrew, Anne experienced it as a repetition of the withdrawal of her first husband, Albert. She became angry and demanding and was convinced that Greg was planning to leave her. "She would go really crazy," says Greg. "She would have all kinds of suspicions and want to know what I was planning. Well, I wasn't planning anything. I was just licking my wounds to get ready for the next offensive." The independence that Anne admired in Greg and the aggressiveness that Greg admired in Anne were now developing into a power struggle.

Anne remembers one significant episode. "I was really upset about something. Something had happened at work that was really painful. I was talking about it with Greg, and I started crying. He looked at me and said, 'I don't console people. I'm not good at it, so I don't do it. Don't turn to me for comfort.' And, of course, that's what I wanted from him more than anything else."

Soon there were other difficulties. Having four teenaged children between them, they had a relationship that was fraught with complexity. There were numerous times when they both wanted to call it quits. The only reason she stayed in the relationship, says Anne, is that "I was very aware of the fact that, if I broke up with Greg, I would be bringing the same issues to another relationship. And when I looked at him, I realized that he was someone I wanted to be with. He was worth the effort. The pain we caused each other was intense, but the attraction between us was very strong."

Knowing that they would not be able to deal with their problems without outside help, Anne invited Greg to one of my weekend couples seminars. Although she was well acquainted with my theories, she had been reluctant to introduce them to Greg. "Because I was a therapist myself," she explained, "I was afraid of getting into the position of telling him what he was doing right and wrong. That had gotten me into trouble with earlier relationships. I wanted to have the ideas presented to him by a third person."

Greg had two important insights at the seminar. First of all, he was very moved by the exercise that helped him envision Anne as a hurting child. "I had never understood her pain before," he said. "All of a sudden I understood what she was going through. She used to tell me that, when I wouldn't talk to her, she felt abandoned, but I didn't know what she meant. How can a grown woman feel abandoned? I had never experienced that kind of insecurity before. Suddenly, during this guided-imagery exercise, I began to see her as a hurting four-year-old child. As an eight-year-old waking up to find no one home. Here was this child being formed and I could see that and feel that—get in touch with Annie as a child. It was real touching to me, and it made me more willing to listen to her complaints and to try to change my tendency to withdraw."

The other insight Greg had at the workshop had to do with communication skills. When he saw the Mirroring exercise demonstrated in front of the group, he realized that it would help him cope with his wife's intense emotions. Greg remembers the first time he tried it out. "Annie and I were driving in the car," he says, "and she was really angry. I think it was about my relationship with one of the kids. I remember that she was all fists and fury. I felt that she was throwing these lightning bolts in all directions, and all I could do was dodge them. My instinct was to throw some lightning bolts in *her* direction or just close down—that's what I would have done in the past— but instead I made a conscious choice to mirror her. I didn't react. I didn't accuse. I just listened and repeated back to her what she was saying. As I listened to her, it was as if I absorbed some of her fury. She got smaller and smaller, until finally she was in a contained package. Then we were able to talk calmly and rationally. By not hooking into her anger, I was able to contain her." This experience made Greg feel good about himself and gave him renewed hope for the future of their relationship. "I was able to defend myself without attacking her or crawling inside my shell."

Eventually Greg got so good at the mirroring technique that it became second nature to him. Whenever he felt threatened by Anne's intensity, he would put on his armor, listen, and stay in touch. "The result of all this," says Greg, "is that Anne has stopped getting so angry. She simply won't do it. It doesn't work anymore. We've progressed way beyond that. We can communicate now."

Another tool that Anne and Greg brought home from the workshop was the Behavior Change Request Dialogue. "Instead of fighting, we started asking for what we wanted," says Anne. "It's made all the difference." Initially this exercise was difficult for both of them, though for different reasons. Greg's problem was that he prided himself on being self- sufficient. It was very difficult for him to admit that he needed anything from anybody, but especially from Anne. However, one need that Greg couldn't deny was that he wanted to have more frequent and more spontaneous sex. "I had this fantasy of coming home and finding Anne in a negligee, eager for sex. But it rarely happened." He finally learned that, if he wanted more sex, he would have to ask for it. "I had to be more direct about my needs. She wasn't going to read my mind."

Anne's problem with the exercise was of a different nature. She had no problem asking for what she wanted. Because of revelations that had come out of her individual therapy, she was well acquainted with her unmet childhood needs, and she didn't hesitate to ask Greg to change his behavior to help meet those needs. What she had a hard time doing was accepting his attentions once he responded to one of her requests. Anne gave the following example. Greg is the owner of an engineering firm and has to leave town frequently on business trips. This separation fuels Anne's fear of abandonment. To ease her anxiety, she asked him to call her up every single day, especially when he was out of town. Greg readily agreed to do this. After a few weeks of receiving these daily calls, however, Anne began to feel anxious. She began to think up reasons why Greg should stop calling her. "It's too expensive," she would say. Or "It takes up too much of your time." Greg was persistent, however, and called every day, despite Anne's unconscious attempts to sabotage his efforts. Eventually she was able to relax and accept the gift.

In the past year, Anne and Greg have gotten better at expressing their needs and asking for what they want. One of the payoffs for Greg is that he spends less time trying to guess what Anne wants. "I used to always be trying to anticipate her needs," says Greg. "I would do all these things that I hoped would make her happy. But she rarely noticed, and I would be exhausted from trying to figure her out. Now I can relax, knowing that, if she wants something, she will ask for it. I like it much better this way. I take care of my own needs. She takes care of hers. We both will go out of our way to meet each other's needs, but we don't do so much mind reading."

One need that Anne has made abundantly clear to Greg is her need for security and affirmation. "I need and want massive doses of reassurance," Anne says. To help meet this need, she informed Greg one day that, whenever she was being overly emotional—whether angry or withdrawn or tearful—what she really wanted was to hear how much he loved her. She wrote down on a card the exact words that she wanted him to say. She handed him the card and said, "Here are your lines." The card read: "I love you. You're the person I want to be with. I want to live with you for the rest of my life." Greg, the man who had once proclaimed that he was not able to console anyone, has been able to deliver his lines with utter sincerity.

Anne and Greg have also learned a new way to fight. Essentially, they do a modified version of the Full Container called the Container Transaction exercise. "We fight in a very healthy manner," says Anne. "We get the anger out, but we don't get into the old garbage. We're real honest and direct." Anne gave me an example. "I looked at Greg's hand the other day and noticed that he wasn't wearing his wedding ring. I felt hurt and betrayed. But instead of stewing about it, I spoke up immediately. I said, 'I'm really hurt that you're not wearing your ring. A ring is a visible sign to other people that we're married, and it's really important to me. I'm really upset. I don't know what it means that you're not wearing it. I don't like it, and I want you to wear it.' Instead of getting defensive or abusive, Greg listened to me and said, 'It makes sense that you feel that way. I understand that you're angry.' Later he explained to me why he wasn't wearing it. It had to do with the fact that I had reverted to using my maiden name, and he was hurt about that. In his mind, not wearing the ring was kind of tit for tat. We didn't resolve the problem immediately, because the issues were complex. But the important thing is that we both got our feelings out. We listened to each other. We defused all the bad energy. And we're not angry anymore. Before, we would have gotten obsessed about it and gone on and on."

Through these efforts, Anne and Greg have been able to meet enough of their needs to attain a new level of acceptance. "I am secure enough in our relationship that I can now accept the fact that Greg is basically a self-contained person," says Anne. "It no longer threatens me. I can wait for him to reveal his feelings. I don't have to press him. When he's upset, my instinct is to make him tell me right now what is bothering him. I just want to get it over with. But that always puts me in the facilitator role. The other thing I found is that, if I wait before I make demands, he usually resolves things himself in his own way. And even when he doesn't, I can live with things the way they are. I've learned that I don't have to fix everything."

Anne and Greg are the first to admit that working to achieve a conscious partnership is not easy. In fact, Anne wants to go on record as saying, "Working things out with Greg is the hardest thing I've ever done." Greg voices a similar opinion. "Marriage is like growing flowers," he says. "You always have to work on it. If you don't, the weeds start to grow and choke out the flowers." He makes another comparison. "When you garden, it's important to have good tools. You can carry water by hand and dig in the dirt with your hands, but it's much much easier to use a hose and a shovel. That's how I feel about living with Annie. We have the right tools and skills to make the kind of marriage we want."

The reason Anne and Greg are willing to put so much effort into their relationship is that they reap daily rewards. Greg thinks that one of the most obvious changes has been in their emotional states. "Early on in our relationship," says Greg, "we were both volatile people, only I kept a lid on my feelings and Anne was too free with hers. Now she's become less crazy, and I'm more emotional. Not that we're trying to become what the other person was—we've just reached a balance. We tend to oscillate around a mean. Sometimes she's more emotional than I am. Sometimes I'm more emotional than she is. But it's like we've established middle ground. Which is very reassuring."

Greg finds that what he's learning in this relationship has helped him become a more effective manager. "I've gotten quite adept at spotting hidden agendas," he says. "I know that the issue that people are talking about is not always the real issue. I look for the underlying problems." He also is better at putting himself in others' shoes. "I say to myself, 'If I were that person, what would I be wanting or needing at this moment?' Being able to empathize with Anne has given me that skill. My marriage has also made me a better communicator and able to withstand more pressure. If someone at work has a problem or becomes angry, I am able to keep from getting defensive. I am able to get things done."

Anne finds that her relationship with Greg has made her a more spiritual being. "The strongest force in the universe is what I would call 'Christ in us' or the Holy Spirit," says Anne. "And to me that's the same thing as the drive to completion. In my mind, our purpose on earth is to be the best that we can be in terms of loving and living and being kind to other people and developing our talents and our skills. I think the best way I can do this is to have full access to who I am. And that means being honest about who I am, the negative part of me as well as the positive. Being free to be complete. That has happened in this relationship. It's a great paradox. Because before I thought I was feeling self-confident, but in reality it was grandiosity. Now I just feel good about myself. All of me. I like being who I am. I can be alone and be happy. I'm more comfortable in my own skin than I have ever been. I'm walking around better on a moment-to-moment basis. My anxiety level is so low. That's a real difference. I feel truly happy and secure for the first time in my life."

I asked Anne if she had any advice for people who would be reading this book and perhaps confronting some of these ideas for the first time. "My advice would be to focus on yourself," she said. "And when I say that, I mean you should realize that what you are doing for your partner is what you're doing for yourself. It's about your own personal growth. I finally learned that, when I was stretching to meet one of Greg's needs, I was reclaiming a part of myself. So, any time your partner asks you to do something, say to yourself, 'Does this make sense? Does it behoove me as an individual to do this?' And if it makes good sense and if it behooves you to do it, then do it, regardless of how you feel about it, because in meeting the needs of your partner you will be recapturing a part of yourself."

KENNETH AND GRACE

KENNETH AND GRACE met in the 1940s, when they were both in college. Kenneth was a premed student, and Grace was studying art history. They became friends when they happened to sit next to each other on the bus going home for spring vacation. Kenneth has a clue to what attracted him to Grace. "A woman in the seat in front of us had a screaming baby and was having a tough time comforting her. Grace asked the woman if she could hold the baby. Soon after Grace got the baby, it started to settle down. I remember thinking to myself, 'That's the kind of woman that I would like to have as the mother of my children.' Deeper down—although I certainly didn't know it at the time—I was wanting some of that tenderness for myself."

Grace had a positive first impression of Kenneth. "He seemed like such a gentle, kind man." She was also pleased that during the long bus ride he expressed genuine interest in a paper she had written at school. "I liked the fact that he respected my intellect, something that other men hadn't done." She remembers telling her parents as soon as she got home that she had met a young man who was "as good as gold."

UNDERLYING THESE CONSCIOUS impressions were more powerful, hidden sources of attraction. What unfinished business did Grace unwittingly bring to their romance? Grace was the oldest in a family of three children, two girls and a boy. She described her family as "a mixture of love and tumult." They prided themselves on being offbeat and doing unusual things. "We were all artists or musicians," said Grace. "There was a lot of spontaneity. Dad would say, 'Let's take a drive after supper. Leave the dishes!' Mother would say, 'Let me do the dishes first.' And Dad would say, 'If we don't leave now, we'll miss the sunset.' So we would all pile in the car and go off for a drive. We sang in the car, in harmony. We sang in church as a family, so we traditionally ended our family singing with the song 'Blessed Be the Tie.'"

Grace has fond memories of her early childhood. She remembers being her father's "little darling." When she was five years old, her younger sister, Sharon, was born, and she had a rude awakening. "All of a sudden I wasn't the center of attention anymore. I felt cast out. I remember thinking, 'What in the world has happened? Aren't I as cute as I used to be? Why am I not loved?' I just couldn't accept the fact that I was no longer the favorite."

Grace described her mother as a confusing mixture of warmth and petulance. She and Grace rarely got along. "She was so strong that I felt that I had to fight her to maintain my own identity," she recalls. "I think this is why I became a rebel." Her father was warm and caring and a good listener. She remembers having a very close relationship with him. "Some would say too close," says Grace. "I remember coming home from high school and lying down on the couch and having my dad rub my back. It felt perfectly comfortable and normal to me, but I know that it made Mother jealous." In later years she would look back on her relationship with her father with some anxiety. "In a way, it was scary to be that close to him. When I got married, I remember that it was very hard on him. Right before my wedding, he told me, 'I always thought you would stay home and never get married.' He was partly kidding, but I think there was some truth to that." Besides experiencing some discomfort over the closeness of their relationship, Grace wished that her dad had a more forceful personality. "He was not very strong," she said. "He would disappear when things got rough. When Mother and I got into an argument, he would go polish the car or tend to his flowers. He would never defend me."

When Grace was about twelve or thirteen, she experienced a religious awakening. She went to a special youth service and was overwhelmed by the presence of God. She remembers feeling a confusing mixture of elation and guilt. Elation at "having God on my side, but guilt for being a wicked girl, for sassing my mother." Around that time, she remembers a day when her family was scheduled to go on a trip, and Grace stubbornly refused to go with them. "I remember going to my room and praying and crying and carrying on. I have no idea what it was really about, but I remember an awful feeling. Some kind of emotional crisis. I remember feeling 'bad' or 'wicked.'" This negative view of herself was to be a refrain in later years.

Grace often worried about being "dumb." She got this idea from her parents, who would criticize her for doing "stupid" things. "It wasn't that I was really dumb," she says in self-defense. "I would just be thinking about something else and do dumb things." Perhaps another reason Grace developed this idea about herself is that she is by nature a "doer rather than a thinker." As a young girl she had an assertive, take-charge personality and could be counted on to get things done with little wasted effort. After a minimum amount of planning and organizing, she would plunge right in. Sometimes Grace would pride herself on her ability to get the job done, but at other times she would agonize about not being as deliberate and contemplative as others.

One of Grace's strengths is that she is very artistic, something that was important to her as a young adult. When she was in high school, she was an assistant to the art teacher at summer camp and enjoyed helping children express themselves through art. In following years she won prizes for her free-form designs and surrealistic paintings, and art gradually became a primary focus in her life.

KNOWING THESE FACTS about Grace, let's take a look at Kenneth's early years. Kenneth has had extensive counseling throughout his life. During our initial interview, he told me that he could "tell my life story with one hand tied behind my back." True to his word, in just a few minutes he was able to give a comprehensive synopsis of his upbringing. "My mother was an intense, energetic, passionate woman," he began, "who wanted a lot from life and wanted a lot from my father, who was a passive, quiet, gentle man. My father was a model for me. I learned to be passive and quiet from him. My mother also wanted a lot from me. I experienced her as being hungry with me. Now, as an adult looking back on my childhood, I can see it was because she wasn't being nourished by my father. She had a sharp tongue that could cut, and she was often critical and angry at me. I didn't understand why, and often thought she was being unfair. I can remember as a kid wishing that I had a different mother. We would have some warm times, but I couldn't trust myself to get too close to her; I was afraid she would eat me for breakfast. I didn't even want to share my achievements with her, because I thought she would take them as a feather in her cap. And I wasn't going to let her do that."

There appears to be a basic similarity between Grace's and Kenneth's upbringing. Both had fathers who were passive and withdrawn and mothers who were aggressive and dominant. Kenneth, however, was not close to either parent. Though he greatly admired his father, his father remained at a distance. "We had some nice times together, but he was shy about talking about feelings. I wanted him to like me and be proud of me, but he never told me that he loved me. I learned from other people that he respected me, not from him." His father was especially wary of anger. "If I was ever angry, he would back away. He used the same technique with my mother. When she was angry at him, he would just withdraw. When my mother was angry at me, I tried to copy his evasive maneuver, but I could never back away far enough." Because of this early indoctrination, Kenneth learned to be afraid of his own anger: anger got him in trouble with his mother and alienated him from his father. "I decided at a young age to be nice," he says. But this persona, this "false self," was covering a desperate longing for, in his words, "some tender mothering and some firm and affirming fathering." And underneath this longing was a reservoir of anger at being denied those needs.

Kenneth and Grace exemplify a principle that I talked about earlier, which is that husbands and wives are often injured in the same way but develop opposite defenses. Kenneth and Grace both felt that they had to carve out a separate identity from an overbearing parent. This suggests that their key developmental struggle was in the stage that child psychologists would label "the stage of individuation and autonomy." Kenneth created his psychic space by being passive and "nice," hoping to sidestep his mother's anger; Grace established her identity by being rebellious and angry, trying to counter her mother's invasiveness. Because of their opposite solutions, it makes sense that they would be attracted to each other. Grace admired Kenneth's gentleness and goodness; Kenneth admired Grace's strength and aggressiveness. They saw in each other parts of their own essential nature that were poorly developed. What they didn't realize was that these opposite character traits were an effort to heal the very same wound.

From a vantage point of thirty-five years of marriage, Kenneth and Grace have some astute observations on why they were initially attracted to each other. "I made arrangements to take care of myself," says Kenneth. "I picked up Grace to remother me. She was full of warmth and vitality and tenderness." Grace has an equally succinct explanation for marrying Kenneth: "I was a 'bad,' 'dumb' girl looking for a 'good,' 'bright' boy. Kenneth was exactly what I needed." While these undoubtedly were some of their positive reasons for marrying each other, there were some negative ones as well. The most obvious one is that they had each chosen a mate who would perpetuate their struggle with the opposite-sex parent. Grace was dominant and aggressive—like Kenneth's mother—and Kenneth was passive and gentle—like Grace's father. They had chosen partners who had character traits that had caused them a great deal of anguish in childhood.

It was a full year, however, before these negative factors became evident. "The first year was pretty idyllic," says Grace. Problems developed in the second year of their marriage, shortly after the birth of their daughter. Kenneth was a physician at a struggling family-practice clinic. Grace was concerned that he wasn't aggressive enough about attracting new patients. "I kept seeing all of these ways that he could help the clinic," recalls Grace, "but he was content with things the way they were. I kept seeing all these possibilities that he was not seeing."

They had their first real fight when Grace realized that the clinic was losing patients. "For two years Kenneth had ignored all the signs that the clinic was going downhill. Now it was getting too late to do anything about it. Two of his colleagues left to find more lucrative employment. One night I finally blew up." Kenneth remembers the fight and recalls that he appreciated Grace's concern for the clinic but resented her intrusion. "On the one hand, I kind of looked to her for leadership," he says. "But, on the other hand, I was furious with her for being so demanding. She seemed to think that she knew what I should be doing and that she had a right to tell me. I felt like she was my mother, making heavy demands on me."

Looking back on the episode, Grace, too, recalls having mixed emotions. "I was concerned about being too strong, too willful. I wondered whether downplaying my personality would make him more dominant. But I couldn't let things lie." The very factors that had been the key to their mutual attraction—Grace's assertive, outgoing nature and Kenneth's passive, gentle nature—were becoming the basis for a thirty-year power struggle.

Kenneth began to have some additional misgivings about Grace. "I was becoming aware of some things that I wished were different in Grace. For one thing, she didn't have the same intellectual interests that I did. I wanted her to read more and be able to discuss issues." Once again Grace was getting the message that she wasn't "smart" enough. The young man who had once seemed so interested in her academic work was now criticizing her for not being intellectual.

When their daughter was in the first grade, Grace began teaching art part-time at a local high school. In the winter of that year, Kenneth's mother came to visit, and Kenneth and Grace had another significant confrontation. At the time Grace was very involved in the school and was putting out a newsletter at their church as well. She was pleasant with her mother-in-law, but went about her business as usual. "I was too busy to be a good hostess," she recalls. Furthermore, she refused to live up to her mother-in-law's expectation that she be a traditional homemaker and spend all her hours after work "cooking, cleaning, and mending." Kenneth's mother had to entertain herself during most of her visit and was so irate at this treatment that she left two days early, complaining bitterly to Kenneth as he drove her to the train. Being trapped in the car with his angry mother made Kenneth extremely anxious. "There I was, listening to my mother attack Grace and not daring to defend her. I didn't have the nerve to stand up for my own wife."

For Grace this visit was an unpleasant replay of her childhood. Once again she was relying on an ineffective, passive male to defend her against a critical, hostile mother figure. "I wanted Kenneth to stand up for me," she says, "to explain to his mother how busy I was. But he was afraid to ruffle her feathers, and then he had the nerve to be angry at me for failing to placate her!"

As Grace was recounting this episode to me, she remarked on the resemblance between Kenneth and her father. "My dad was a very kind, loving man, but he was not strong. I wanted him to be protective of me, to take leadership—the very same things I wanted from Kenneth." Interestingly, when she was angry with Kenneth, she treated him the same way her mother treated her father. "I would rant and rave, cry and yell, generally terrorize him with my anger. Kenneth would do his best to placate me. But the 'nicer' he got, the angrier I got. It all became quite poisonous." Unknowingly, Grace had introjected her mother's negative traits, the very ones that had plagued her as a child.

On the surface Kenneth and Grace, like many couples, appeared to be polar opposites. Grace as the outgoing, angry one; Kenneth was the passive, pleasant one. However, underneath his superficial "goodness," Kenneth was just as angry as Grace. The way his anger revealed itself was through criticism. This tendency showed up early in their marriage. "From the word 'go,' Kenneth never gave me the feeling that he admired me," says Grace. "Other fellows that I had dated treated me much more kindly. Kenneth was critical of my housekeeping, my parenting, my moods, my lack of intellect. And he was always playing teacher. He would ask me, 'Do you know such and such?'—some obscure fact that had no relevance to me. When I admitted that I did not, he would proceed to lecture me as if I were a high-school student. I was able to put a stop to that particular behavior in the first few years. But he never gave me the feeling that he cherished me. He never loved me the way I wanted to be loved. Gradually I think I lost much of the self-esteem that I had brought into the marriage."

Today Kenneth can be quite candid about the way he used to criticize his wife. "I wanted a lot from her, and I was getting a lot. But I seemed determined to bite the hand that fed me. I needed to keep her unsettled, even though I knew how much this hurt her."

Why was Kenneth so critical of Grace? If you will recall, Kenneth's goal in life was to get tender nurturing from a dominant mother figure, but at the same time he had to stay far enough away so that he would not be absorbed. Unconsciously, he accomplished this delicate maneuver by giving Grace enough love and affection to keep her interested, but maintaining a crucial distance through the use of constant criticism.

Because Grace was getting so little affirmation from Kenneth, she was understandably insecure about the relationship. She felt jealous and suspicious of his outside activities, especially his contacts with women. "There are so many women who fall in love with their doctors," she says, "I was sure he was having an affair." Kenneth admits that for a very long time he had "one foot in the marriage and one foot out. Like maybe somebody better would come along. Like maybe I hadn't picked the best one. It hurts me to say this, but I had only a partial commitment to Grace."

It's no wonder that Grace often felt angry. "The one thing I can't deny," Grace says, "is that there was a constant surge of anger in me." But at the time Grace didn't know where it was coming from. The time that she was most aware of her anger was when she went to bed at night. She would say to herself, "Why am I so angry? Why is this?" But she didn't have any answers. Now, when she looks back on this period of their relationship, it is plain to her that Kenneth was the source of her anger. She remembers that he often had to put in late nights delivering babies or responding to medical emergencies. When she heard the sound of his car coming down the gravel driveway, she would have a rush of what she calls "romantic feelings." She would be eager to see him and she would greet him with an air of expectancy. But within a very few minutes she would be angry. The romance would crumble. "I felt disappointed," says Grace. "Yet I wasn't even sure what it was that I wanted from him."

Kenneth and Grace's relationship went through many changes in those first twenty or so years. They raised four children, lived in three different cities, and had good years and bad years. But the emotional undercurrents were the same. Grace kept wanting more love, strength, and commitment from Kenneth. Kenneth kept wanting more love, softness, and, at the same time, more distance from Grace. The underlying tension was so great that, had they been born in a more permissive era, they probably would have gotten a divorce. "I was always threatening divorce," says Grace. "After the first year of marriage, divorce was a frequently occurring issue. We were very different people, and we weren't willing to accommodate each other." One of Grace's deepest regrets is that she shared her anger at Kenneth with her oldest daughter. "From the time she was old enough to listen, I would complain to her about her father," she says. "To this day, I'm afraid she thinks less of him because of this."

The lowest ebb of their relationship took place when they were in their forties and Kenneth was going through a midlife crisis. Until this point in his life, he had always thought of himself as a "promising young man." Life was an adventure, and there were many avenues open to him. Now he looked around and saw that he was in a lackluster marriage, that he was a "mediocre" doctor, and that he didn't have much enthusiasm for his profession. "I was just delivering babies. I could no longer maintain the fantasy of a promising future," he says. This realization led to a long depression.

Meanwhile, Grace was going through a religious crisis. The church had always been very important to her; suddenly the beliefs that she grew up with no longer made any sense to her. She began to search for new meaning, but the more she searched, the less she found to hold on to. She turned to Kenneth in desperation. "I would say to him, 'Tell me what *you* believe and I'll believe it!' But he would only give me books to read. He gave me Paul Tillich and I would sit and read and cry.

I couldn't understand it. I finally decided that I was going crazy. I was going insane. I was too smart to be taken in by the conservative evangelists, and I was too dumb to understand the liberal theologians. I was in a religious vacuum."

Kenneth remembers Grace's tumult. "She wanted me to sort out her moral and religious confusion," he says. "I would try and fail, and there would be a storm of pain and rage from her. She was in anguish for her soul. I felt as if she had her hands around my throat, begging me for answers. I was supposed to provide something for her, and I was failing." He was distressed that he couldn't help Grace, but he was also aware that he was deliberately holding back from her something that she wanted. "She wanted me to be strong, to be decisive. And it wasn't just about religion. It was everything. She wanted to be a little girl and have me be the daddy. But that felt like an unfair position to me. I didn't want to be too strong. Then I would have to give up forever my wish to get what I needed. I wanted to be the child, too."

Gradually the crisis began to diminish. Grace joined a church that was willing to accept her confusion and questioning, and she was deeply relieved to discover that her husband, a very religious man, stuck by her, "even though I was next thing to an atheist." At the same time, Kenneth sought help for his depression by joining a therapy group. In the course of his therapy, he made some important discoveries about himself. One of the most important ones was that he was making Grace carry all the anger in the relationship. "I was projecting all my anger onto her. I was the good, gentle one. She was the bad, angry one. Meanwhile, I had a lot of unexpressed anger of my own, and keeping it inside of me was one of the things that kept me remote and made Grace so angry."

Slowly Kenneth began to test out his capacity for anger. "It was while he was in therapy," recalls Grace, "that Kenneth dared to get mad at me for the first time. I don't even remember what it was about. But I distinctly remember that he actually raised his voice at me. He was dumbstruck that I didn't turn around and kill him. He didn't think he was going to survive his own anger." This was a crucial experience for Kenneth. He had challenged his internal prohibition against anger and lived to tell about it. He began to test his newfound ability. "I got mad at Grace four or five times in one week, just to prove that I could do it. Then I got so that any time she started yelling at me I began to yell back. Only I made sure that I yelled louder." Even though she had always wanted Kenneth to be more assertive, once he started standing up for himself Grace found it hard to get used to. At times she yearned for the old, passive Kenneth.

Despite his wife's apprehensions, Kenneth continued to become more self-confident and aggressive, growth that was supported and encouraged by his therapy group. One of the messages that Kenneth was getting from the members of the group was that he wasn't asking enough for himself. "You act as if you're not entitled to much in life," they told him. Kenneth felt there was some truth to this observation, and he began searching for ways to feel more fulfilled. It was during this time that he had an affair. "I don't blame the group for what I did," he says. "They did nurture in me the notion that I was too self-effacing, but it was my idea to have this affair. I saw it as an opportunity to go for something for me. To spread my wings and fly. It wasn't that Grace and I were at odds with each other. We were actually doing OK at the time—not great, but OK. It's just that I wanted an exciting adventure. This was a way to prove myself."

The affair lasted only a couple of weeks. Grace found out about it when she discovered a motel receipt that had fallen from his pocket. She knew right away what had happened. "I had been suspicious of him for years. Now it had really happened." Grace reacted to the affair in a typical fashion: "I was furious. I yelled and screamed." Two days after her discovery of the receipt, she arranged for an appointment with a relationship counselor. "I wanted help dealing with this," she says. "I felt like I was going to explode. Also, I suppose, I saw therapy as a way to take him to court, make him acknowledge the pain he had caused me."

Through the therapy, Kenneth and Grace were able to come to a resolution. Kenneth agreed to stop seeing the other woman, and Grace agreed to try to rebuild her trust. In the process, Kenneth gained some important insights about Grace. "Her anger over the affair was threatening to me, but it was also very affirming. It showed me how much she cared about our marriage, and that she was willing to pick up the pieces and continue to work on our relationship. We had talked about divorce for so long that I was gratified that she was still willing to see if anything good could come of a bad situation."

Understandably, it took Grace a long time to rebuild her trust. When Kenneth came home at night, she would ask him about his comings and goings in great detail. Kenneth patiently put up with her cross-examination for months, accepting full responsibility for betraying her trust. It was during this critical period of their relationship that the final crisis occurred: Kenneth had to have quadruple-bypass surgery. Even though he responded well to the surgery, Grace was more shaken by his heart condition than by the affair. "One evening," says Kenneth, "we were lying in bed and Grace told me that, if getting out of my life would make my recovery easier for me, she would be willing to leave. She knew that our marriage had not been very satisfying to either of us and thought maybe my heart problem was a sign of my 'disease.' If living apart would be a benefit to me, she would agree to a divorce. She made it clear that she didn't *want* to leave me, but she was afraid that living together was only making matters worse."

Grace's willingness to make this sacrifice was the turning point for Kenneth. "It was then that I decided to put both of my feet into the marriage," he says. "I knew I wasn't going to find a better woman than Grace. She was a remarkable woman.

She had been hard to live with at times. But, then, aren't we all? I finally made a full commitment to our marriage."

I suggested to Kenneth that maybe his decision to commit himself to Grace had something to do with her offering him an accepting, nonpossessive love, something that he had always wanted from his mother. He thought about it for a minute. "Yes. Yes. I believe that's exactly what it was. My mother's love always had strings attached. Grace was offering me a selfless love."

Kenneth and Grace didn't have an official ceremony to celebrate their remarriage, although there was one conversation in a restaurant that felt very significant to them. A pianist was playing the song "Someone to Watch over Me" and Kenneth took hold of Grace's hand and said to her, "Let's make a deal. I'll watch over you, and you'll watch over me." It was a simple declaration of love: Let's agree to be each other's protectors, each other's best friends.

Finally, after thirty years of an intimate love relationship, Grace was getting Kenneth's full attention and commitment. Spontaneously, along with his commitment, Kenneth gained new appreciation for Grace's good qualities. "I think he began to realize that I was intelligent. I wasn't an academic, but I was a gifted artist. I began to feel for the first time that Kenneth truly admired me." The anger that had consumed her for so many years became less intense—because, as Grace put it, "He truly loved me, and I knew it."

It was at this advanced stage of love and acceptance that Kenneth and Grace first came to one of my workshops. On their own they had managed to work through their major impasse, but they still were able to acquire some new insights and skills. For Grace, the most significant part of the couples workshop was watching a demonstration of the Container Transaction exercise. She was deeply moved to see the couple learn how to handle their anger. It was, she says, the first time that her anger had made any sense to her. "I suddenly realized that I wasn't a 'bad' or crazy person to be angry. Anger had a reason and a purpose. I wouldn't need to deny my explosiveness to be lovable, only channel it and make it a productive part of our relationship. It was a marvelous revelation to me!"

Since the workshop, Kenneth and Grace, like Anne and Greg, have developed their own version of the Container Transaction exercise. They both feel free to "rant and rave," as they put it, when they have strong feelings. But they are very conscious of what they are doing and are careful not to hurt each other in the process. "We never call each other names," says Kenneth. "We just express our anger and irritation. And the other person knows that this is an important part of keeping our relationship healthy. We don't harbor grudges." Grace feels that this process has dramatically increased Kenneth's acceptance of her emotional nature. "It seems that his attitude toward my anger changed at that workshop. He had already learned to accept his own anger in his therapy group, but he hadn't accepted mine. Now he has. I yell and I scream and I'm still loved. We go through it, and we come back together. It's been a very important change in our relationship."

Grace believes that Kenneth's increased acceptance of her has been the determining factor in her own acceptance of herself. "I think the fact that Kenneth accepts my energy and determination and my anger helps me accept what I call 'my mother' in me, the part of me that is like my mother, which I have always tried to deny. Because he likes who I am, I don't have to wage that battle anymore. I don't have to deny who I am."

For Kenneth, the biggest improvement in their relationship has been an increased sense of caring and safety. "We're friends now," he said. "Not antagonists. The key is that I feel safe. She's on my side, committed to my well-being. She is valuing me. Liking me. And I'm committed to liking her. Supporting her and affirming her. It just feels a lot different. The struggle with my mother is over. A woman is on my side, and it happens to be Grace. I can relax with her and feel safe with her." Grace echoed this last sentiment. "That's important to me, too. I can relax and feel safe with Kenneth." For both of them, the primitive need of the old brain to be in a safe, secure, and nurturing environment has finally been met.

Kenneth and Grace attended two more couples workshops. During these, they noticed that I described the conscious partnership as a journey, not a destination, explaining that even in the best love relationships there would always be struggle and the need to adapt and change. To some degree, their experience confirms this observation. "We still have problems," says Grace. "For example, Ken wants me to be more cautious in the things I tell him. To rehearse what I'm going to say, so that I don't risk hurting his feelings. But that's difficult for me to do. I'm an impulsive person. It would feel very strange to filter all my thoughts before I revealed them. And I want the opposite of him. I want him to be more spontaneous, less calculated. But that feels risky for him." They both express ambivalence about the challenge to keep growing. "Perhaps it has something to do with our age," says Kenneth. "Part of me wants life not to be a struggle anymore. Grace and I have arrived at a place that feels very comfortable. It's not that we've stopped growing and changing altogether, but this just feels like a nice place to be." In a way, they were questioning my description of reality love as a journey without end. It may be an endless journey, they are telling me, but it is a journey that becomes more and more effortless as time goes on.

THESE TWO RELATIONSHIPS offer an excellent description of what I call "the conscious partnership." Anne and Greg, along with Kenneth and Grace, reveal it to be a state of mind and a way of being based on acceptance, a willingness to grow and change, the courage to encounter one's own fear, and a conscious decision to treat each other as separate, unique inidivuals who are worthy of the greatest level of respect. They are relationships built on a solid foundation, no longer just the infatuation of romantic love, but the feelings are just as joyful and intense.

When we look at love relationships in more detail, it is clear that the simple word "love" cannot adequately describe the wide variety of feelings two individuals can have for each other. In the first two stages of a love relationship, romantic love and the power struggle, love is reactive; it is an unconscious response to the expectation of need fulfillment. Love is best described as eros, life energy seeking union with a gratifying object. When a husband and wife make a decision to create a more satisfying relationship, they enter a stage of transformation, and love becomes infused with consciousness and will; love is best defined as agape, the life energy directed toward the partner in an intentional act of healing. Now, in the final stage of a conscious partnership, reality love, love takes on the quality of "spontaneous oscillation," words that come from quantum physics and describe the way energy moves back and forth between particles. When partners learn to see each other without distortion, to value each other as highly as they value themselves, to give without expecting anything in return, to commit themselves fully to each other's welfare, love moves freely between them without apparent effort. The word that best describes this mature kind of love is not "eros," not "agape," but yet another Greek word, "philia,"[2] which means "love between friends." The partner is no longer perceived as a surrogate parent, or as an enemy, but as a passionate friend.

When couples are able to love in this selfless manner, they experience a release of energy. They cease to be consumed by the details of their relationship, or to need to operate within the artificial structure of exercises; they spontaneously treat each other with love and respect. What feels unnatural to them is not their new way of relating but the self-centered, wounding interactions of the past. Love becomes automatic, much as it was in the earliest stage of the relationship, but now it is based on the truth of the partner, not on illusion.

One characteristic of couples who have reached this advanced stage of consciousness is that they begin to turn their energy away from each other toward the woundedness of the world. They develop a greater concern for the environment, for people in need, for important causes. The capacity to love and heal that they have created within the relationship is now available for others.

I have found no better description of this rare kind of love than in I Corinthians 13:

Love is patient, love is kind. It does not envy, it does not boast, it is not proud. It is not rude, it is not self-seeking, it is not easily angered, it keeps no record of wrongs. Love does not delight in evil but rejoices with the truth. It always protects. It always trusts, always hopes, always perseveres. Love never fails.

part III

THE EXERCISES

TEN STEPS TOWARD A CONSCIOUS PARTNERSHIP

THIS PART OF the book describes a ten-step process based on Imago Relationship Therapy that will help you achieve a conscious, loving, and deeply connected relationship. It contains eighteen exercises that will assist you in translating the insights you have gained about marriage into effective skills.

I have some general comments to make before I describe them. All of the exercises have been thoroughly tested. With a few exceptions, they are the same exercises I have been assigning to couples for the past twenty years. These exercises have been shown to be very effective. An independent researcher concluded that couples who attended one of my weekend workshops, which contain approximately the same material as this book, improved their relationships as much as those who had been in private marital counseling for as long as three to six months.[1]

Most of the exercises follow the principle of graduated change, which means that you will begin with an easy task first and move on to progressively more difficult ones. You will be in control of how fast you go and how much you learn. Keep in mind that, the more difficult a particular exercise seems to you, the more potential it contains for growth.

You will discover that doing the exercises requires a significant amount of time and commitment. To complete them all, you will need to set aside an hour or two of uninterrupted time each week for several months. You may even have to hire a babysitter or give up some other activity to find the necessary time—just as you would if you were going to a weekly appointment with a therapist. This degree of commitment requires a clear understanding of how important a good marriage is to you, and a continual affirmation of your priorities.

You may want to do these exercises but don't have the support of your partner. If you are the only one interested at present, do as many of the exercises as you can by yourself. A relationship is like a balloon filled with water: push on one part of it and you change the shape of the entire balloon. When you practice the exercises by yourself, you will begin to listen to your partner more objectively, share your feelings with more candor, block your defensive and aggressive reactions, and make more of an effort to please your partner. As a result, your relationship will improve. Eventually your partner's resistance to change might diminish, and you will be able to go through the rest of the process together.

You can do these exercises as a couple or in a group setting where you have the support of other couples with similar goals. A group study guide and a couples' study guide are available to help you structure these sessions. For more information about the study guides and other resource materials, call 1-800-729-1121 or visit the Web site, www.HarvilleHendrix.com.

As you work your way through the exercises, you will discover that the journey toward a conscious partnership is never a straight line. There will be moments of great joy and intimacy, and there will be detours, long periods of stagnation, and unexpected regressions. During the periods of regression, you may feel despondent or criticize yourself for backsliding. My clients often tell me, "Dr. Hendrix, we've done it again. We've fallen back into the same old patterns. We thought this phase of our lives was over and done with! What is wrong with us?" I respond that there is nothing linear about love and marriage. Relationships tend to move in circles and vortices; there are cycles, periods of calm and periods of turbulence. Even when you feel as if you are going through the very same struggles over and over again, there is always some degree of change. What is happening is that you are deepening your experience or participating in a particular phenomenon in a different way or on a different level. Perhaps you are integrating more unconscious elements into your relationship, or enlarging your consciousness of a change that has already taken place. Perhaps you are reacting more intensely to a familiar situation because you have opened up new feelings. Or, conversely, you may be reacting less intensely because you have managed to work through some of your feelings. These changes may seem imperceptible, but there is movement all the same. By continually affirming your decision to grow and change, and by diligently practicing the techniques described in the following pages, you will be able to make sure and steady progress on your journey to a conscious partnership.

DOING THE EXERCISES

AS I DISCUSSED in chapter 7, making a firm commitment to work on your relationship before you begin the process will help you overcome any potential resistance to change. Take the time now to examine your priorities. How important to you is creating a more loving, supportive relationship? Are you willing to take part in a sometimes difficult process of self-growth? If you are, take out a separate sheet of paper and write a statement indicating your willingness to participate. You may wish to use words like the following:

> Because our relationship is very important to us, we are making a commitment to increase our awareness of ourselves and each other and to acquire and practice new relationship skills. Toward this end, we agree to do all the exercises in this book in a careful, conscientious manner.

As you work on the exercises, keep in mind these two cardinal rules:

1. The information you gather in the process of doing the exercises is designed to educate you and your partner about each other's needs. Sharing this information does not obligate you to meet those needs.
2. When you share your thoughts and feelings with each other, you become emotionally vulnerable. It is important that you use the information you gain about each other in a loving and helpful manner.

Suggested Ten-Session Timeline

First session: Exercise 1

Second session: Read or recite Relationship Vision
                  (Exercise 1)
                  New material: Exercises 2–5

Third session: Read or recite Relationship Vision
                  Do another Parent-Child Dialogue
                  (Exercise 5)
                  New material: Exercises 6–7

Fourth session:
Read or recite Relationship Vision
New material: Exercise 8

Fifth session:
Read or recite Relationship Vision
Review the need to close additional exits
New material: Exercise 9

Sixth session:
Read or recite Relationship Vision
Review the need to close additional exits
Continue with 2–3 caring behaviors a day
New material: Exercises 10–13

Seventh session:
Read or recite Relationship Vision
Review the need to close additional exits
Continue with 2–3 caring behaviors a day
Continue to give surprises and engage in
high-energy pleasurable activities and do
the positive flooding exercise again
New material: Exercise 14

Eighth session:
Read or recite Relationship Vision
Review the need to close additional exits
Continue with 2–3 caring behaviors a day
Continue to give surprises and engage in
high-energy pleasurable activities

Start daily short positive flooding
Continue with 3–4 behavior changes a week
New material: Exercise 15

Ninth session:
Read or recite Relationship Vision
Review the need to close additional exits
Continue with 2–3 caring behaviors a day
Continue to give surprises and engage in
high-energy pleasurable activities.

Continue daily positive flooding
Continue with 3–4 behavior changes a week
New material: Exercise 16

Tenth session:	Read or recite Relationship Vision
	Review the need to close additional exits
	Continue with 2–3 caring behaviors a day
	Continue to give surprises and engage in high-energy pleasurable activities.

Continue daily positive flooding
Continue with 3–4 behavior changes a week
New material: Exercises 17–18

Subsequent sessions:	Read or recite Relationship Vision
	Review the need to close additional exits
	Continue with 2–3 caring behaviors a day
	Continue to give surprises and engage in high-energy pleasurable activities.

Do positive flooding daily from now on.
Continue with 3–4 behavior changes a week
Review Exercise 16
*New material: Add additional caring
behaviors and behavior changes as they
occur to you.*

Note: You will need to save your responses to the exercises so you can refer to them later on in the process. I suggest that before you begin work you prepare two loose-leaf notebooks, one for each of you, each containing thirty or forty sheets of lined notebook paper. Do all your work in these notebooks.

EXERCISE 1: YOUR RELATIONSHIP VISION

Time: Approximately 60 minutes.

Purpose: This exercise will help you see the potential in your relationship.

Comments: Do this exercise together.

Directions

1. Take out two sheets of paper, one for each of you. Working separately, write a series of short sentences that describe your personal vision of a deeply satisfying love relationship. Include qualities you already have that you want to keep and qualities you wish you had. Write each sentence in the present tense, as if it were already happening. For example: "We have fun together." "We have great sex." "We are loving parents." "We are affectionate with each other." Make all your items positive statements. Write: "We settle our differences peacefully." rather than "We don't fight."

2. Share your sentences. Note the items that you have in common and underline them. (It doesn't matter if you have used different words, as long as the general idea is the same.) If your partner has written sentences that you agree with but did not think of yourself, add them to your list. For the moment, ignore items that are not shared.

3. Now turn to your own expanded list and rank each sentence (including the ones that are not shared) with a number from 1 to 5 according to its importance to you, with 1 indicating "very important," and 5 indicating "not so important."

4. Circle the two items that are most important to you.

5. Put a check mark beside those items that you think would be most difficult for the two of you to achieve.

6. Now work together to design a mutual relationship vision similar to the following example. Start with the items that you both agree are most important. Put a check mark by

those items that you both agree would be difficult to achieve. At the bottom of the list, write items that are relatively important. If you have items that are a source of conflict between you, see if you can come up with a compromise statement that satisfies both of you. If not, leave the item off your combined list.

Our Relationship Vision

Bill		Jenny
I	We have fun together.	I
I	We settle our differences peacefully.	I
I	We have satisfying and beautiful sex.	I
I	We are healthy and physically active.	I
I	We communicate easily and openly.	I√
I	We worship together.	I
I	We are each other's best friends.	I
I	We have secure and happy children.	I
2	We trust each other.	I
I	We are sexually faithful.	I
2	We both have satisfying careers.	2√
2	We work well together as parents.	I
2	We share important decisions.	2
2	We meet each other's deepest needs.	2
3	We have daily private time.	4
3	We feel safe with each other.	2
3	We are financially secure.	4√
4	We live close to our parents.	5√
5	We have similar political views.	3

7. Post this list where you can see it easily. Once a week, at the beginning of your work sessions, read it aloud to each other.

Exercise 2: Childhood Wounds

(review chapter 2)

Time: Approximately 30 minutes.

Purpose: Now that you have a vision of the future, this exercise will take you back into the past. It is designed to refresh your memory of your caretakers and other influential people so that you can construct your imago.

Comments: You may do this exercise together or at separate times. It is important that you be free from distractions for a period of thirty minutes. Read all of these instructions before carrying them out.

Directions

1. First do some slow stretching exercises to help you relax. Then settle into a comfortable chair. Breathe deeply ten times, becoming more relaxed with each breath.

2. When you are feeling peaceful, close your eyes and imagine your childhood home, the earliest one you can recall. Imagine yourself as a young boy or girl. Try to see the rooms from the perspective of a small child. Now wander around the house and find the people who influenced you most deeply as a child. As you encounter these people, you will be able to see them with new clarity. Stop and visit with each one. Note their positive and negative traits. Tell them what you enjoyed about being with them. Tell them what you didn't like about being with them. Finally, tell them what you wanted from them but never got. Don't hesitate to share your angry, hurt, or sad feelings. In your fantasy, your caretakers will be grateful for your insights.

3. When you have gathered this information, open your eyes and record it according to the instructions in Exercise 3.

EXERCISE 3: IMAGO WORKUP

(review chapter 3)

Time: Approximately 30–45 minutes.

Purpose: This exercise will help you record and summarize the information you acquired in Exercise 2.

Comments: You can do this exercise individually.

Directions

1. Take out a blank piece of paper and draw a large circle, leaving about three inches below the circle. Divide the circle in half with a horizontal line. Put a capital letter "B" above the line on the left side of the circle, and a capital letter "A" below the line on the left side of the circle. (See illustration below.)

2. On the top half, next to the "B," list all of the positive character traits of your mother, father, and any other people who influenced you strongly when you were young. Lump all the positive traits of all these people together. (Don't bother to group them according to individuals.) List these traits as you recall them from childhood. Do not describe your caretakers as they are today. Describe them with simple adjectives or phrases like the following: "kind," "warm," "intelligent," "religious," "patient," "creative," "always there," "enthusiastic," "reliable," etc.

3. On the bottom half, next to the "A," list the negative traits of these key people. Once again, lump all the traits together.

This list of positive and negative traits is your imago.

4. Circle the positive and negative traits that seem to affect you most.

5. In the blank space below your circle, write down a capital letter "C" and complete this sentence: "What I wanted most as a child and didn't get was . . ."

6. Now write down a capital letter "D" and complete this sentence: "As a child, I had these negative feelings over and over again: . . ."

(For the moment, ignore the capital letters. They will be referred to in Exercise 5.)

EXERCISE 4: CHILDHOOD FRUSTRATIONS

(review chapter 2)

Time: Approximately 30–45 minutes.

Purpose: This exercise will help you clarify your major childhood frustrations and describe the way you reacted to them.

Comments: You can do this exercise individually.

Directions
1. On a separate sheet of paper, list the recurring frustrations you had as a child (see example below).

2. Next to the frustrations, briefly describe the way you reacted to the frustrations. (You may have responded in more than one way. List all your common responses.) Put the capital letter "E" above your reactions as in the example.

Matt's Chart

Ⓔ

Frustration	Response
Didn't get enough attention from my older brother.	Was a pest. Kept trying to get his attention.
Father often gone.	Sometimes I was angry. Usually tried to please him.
Felt inferior to older brother.	Resigned myself to my inferiority. Tried not to compete directly.
My father drank too much.	Tried to ignore it. Sometimes I would get stomachaches.
My mother was overly protective.	I kept things to myself. Sometimes I was defiant.

EXERCISE 5: PARENT-CHILD DIALOGUE

(review chapter 9)

Time: Approximately 30 minutes.

Purpose: The Parent-Child Dialogue is designed to help you deepen your memory of your childhood and increase your empathy for each other.

Comments: Decide who will be the Child and who will be the Parent. The partner playing the Child role acts as if he or she were a young child of a specific age and talks in the present tense. The Child selects which parent he or she wants to talk to. The Child may select both parents or any other significant caretaker. The partner playing the Parent takes the role assigned but responds with more compassion than the real-life parent.

Directions

1. Sit face to face. The Parent says: "I am your mom/dad. What is it like living with me?" (If the parent is dead, use the past tense.) The Child (regressed to a specific age) then describes painful childhood experiences with the parent by saying: "I am X years old. Living with you, mom/dad is ..." The Parent mirrors those memories in an empathic tone that, most likely, contrasts with the behavior of the actual parent.

2. The Parent asks: "What is your deepest hurt with me?" The Child replies: "My deepest hurt with you, mom/dad is ..." The Parent mirrors the Child. The Child continues the converation by filling in the following sentence stems in order. "What hurts me about that is ..." "I'm sad about that because ..." "What I am afraid of is ..."

3. The Parent says: "What do you do when I hurt you?" The Child says how s/he copes with the pain. Examples: "I go to my room and cry." "I get angry and strike out." The Parent mirrors the comments with empathy.

4. Next, the Parent asks: "As your mom/dad, what do you need from me the most that I am not giving to you?" The Child says: "What I need most is ..." The Parent mirrors the statement and then validates the Child's pain and the underlying need by filling in the blanks in the following remark: "It makes sense to me that you feel ... and that you need ..., given that I ..." As an example, "It makes sense to me that you feel alone and frightened and that you need me to pay more attention to your needs and feelings given the fact that I am so emotionally distant from you."

5. Now, step out of your roles. The Parent says, "I am no longer your mom/dad. I am your partner. Thank you for

sharing that with me." The partner responds, "I am no longer your child. I am your partner. Thanks for listening to me."

6. Switch roles and go through the exercise again.

7. Now, on a sheet of paper, write a summary of what you learned about your partner's pain and frustrations from childhood and what your partner needs to heal those wounds. Review each other's summary statements for accuracy. Do not criticize your partner for any inaccuracy. Just correct the text until it fully reflects your experience.

8. When you are through, share what it was like to do the exercise.

EXERCISE 6: PARTNER PROFILE

(review chapter 3)

Time: Approximately 30–45 minutes.

Purpose: This exercise will help you define the things you like and don't like about your partner and compare your partner's traits with the traits of your Imago.

Comments: Do this exercise individually. Do not share this information at this time. The Behavior Change Request Dialogue exercise on pages 280–84 will help you make constructive use of this information.

Directions
1. On a separate sheet of paper, draw a large circle, leaving three inches of blank space below the circle. Divide the circle in half with a horizontal line, as you did in Exercise 3. Put the capital letter "F" above the line on the left side of the circle. Put the capital letter "G" below the line on the left side of the circle.

F
_____
G

2. On the top half of the circle (beside the "F") list your partner's positive traits. Include traits that first attracted you to your partner.

3. List your partner's negative traits beside the "G" on the lower half of the circle.

4. Circle the positive and negative traits that seem to affect you the most.

5. Now turn back to Exercise 2 and compare your imago traits with your partner's traits. Star the traits that are similar.

6. On the bottom of the page, write the letter "H" and complete this sentence: "What I enjoy most about my partner is . . ."

7. Now write the letter "I" and complete this sentence: "What I want from my partner and don't get is . . ."

Note: Your comments will make sense to you when you complete the next exercise.

EXERCISE 7: UNFINISHED BUSINESS

(review chapter 2)

Time: Approximately 15–20 minutes.

Purpose: This exercise organizes the information from Exercises 2–6 into a description of your unfinished business, the hidden agenda that you brought to your love relationship.

Comments: Do this exercise separately.

Directions

On a separate piece of paper, write down the words below that are written in boldface. Complete the sentences by filling in what you wrote beside the appropriate letters in the exercises cited in brackets.

I have spent my life searching for a person with these character traits [the traits that you underlined in A and B from Exercise 3, pages 262–63]:

When I am with such a person, I am troubled by these traits [the traits that you underlined in A in Exercise 3, step 3, page 262]:

And I wish that person would give me [C from Exercise 3, step 5, page 263]:

When my needs aren't met, I have these feelings: [D from Exercise 3, step 6, page 263]:

And I often respond this way [E from Exercise 4, page 264]:

Exercise 7 completes the first portion of the exercises. You now have a relationship vision, a description of your imago, a record of your early frustrations and coping patterns, a chart listing the things you like and don't like about your partner, and a sheet that describes the hidden agenda you brought to your relationship.

EXERCISE 8: THE IMAGO DIALOGUE

(review chapter 9)

Time: Approximately 45–60 minutes.

Purpose: This three-step exercise will train you to: 1) listen accurately to what your partner is saying, 2) understand and validate your partner's point of view, and 3) express your empathy for your partner's feelings.

Comments: Do this exercise together and often. The Imago Dialogue is a very effective tool for communication, mutual healing, and deep connection. It is the central therapeutic process in Imago Relationship Therapy. At first, it will feel like an unnatural, cumbersome way of talking, but it is an excellent way to assure accurate communication. With practice, the exercise will seem less mechanical. When you have the exercise down pat, you will discover that you do not need to use the structured process all the time. The three steps will be necessary only when you are discussing highly charged subjects or when communication breaks down. Eventually, through months of practice, you will feel safer, become less reactive to your partner's comments, and experience a deeper sense of connection and communication.

Directions

1. Choose who will be the sender and the receiver. The one who decides to be the sender starts the dialogue by saying: "I would like to have a Dialogue. Is now an OK time?" (When using this process in your relationship, it is important that the receiver respond as soon as possible. If that is not possible, set a time in the near future when you will be available so your partner will know when he or she will be heard.) The sender signals his or her readiness by saying: "I am available now."

2. The sender now talks very briefly, sending the simple message he or she wants the receiver to hear. The message should start with "I" and describe what the sender is thinking or feeling. The first time you do this exercise, choose a message that is neutral and very simple. Example: "I woke up this morning with a sore throat and didn't feel like going to work. I decided to stay home."

3. The receiver then mirrors (paraphrases) those words, starting with the words, "If I got it . . ." or "If I heard you accurately . . ." Example: "**If I got it**, you awakened with a sore throat, and since you don't feel well, you decided to stay home from work. **Did I get it?**" The sender indicates whether or not the message was correctly received. If the answer is "Yes," go on to step 4. If the answer is "No," the sender explains what was missing or added without a hint of criticism. The receiver mirrors back again. This continues until the sender acknowledges that the message was received as sent.

4. The receiver then asks: "Is there more you want to say about that?" If the sender has more to say, he or she sends an additional message. The receiver continues to mirror back the added information and then ask **"Is there more about that?"** until the sender has completed the message. (The question "Is there more about that?" is important. It helps the sender complete all the thoughts and feelings linked with the first statement and prevents the receiver from responding to an incomplete message. And, since it is limited to "more about *that*," it helps the sender limit the message to *one* subject at a time.)

5. When the sender has completed the message, the receiver then summarizes all of the sender's message with this lead-in sentence: **"Let me see if I got all of that . . ."** When the receiver finishes the summary, he or she asks, **"Did I get it all?"** The summary is important because it helps the receiver understand the sender more deeply and to see the logic in what was said. This helps with the next step, validation. When the sender indicates that all of the message has been heard accurately, go on to step 6.

6. Now the receiver validates the sender's message starting with words such as these: **"You make sense, because . . ."** or

"It makes sense to me, given that you . . ." or "I can see what you are saying . . ." Example: "What you say makes sense. Given the fact that you had a sore throat and felt bad, I can understand why you didn't go to work today." (This response indicates that the receiver understands the logic of what the sender is saying. It is the sender's "truth." The receiver does not have to agree with the sender, but it is essential that the receiver "sees" the logic or "truth" of the sender's experience. The receiver checks to see if the sender feels validated. If so, then move on to step 7.

7. The sender expresses his or her empathy by starting with the following sentence stems: "I can imagine that you might be feeling . . ." or "I imagine that you felt . . ." Example. "I can imagine that you might be feeling frustrated that you had to miss a day of work." Feelings are best stated using one word such as angry, upset, happy, etc. If you use more than one word, such as: "you feel you don't want to go to work" you are probably expressing a thought. Then the receiver checks for accuracy by asking, "Is that what you are feeling?" or "Did I get your feeling right?" If the receiver did not imagine the right feeling or misperceived the expressed feeling, then the sender explains what the feeling is. Once the feeling has been identified correctly, the receiver asks, "Is there more about that feeling?" Continue the process until the exchange is completed.

8. When the receiver has gone through all three steps—mirroring, validation, and empathy—the partners switch roles. The new sender (the former receiver) can respond to the partner's original message or may express an unrelated thought or feeling. Go through all the steps, as before.

9. Now use the three-step Imago Dialogue to share what each of you learned about yourself when doing Exercise 2,

Childhood Wounds. As you listen, try to visualize your partner's childhood frustrations or pain. When it's your turn to talk, divide your comments into simple, easy to remember statements.

EXERCISE 9: THE COMMITMENT DECISION

(review pages 100–115)

Time: Approximately 60–90 minutes.

Purpose: This exercise serves two purposes: (1) it assures that you will stay together while you are working through these exercises, and (2) it creates a sense of safety that gradually increases your level of intimacy.

Comments: Do this exercise together.

Directions

1. Imagine that your relationship is represented by a rectangle with perforated sides. The open spaces are your "exits," by which I mean all the inappropriate ways that you seek safety, gratify your needs, or drain the energy away from your relationship. In essense, you use an exit to act out your feelings rather than talking about them with your partner.

Each of the four corners of the rectangle is a catastrophic exit—suicide, divorce (or separation), murder, and insanity. Examine your thoughts and feelings to see if you are contemplating leaving the relationship through any of these corner exits. If so, I urge you to make a decision now to close them for the period of time that you are working together on these exercises. If you cannot make that decision, than I urge you to call an Imago therapist and begin therapy. (Go to www.HarvilleHendrix.com to locate a nearby therapist. If you cannot find an Imago therapist, find a couples therapist in your area.)

2. Now take out four sheets of paper, two for each of you. On your first sheet of paper, make a comprehensive list of your ordinary exits. Ordinary exits are such things as overeating, staying late at work, spending too much time with the children—anything that you do primarily to avoid your partner. (See page 109 for a more comprehensive list.)

3. Using the mirroring technique described in Exercise 8, the Imago Dialogue, take turns sharing the list of exits you are using. (You do not have to use all the steps in the Imago Dialogue, just the mirroring portion.) Example:

PARTNER A: I am aware that I bring work home for the weekend, and that I do that because I am afraid to spend time with you and get into conflict about something.

PARTNER B: You think you bring home work from the office because you are afraid to spend time with me. Did I understand you correctly?

PARTNER A: Not completely. I said that I think that one of the reasons that I bring work home is to avoid spending time with you because we get into conflicts and that is unpleasant for me. I have other reasons, too.

PARTNER B: OK. You are saying that one of the reasons you work over the weekends is to spend less time with me because we get into conflicts and that is unpleasant for you. And you have other reasons, too. Did I get you this time?

PARTNER A: Yes, you heard me correctly.

4. Now, working with your own list, put a check mark by exits that you are willing to eliminate or use less frequently at the present time. Put an "X" by those that would be difficult for you to change.

5. Write out the following agreement and fill in the blanks: "Starting this week [insert date], rather than bringing work

home, I agree to ask you for a dialogue to talk about why I work on the weekends and my fear of being in conflict with you.

Note: It is important to talk about the fear behind your exit. Talking about your fear in the safety of Imago Dialogue paradoxically closes the exit of avoidance. After you talk about your feelings, it may be important also to close an exit if it is draining energy that belongs to your relationship.

EXERCISE 10: REROMANTICIZING

(review chapter 8)

Time: Approximately 60 minutes.

Purpose: By sharing specific information about what pleases you and agreeing to pleasure your partner on a regular, consistent basis, you can turn your relationship into a zone of safety.

Comments: You can do steps 1–3 separately if you wish. Do the remaining steps together.

Directions

1. The first step in this process is to identify what your partner is already doing that pleases you. Get out separate sheets of paper and complete this sentence in as many ways as possible, being specific and positive and focusing on items that happen with some regularity: *I feel loved and cared about when you . . .*

> Examples: fill my coffee cup when it's empty.
> let me read the front page of the paper first.
> kiss me before you leave the house.
> call me from work just to chat.
> tell me important things that happen to you.
> massage my back.

tell me you love me.
ask if I want a treat from the store.
bring me surprise presents.
sit close to me when we're watching TV.
listen to me when I'm upset.
check with me first before making plans.
pray with me and for me.
make special Sunday dinners.
want to make love to me.
compliment me on the way I look.

2. Now recall the romantic stage of your relationship. Are there any caring behaviors that you used to do for each other that you are no longer doing? Once again, take out separate sheets of paper and complete this sentence: *I used to feel loved and cared about when you . . .*

Examples: wrote me love letters.
brought me flowers.
held my hand as we walked.
whispered sexy things into my ear.
called me up on the phone to say how much
you loved me.
cooked me special dinners.
stayed up late talking and making love.
made love more than once a day.
kissed me when you went out the door and
hugged me when you came home.

3. Now think about some caring and loving behaviors that you have always wanted but never asked for. These may come from your vision of a perfect mate or from prior experience. (They should not, however, refer to activities that are a present source of conflict.) These may be very private fantasies. Whenever possible, quantify your request. Complete this sentence: *I would like you to . . .*

Examples: massage me for thirty minutes without
            stopping.
            take a shower with me.
            buy me some silver jewelry as a surprise.
            go backpacking with me three times each
            summer.
            sleep in the nude.
            go out to brunch with me once a month.
            read a novel to me over Christmas vacation.
            eat dinner on the deck.

4. Now combine all three lists and indicate how important
each caring behavior is to you by writing a number from 1 to 5
beside each one. A "1" indicates "very important"; a "5" indicates "not so important."

5. Exchange lists. Examine your partner's lists and put an
"X" by any items that you are not willing to do at this time.
(Make sure that you are willing to do all the ones you have not
checked.) Starting tomorrow, do at least two of the caring
behaviors each day for the next two months, starting with the
ones that are easiest for you to do. Add more items to your list
as they occur to you. When your partner does a caring behavior for you, acknowledge it with an appreciative comment. As
you will recall from reading chapter 8, these caring behaviors
are gifts, not obligations. Do them regardless of how you feel
about your partner, and regardless of the number of caring
behaviors your partner gives you.

6. If either you or your partner experiences some resistance
to this exercise, keep on doing the caring behaviors until the resistance is overcome. (See pages 127–30 for an explanation of
the fear of pleasure.)

Exercise 11: The Surprise List

(review pages 124–26)

Time: Approximately 15–20 minutes.

Purpose: The purpose of this exercise is to augment the caring behaviors in Exercise 10 with unanticipated pleasures, which adds to your feelings of safety and bonding.

Comments: This exercise is to be done separately and must be kept secret from your partner.

Directions

1. Make a list of things you could do for your partner that would be especially pleasing. Don't guess. Draw up your list from your memory of things that have pleased your partner in the past or from hints or comments your partner has made. Become a detective and ferret out your partner's hidden wishes and desires. Keep your list hidden from your partner at all times.

2. Select one item and surprise your partner with it this week. Be sure to do this at least once a week and at random times, so that your partner will have difficulty anticipating the surprise.

3. Record the date when you gave each surprise.

4. On a separate sheet of paper, record and date the surprises you receive from your partner. Thank your partner for surprising you.

EXERCISE 12: THE FUN LIST

(review page 126)

Time: Approximately 20–30 minutes.

Purpose: This exercise is designed to intensify your emotional bond and deepen your feelings of safety and pleasure.

Comments: Do this exercise together.

Directions

1. Make separate lists of fun and exciting activities you would like to do with your partner. These should include face-to-face experiences and any body contact that is physically pleasurable. Examples: tennis, dancing, wrestling, showering together, sex, massage, tickling, jumping rope, bicycling.

2. Now share your lists and compile a third list that combines all of your suggestions.

3. Pick one activity from the list and do it each week.

4. You may experience some resistance to taking part in such exuberant, childlike activities—especially if you have a conflicted relationship. It is important that you do this exercise nonetheless. Go against your natural inclination and experiment with this brief return to childhood.

EXERCISE 13: POSITIVE FLOODING

(review chapter 11)

Time: Approximately 45 minutes.

Purpose: This exercise will help you and your partner experience emotional intensity connected to specific physical features, traits, and behaviors you appreciate and love. Speaking with intensity about the positive will also reduce your sensitivity to negative comments that are spoken with intensity.

Comments: Use the first 30 minutes working alone to make your lists and then do the exercise together.

Directions:

1. Take out two sheets of paper, one for each of you. Each of you takes one piece and divides the sheet into four columns. Write in the following four headings: "Physical Traits," "Character traits," "Behaviors," "Global Affirmations." Now under the respective columns, write down the physical traits you appreciate about your partner, the positive character traits you adore, the behaviors your partner has done that you appreciate, and global expressions of love such as "I love you," "I can't believe I married someone as wonderful as you!"

2. Now, one of you sits in a chair while the other circles around saying the words he or she has written on the paper. Use about one minute for each column, and increase the intensity of your voice as you go from column to column. When your reach the global affirmations column, jump up and down, your feet leaving the floor.

3. Take out two more sheets of paper and design it exactly as the one above, including the same column headings. This time, each of you lists the praises you would like to hear from your partner. Examples: "Tell me that I have long, beautiful legs." "Tell me that I am a trustworthy friend." "Tell me that I do an excellent job of managing the house." "Tell me that I am a patient, loving parent." "Tell me that you love to touch my skin." "Tell me that you love to see me undressed." "Tell me

that I am the best partner you have ever had." "Tell me how lucky you are to be with me."

4. Now repeat the circling exercise and take turns flooding each other with these new lists of praise. End the exercise with an intense hug. Let your self feel all the powerful feelings the exercise evokes.

5. Talk with your partner about what the exercise meant to you, using the Imago Dialogue.

6. Repeat this exercise once a week for four weeks. Then, make a practice of flooding your partner for a few moments every day.

EXERCISE 14: THE BEHAVIOR CHANGE REQUEST DIALOGUE

(review chapter 10)

Time: Approximately 60–90 minutes.

Purpose: The purpose of this exercise is to learn more about each other's deepest needs and to give you the opportunity to change your behavior to meet those needs. As you stretch against your resistance to change, your partner will experience emotional healing, and you will become a more whole and loving individual.

Comments: This is a very important exercise. I recommend you give it your highest priority.

Directions
1. The first step in this exercise is to identify the desires that lie behind your frustrations. On a separate sheet of paper, each

of you makes a comprehensive list of all the things that bother you about your partner. What does your partner do that makes you feel angry, annoyed, afraid, suspicious, resentful, hurt, or bitter? After you list the frustrating behavior and the feelings that go with it, see if you can remember feeling that way as a child. Here is an example:

Jenny's List

I don't like it when you . . .

drive too fast. I feel scared.
leave the house without telling me where you are going. I feel abandoned.
criticize me in front of the children. I feel shamed.
undermine my authority with the children. I feel humiliated.
read the newspaper during dinner. I feel ignored and unimportant.
criticize me in a joking manner in front of friends. I feel shamed.
don't pay attention to what I'm saying. I feel ignored.
turn away from me when I'm upset or crying. I feel abandoned.
criticize me for being indecisive. I feel guilty.
criticize me for being a poor housekeeper. I feel shamed.
keep pointing out the fact that you earn more money than I do. I feel shamed.

2. Now get out a second sheet of paper and write down the global desire that lies hidden within each of your frustrations. Skip several lines after each desire. Do not write down the frustration, only the desire. (This is necessary, because you will be showing this second sheet to your partner.)

Example:

Global Desire (corresponds to the first frustration listed above): I would like to feel safe and relaxed when you are driving.

3. Underneath each global desire, write three specific requests, each of which would help you satisfy that desire. It is important that your requests be positive and that they describe a specific, doable behavior. Remember the acronym SMART. Each behavior should be specific, measurable, achievable, relevant to the desire, and time-limited. Then ask your partner to give you one of your requests as a gift.

Examples:

Global Desire: I would like to feel safe and relaxed when you are driving.
Specific Request 1: For the next month, when you are driving, I would like you to obey the speed limit. If the road conditions are bad, I would like you to drive even more slowly.
Specific Request 2: For the next two weeks, before we get into the car, tell me that you will drive within the speed limit, and give me a hug.
Specific Request 3: Two times next week, have a dialogue with me for 15 minutes and ask me how I feel when you drive beyond the speed limit and help me connect my fear to childhood.

Global Desire: I would like you to always comfort me when I'm upset.
Specific Request 1: For the next month, when I tell you that I am upset, I would like you to put your arms around me and give me your full attention for five minutes.

Specific Request 2: Twice this week, I would like you to go for a walk with me after dinner so we can talk about each other's day without interruption.

Specific Request 3: This week, whenever I tell you that I am upset, I would like you to look directly at me, listen carefully, and reflect back to me what I said.

Notice that these requests are for specific, positive behaviors. The following request is a bad example because it is not specific.

Vague Request: I would like you to be more attentive.

It should be rewritten to make it more detailed:

Specific Request: For the next two weeks, I would like you to give me a warm hug as soon as you come home from work and hold me for one full minute.

This next request is a bad example because it is negative:

Negative Request: I would like you to stop yelling at me when you're upset.

This should be rewritten so that it describes a positive behavior:

Positive request: For the next month, when you are mad at me, I would like you to ask me for what you want in a normal tone of voice. Give me a specific, time limited, and positive request.

4. Share your second list (the one that lists desires and requests but not frustrations) with each other. Use your communication skills to clarify each desire and request so that it is

clearly understood using SMART behaviors. Rewrite the request if necessary so that the partner knows exactly what kind of behavior you want, how often you want it, how long you want it, and when you want it.

5. Now take back your own list and rank each request on the left side of the page with a number from 1 to 5 indicating its relative importance to you, 1 indicating "very important," and 5 "not very important."

6. Exchange lists once again so that you now have your partner's requests, and assign a number from 1 to 5 on the right side of the paper indicating how difficult it would be for you to grant each request, with 1 indicating "very difficult," and 5 "not at all difficult."

7. Keep your partner's list. Starting today, you have the opportunity to grant your partner three or four of the easiest requests each week. Remember that these behaviors are gifts. Regardless of how you feel and regardless of how many changes your partner is making, keep to a reliable schedule of at least three or four behavior changes a week. (You are encouraged to add more requests to your lists as time goes on.)

EXERCISE 15: THE HOLDING EXERCISE

(review pages 190–93)

Time: Approximately 30 minutes.

Purpose: This exercise is designed to deepen your empathy and connection with your partner. It may also allow you to reexperience and release stored pain or sadness from your childhood.

Comments: Find a place where you can sit comfortably for as long as 15 minutes. (You may want back support.) Then, take turns holding each other and following the directions below. The person being held lies across the partner's lap with his or her head against the heart of the holding partner. Let yourself be aware of your experience of holding and being held in this way.

Note: This is not what is called a "regression exercise." Each of you will be speaking as an adult, not as a young child.

Directions:

Decide who will be the holder and who will be held. Get into a comfortable position, with the head of the person being held close to the heart of the holder.

1. The holder begins the exercise by asking: "Tell me about the pain and frustration of your childhood." The person being held talks about early, hurtful experiences. After every few sentences, the holder mirrors back what the partner has said. (If the person being held cannot remember any pain from childhood, he or she can talk about any relationship pain outside of the current relationship.) If the person being held cries or sobs, the holding partner encourages those feelings and mirrors them. "You must have felt so sad." "You went through so much pain." "I can see how much it hurt." "Your tears make me want to cry."

2. Once the memories are over, the holder says: "What was the worst part of that . . . ?" The person being held responds: "The worst part was . . ." The holder listen empathetically, and then says, "Thank you for telling me." The person being held says, "Thanks for listening."

3. Change roles and repeat the exercise.

4. Now write down your own childhood pain and injury and your partner's pain and injury. In the days to come, bring to mind your partner's early experiences and visualize your partner's hurts when he or she was a child.

EXERCISE 16: OWNING AND ELIMINATING YOUR NEGATIVITY

(review chapter 11)

Time: Approximately 45 minutes.

Purpose: This exercise will help you create more safety and passion in your relationship by helping you let go of your negative thoughts and behaviors toward your partner and replace them with loving thoughts and behaviors.

Comments: When you focus on your partner's negative qualities, your tend to ignore the positive traits. If you go one step further and criticize your partner for having those negative traits, your partner becomes defensive and may go on the attack. This climate of negativity feeds on itself. This exercise turns the tables. It focuses your attention on your partner's positive traits and encourages you to praise your partner more often. The result? You begin to feel much more positive toward each other and to treat each other with more love and respect. This positive climate is also self-reinforcing. What you pay attention to is what you get.

Directions

Do this exercise separately and then, using the Imago Dialogue, talk about what you learned about yourself with your partner. Work alone through point 5. Then invite your partner into dialogue for point 6. Do the remaining steps on your own at a later date. It is important that you follow the instructions exactly as stated.

1. Take out several sheets of lined paper. Think about all the negative words you use to describe your partner. Include words that you have spoken in a heated situation, when name calling, and negative words you have thought about your partner but not spoken out loud. Write down these words in a column on the left side of your paper, one word or phrase on every second line. (This leaves room to write a sentence or two by each trait.)

2. Now recall a behavior your partner has done that illustrates each negative word or phrase. Write it beside the word. Here is an example:

Negative Trait	Related Behavior
Always late	Last night, she was late coming home for dinner.
Neglectful	She forgot to get me anything for my birthday.
Controlling	She always wants things her way. We always watch the movies that she wants to see.

3. Look through your list and circle the trait that bothers you the most.

4. Now write a second list of your partner's positive traits and behaviors. Write down as many positive traits as you wrote down negative traits.

Example:

Positive Trait	Related Behavior
Kind	Yesterday she drove our elderly next-door neighbor to his doctor appointment.

Funny   When we were out to dinner with friends,
                       she had everyone laughing.

Hardworking   Last weekend she painted both bedrooms.

5. Now go back to your list of criticisms. Look at the first negative behavior on your list. Close your eyes and visualize your partner doing that behavior. When you have it clearly in mind, release the image and then bring to mind a positive behavior your partner has done that you do like. (Look at your list of positive traits for suggestions.) Hold the positive image in your mind and note how you feel. Do this for all the negative words on your list.

6. Use the Imago Dialogue to discuss with your partner what you learned about yourself doing this exercise. (This is not a time to talk about what you don't like about your partner. You are sharing self-discoveries.)

7. In the next few days, when you have a negative thought about something your partner has done, release it and think of something he or she has done that you do like.

8. In the next few days, make it a point to tell your partner about only the positive things he or she has done that you appreciate. If you have a negative thought or memory, release it.

9. When your partner does or says something that you wish hadn't happened, refrain from criticism. Instead, use the Behavior Change Request Dialogue (Exercise 14 above) to make a request for a positive change in behavior.

EXERCISE 17: SELF-INTEGRATION

(review chapter 2)

Time: Approximately 15–30 minutes.

Purpose: The purpose of this exercise is to integrate aspects of your disowned self, your false self, and your lost self, making you more aware of your essential wholeness.

Comments: Because you have been faithfully performing these exercises for several weeks, you have been enlarging your sense of self by eroding your false self, integrating your denied self, and recovering your lost self. This exercise is designed to help you become more conscious of these changes. You can do the exercise separately or together.

Directions

1. Take out a sheet of paper and draw a vertical line down the middle.

2. Now draw two horizontal lines across the paper so that the sheet is divided horizontally into thirds. Your page should now be divided into six equal boxes, as in the illustration below.

3. Flip through your notebook until you find your response to the Imago Workup (Exercise 3) and the Partner Profile (Exercise 5). In the top left box of the paper you have just divided into six boxes, list the predominant negative traits of your caretakers and your partner. Label these traits "My Disowned Self." Think about the extent to which these negative traits may be true of you. Has anyone, especially your partner, told you that you possess these traits? For the moment assume that these traits are descriptive of you. What would you be like or how would you behave if you didn't have these traits? Write a description of the person you would be without these negative traits in the upper right box of your paper. Write them as short, positive statements beginning with the word "I." For example: "I am warm." "I am responsible." "I am nurturing."

4. In the middle box on the left side of your page, list your caretakers' positive traits and your partner's positive traits. It may be that some of these positive traits are a description of your lost self, parts of yourself that you repressed in childhood. Label this box "My Lost Self." Look at this box and ask yourself if you have ever been asked by your partner or other significant people in your life to develop these traits. Assuming that these traits represent repressed aspects of yourself, how would you behave or what would you be like if you had these traits? Write your answers in the middle box on the right side of your page. Once again, use simple, positive statements in the present tense: "I am artistic." "I am spiritual." "I am conscientious." "I am creative."

5. Think about the traits that you had to develop in order to get or keep your parents' love, and think about the kinds of things you do today to try to get people to like you. List those traits in the bottom box on the left side of your page. (Examples: "I try to be perfect." "I am compliant." "I am super-responsible." "I always try to please." "I don't express my anger.") Label this box "My False Self." Now think about

the way you would be and behave if you were free of such adaptive characteristics. List these traits and behaviors you would have in the bottom box on the right side of your page. Use simple, positive statements: "I am assertive." "I can express anger." "I can relax and don't have to try to be perfect."

6. On top of the three boxes on the right-hand side of your page, write the words "My True Self." These three right-hand boxes are a description of your true potential. Read this description once a week. As you read it, note areas where the description does not match your current reality. Visualize yourself changing so that the description is a valid one.

EXERCISE 18: VISUALIZATION OF LOVE

Time: One minute, three times each day.

Purpose: This exercise uses the power of visualization to amplify the positive changes you have been making in your relationship.

Comments: This exercise becomes a daily meditation.

Directions
  1. Three times each day, do the following: Close your eyes, take several deep breaths, and visualize your partner. Gradually refine the image until you see your partner as a whole, spiritual being who has been wounded in the ways you now know about. Hold this image in your mind and imagine that your love is healing your partner's wounds.

  2. Now visualize the energy of love that you are sending to your partner coming back to you and healing your wounds. Imagine that this energy flows back and forth between you in a continuous oscillation. When a minute is up, open your eyes and continue whatever you were doing.

Seeking Professional Help

SOME OF YOU MAY WANT to deepen your understanding of your relationship and gain additional skills by working with a couples therapist. Fortunately, couples therapy has lost much of the stigma that it had in earlier years. Years ago only people who were in great pain or who were very courageous signed up for couples counseling. Now more and more couples are deciding to seek help before irrevocable damage is done. They want to enhance the quality of their lives, and they realize that nothing is more important to them than their primary love relationship. They have the healthy attitude that going to a therapist is no different from going to any skilled teacher: you learn faster and better if you get expert supervision.

One of the main benefits of seeing a therapist is that you will speed up the integration of material from your unconscious. A therapist can help you maneuver around your blind spots and assimilate material from your unconscious that might take you months or years to assimilate on your own. As a result, you will spend a lot less time spinning your wheels.

Another good reason to enlist the aid of a therapist is to give you an added measure of safety and support. When you are working on new material and begin to experience some anxiety, a therapist will help you understand your fears. Given reassurance and insight, you will probably be able to plunge ahead instead of retreating to safer ground. This will prove especially valuable for couples who are experiencing a great many problems.

A final reason for seeking professional counseling is to provide a structured environment for growth. If you are short on discipline or motivation, having a weekly appointment and paying a therapist a good deal of money can give you added incentive.

If you are interested in working with a couples therapist, I have some general recommendations. My advice is that you look for a therapist whose primary area of expertise is relationship therapy, not individual therapy, so that he or she will be well versed in the complexities of love relationships. Furthermore, I recommend that you look for a therapist who will work with you jointly, in what is referred to in professional circles as "conjoint" couples therapy. If you see separate therapists or the same therapist at different times, you might inadvertently focus on issues that would help you live more autonomously, not help you live more harmoniously as a couple. Dwelling on matters that are not directly relevant to your relationship may help you as an individual, but there is some evidence that it might not be the best way to strengthen your marriage. When you are seeing a therapist together, you will more clearly see how your personal issues affect the state of your relationship, and both your personal and relationship issues can be resolved together.

How do you go about selecting a couples therapist? A person professing to be a therapist may be a clergyman, a social worker, a psychologist, a psychiatrist, an educator, or, in some states, simply a person with strong views on love relationships. A therapist's training may vary from years of postgraduate training to none at all. In some states, all that's required for a license as a couples therapist is a recommendation by someone who already has a license. For this reason, it is wise to choose your therapist on the basis of a referral. Get recommendations from friends or from the minister of a church who has successfully referred a large number of couples. If you are unable to get a referral, look in your phone book under the headings "American Association of Pastoral Counselors," "American Association for Marriage and Family Therapy," "Association of Clinical Social Workers," "Marriage Counselors," or "Mental Health." If you live in a large city, there may be a special referral service that will match you up with an appropriate therapist.

When you have been given the name of a particular therapist, there are a number of things you should check out. First make sure the therapist is fully accredited by a recognized organization such as the American Association of Marriage and Family Therapists, the American Association of Pastoral Counselors, the American Psychological Association, or the American Psychiatric Association. When you are satisfied that the therapist meets your initial criteria, sign up for a preliminary interview to see if you would feel comfortable working together. (Some therapists will waive the fees for this initial consultation.) Find out the therapist's views on relationship therapy. Most important of all, trust your instincts. You are looking for a therapist who is a caring, warm, sensitive person who gives you a feeling of safety and confidence. Even if you like the therapist, it is wise to interview more than one person, so that you have a basis for comparison.

If you are interested in working with a therapist specifically trained in Imago Relationship Therapy, or wish to attend a *Getting the Love You Want* Couples Workshop, please call 1-800-729-1121 or visit our Web site at www.HarvilleHendrix .com.

Notes

FOREWORD TO THE 20TH ANNIVERSARY EDITION

1. From the U.S. Census document: "Married-Couple and Unmarried-Partner Households: 2000." This sixteen-page report is the first time the Census Bureau has commented on the growing trend of cohabitation.

INTRODUCTION TO THE 1988 EDITION

1. A conscious marriage is created by bringing into awareness the unconscious directives and purposes of a romantic or love marriage. A love marriage is defined as a voluntary union of two individuals based upon romantic attraction that is stirred by unconscious needs that have their roots in unresolved childhood issues.

Love marriages have existed throughout history, but they have not been the dominant cultural form of marriage until the latter part of the nineteenth century, and then largely in the Western world. Romantic relationships are recorded in all the world's mythologies and literature, but they have generally been extramarital and often adulterous. For a discussion of this phenomenon, see Denis de Rougemont, *Love in the Western World*, and Morton Hunt, *The Natural History of Love*.

There are historical indications of the trend toward the fusion of romance and marriage, creating the love marriage, in the Western world in the sixteenth century. Following the Renaissance and the Reformation, which gave birth to the concept of individual rights, to democratic institutions, and to the changing status of women, marriage gradually became a source of personal satisfaction and began to shed its function as a stabilizing unit for society. For a detailed historical analysis of this process, see Robert Bellah et al., *Habits of the Heart*, chapters three and four. He presents a brilliant analysis of the tension between the demands of social roles and social institutions and the emergence of private life, especially in the arena of love and marriage. He sees this tension, which was rampant in the nineteenth century, as "endemic" in our culture today.

Prior to the modern period, from the sixteenth century until the present, the dominant form of marriage in the Western world was the arranged marriage, variously based upon economics, politics, or social position, and serving the purpose of maintaining a particular social reality. This form of marriage is still numerically dominant in the non-Western world today. A second form of marriage that has existed throughout history, and still exists in many cultures, is the slave marriage, in which the spouse, usually the woman, is purchased by the man with whatever "coin in trade" is used in that culture—money, pigs, water buffalo, etc. The purchased spouse usually bears and rears the children, does much of the domestic work, owns no property, has no rights, and can be sold if desired or necessary. (I have recently visited the Dani tribe in Irian Jaya, where a wife could be bought for five pigs, and also the Batak people of Sumatra, where the price of a wife was five water buffalo. At the current exchange rate, that was about five thousand dollars.)

Love relationships can and do exist in all cultures, but marriage based on love and mutual selection requires freedom of choice and gender equality. However, freedom is a relative state, and most marriages in the Western world are still arranged and spouses are still selected because of their value. The arena, however, has shifted from the social and objective world to the private and subjective world. Partner selection in a democratic society is arranged by the unconscious, and the value of the partners is determined by unconscious judgment of their ability to provide psychic satisfaction of specific emotional needs. The romantic or love marriage is influenced, perhaps even determined, by the parents, albeit out of the awareness of the actual parents or the marital partners. But in this case the selection is not to do the bidding of the parents but to make up for their deficiencies as caretakers. The romantic marriage is, therefore, an unconscious marriage, with purposes that suit the unconscious. It is the thesis of this book that this subterranean drama must be brought into consciousness, thus creating the conscious marriage, if the psychic purposes are to be realized. Since we view these purposes as positive and constructive, bringing them into consciousness and intentionally cooperating with them results in a type of healing and wholeness that satisfies deep and universal longing. For the first time in history, marriage can be an arena for personal growth that matches or exceeds the offerings of other forms of personal salvation, such as psychotherapy, religious disciplines, and social revolutions. See Jung, "Marriage as a Psychological Relationship," in *The Portable Jung*, pp. 163ff.

CHAPTER 1: THE MYSTERY OF ATTRACTION

1. This theory, that people tend to select mates who are more or less their equals, also attempts to explain the stability of some couples. In a study of 537 dating men and women reported in the July 22, 1986, edition of *The New York Times* by writer Daniel Goleman, the researchers found that people who perceived their partners to be superior to them felt guilty and insecure. People who perceived their partners to be inferior to them reported feelings of anger. When partners perceived themselves to be equals, their relationships were relatively conflict-free and stable.

2. C. G. Jung, *Two Essays in Analytical Psychology*, pp. 155–56. See also *The Archetypes and the Collective Unconscious*, vol. 9, pp. 122–23.

3. Paul D. McLean, "Man and His Animal Brains." This is one of several ways of looking at the brain distinguished by an evolutionary perspective. I use the terms "old brain" and "new brain" because of their simplicity and illustrative power, as compared with the more familiar terms, the "unconscious" and the "conscious."

4. The question of freedom and determinism divides various disciplines into opposing camps. In philosophy and religion, the question has been debated for centuries with no resolution. Psychological schools are distinguished by their adherence to a mechanistic versus an organismic view of human beings. This question is crucial for marriages, because if we are destined to certain marital fates, then what is the value of therapies that offer hope and change? To my way of thinking, both sides of most polarities are valid. The old-brain/new-brain metaphor offers a resolution to the dialogue—we are both determined and free. The old brain, with its built-in survival programs, determines our basic reactions, and the new brain can become aware of reactions that are not effective and devise new options. The survival directives of

the old brain cannot be overridden, but the new brain can re-educate the old brain with regard to what is dangerous and what is not. We are free within limits, but our limits are not absolute.

5. These primary evolutionary defenses are believed to have evolved in the reverse order of the way I have listed them. Fear, considered the primary affect, is followed much later in evolutionary history by the nurturing response. It is believed that self-preservation as the basic instinct preceded the nurturing response by millions of years.

CHAPTER 2: CHILDHOOD WOUNDS

1. Martin Buber, *I and Thou,* p. 76. The notion that human life includes an awareness of oneness with the universe is endemic in most religions in most cultures and is often referred to by the term "mystical." This experience was reduced by Freud to an "oceanic feeling" reminiscent of prenatal union with the mother, thus polarizing with Buber. Silverman et al., in *The Search for Oneness,* subject Freud's thesis to empirical research and conclude that "unconscious fantasies of oneness can enhance adaptation if a sense of self can be preserved" (pp. 1ff).

I take the position that the search for oneness is multidimensional. It expresses our awareness of our separation from essential aspects of ourselves, a split in the psyche caused by the repressive aspect of socialization, which disturbs our awareness of our union with the universe, which Buber so poetically says "we forgot at birth." The desire for union with the mother, an empirical reality, expresses this deeper desire for union with split-off parts of the self, a search for personal wholeness, which, when achieved, restores our awareness of our essential union with the universe out of which both the self and the maternal matrix arise. From this I hypothesize that in marriage the impulse to unite with the partner is unconsciously an attempt to reunite with the split-off parts of the self, which are projected onto the partner. Since there is a fusion of the partner and the parent in the unconscious, a positive emotional bond with the partner (achieved by loving in the partner that which is split off from the self and projected) restores a sense of personal wholeness and an awareness of our essential union with the universe. This gives marriage an essentially spiritual potential.

2. The brief summary of the developmental stages of childhood is based upon the work of Margaret Mahler, *On Human Symbiosis and the Vicissitudes of Individuation.* I take full responsibility for the liberties I have taken with identifying developmental issues that reappear in

marriage, since this was not her intention. Developmental theories are distinguished by the interests of the theoretician. Current theories include childhood viewed from the perspective of sexual, social, cognitive, moral, and faith development. All these dimensions are involved in the developmental processes of every child, and their fate is reflected in every marriage. The elaboration of this thesis would be book-length itself, and that is not my present intention. I wish only to identify the issues of childhood that appear in marriage as a basis of understanding and grounding the thesis that marriage, at the unconscious level, is an attempt to resolve those issues, and, indeed, must resolve them if the marriage is to be a growth experience.

3. The English language has only one word for the phenomenon of love, and that word is used in so many contexts to describe so many emotions that it has no distinct meaning. We use it to say "I love New York," "I love the movies," "I love sex," "I love you," and everything else about which we may have positive feelings. Consequently, its meaning is determined largely by its context.

Until recently, psychology made little reference to love, and it is noticeably absent in most studies of marriage. Perhaps that is because the association of love and marriage is, as discussed earlier, a recent historical phenomenon. Theories of marriage and marital therapy have focused on contract making, conflict resolution, systems analysis, and restructuring rather than love. Freud and Jung used the Latin word "libido," but in different ways. Freud spoke of a libidinal love and a narcissistic love; the first is a generalized sexual energy directed to others, notably the infant to the mother as a first love object, and later redirected to others. The second, narcissistic love, was a consequence of psychic injury that resulted in focusing libido on the self. He called this "primary narcissism." The resolution of this self-invested love led to the redirection of libido to another, or secondary narcissism. (See Sigmund Freud, "On Narcissism: An Introduction.") Jung used "libido" to refer to a generalized life energy. (For a discussion of love by psychoanalytically oriented psychologists and psychiatrists, see Rollo May, *Love and Will;* Erich Fromm, *The Art of Loving;* Reubin Fine, *The Meaning of Love in Human Experience;* Willard Gaylin, *Rediscovering Love;* and Nathaniel Brandon, *The Psychology of Romantic Love.*)

To avoid the vagueness of the word "love," I have elected to use three Greek words: "eros," "agape," and "philia." These words have precise meanings and refer to various phases of one phenomenon. They also make possible a description of a developmental view of love as a possibility in marriage. "Eros" is the root of the word "erotic," which in our culture has a sexual, even pornographic connotation, but in Greek means "passionate love of the world." (See Bauer, *A Greek-English Lesson,* p. 311.)

The broader meaning of "eros" is "life force," which is directed outward in passionate appreciation of the world. This includes, but is not limited to, sexuality. It also denotes the sense in which the self and its demands and needs are emphasized. In my view, when eros is frustrated or blunted by deficient nurturing or excessive socialization, it turns back upon itself in self-absorption and becomes preoccupied with organismic survival. This condition remains until the experience of romantic love, when eros is redirected to another, the romantic partner, in an attempt to restore the original condition of wholeness. The failure to achieve the original situation results in the power struggle, which is ultimately a defense against death. In this I take issue with Freud, who posits a "death instinct," or "thanatos," as a polarity to eros. (Freud, "The Instincts and Their Vicissitudes.") I see eros as a singular life energy expressing itself in the face of the fear of death, not the "pull" of death. See Chapter 10, note 1, for a further discussion of eros.

4. Plato, *The Symposium,* pp. 143ff.

CHAPTER 3: YOUR IMAGO

1. The reconstruction of the past by selecting a partner who resembles one's parents was originally given the name "repetition compulsion" by Freud. This idea was expanded by Fritz Perls, founder of Gestalt Therapy, and given the name "unfinished business." For Perls, this consists of feelings and memories that are unconscious and avoided but are expressed in behavior. Some view this repetition as an attempt to restore the familiar, thus as a static and nonpurposive process. I side with Freud's view of the purposive character of repetition as an attempt at resolution.

2. In *Webster's Dictionary,* "imago" means the "representation of a person or a thing," "a copy," "likeness," "a mental picture." The term was used in psychology by Freud. In fact, it was the title of a now defunct journal edited by him. Jung also uses the term in his *Collected Works,* vol. 9, pp. 60ff., to mean the "inner representation of the opposite sex." In this book I depend in principle upon Jung rather than the "object-relations" school, who would define it as the "significant other." In either case, the image is formed out of the internalization of all

childhood caretakers, and its projection generates the feelings of romantic love.

In Jungian psychology, the anima image is projected by the man and the animus image is projected by the woman. In this book, the imago is a fusion of the traits of all significant caretakers and may have dominant same-sex or opposite-sex qualities and can be projected by either sex. In other words, from clinical experience it is obvious that a man may choose a woman who is like his father and a woman may choose a man who is like her mother. In all cases the imago selection is a combination of same- and opposite-sex traits.

3. See Wilder Penfield, *The Mystery of Mind,* p. 20.

CHAPTER 4: ROMANTIC LOVE

1. The experience of romantic love, an intensely passionate and often sexual relationship between a man and a woman, is among the oldest recorded experiences of mankind. It inflames the relationship between the ancient gods and goddesses (Zeus and Hera), sometimes between gods and humans (Cupid and Psyche), often between famous persons (Dante and Beatrice, Isaac and Rebekah, Franklin D. Roosevelt and Lucy Mercer), and surely among many ordinary mortals, although history shows little interest in lesser persons. Some of these relationships inspired by the fires of eros have changed the course of history (Antony and Cleopatra, Paris and Helen of Troy); others have inspired great literature (Dante and Beatrice, Tristan and Isolde); all constitute the most endearing and enduring stories of humankind, most of which end in tragedy and death (Romeo and Juliet, Samson and Delilah, Lancelot and Guinevere). (See *Love Through the Ages,* by Robert Lynd.) Explanations of the source of this energy have ranged from the "infusion of the gods" or a "demon" to the result of a disease. People fell in love because they were struck by Cupid's arrow, were tricked into drinking a magic potion, or happened to be born under favorable stars. In every case, something external, even extraterrestrial, was involved. Today, with the decline in the belief of the supernatural, explanations tend to be more psychological and subjective, with the energy believed to be arising from within the persons.

The forms of romantic love seem to have undergone three changes in history, each reflecting changes in the male/female relationship, and its fate has been determined by social structure and cultural practices. Prior to the eleventh century, the dominant form of romantic love was called "heroic love." The major theme in heroic love is the pursuit and capture of the woman by the man. The societies in which this form of love existed were feudal aristocracies in which romantic love was sought and mainly existed either in passionate or extramarital love or in romanticized nonsexual relationships. Contributing factors to this situation were the existence of slavery, the bias of free-born men against labor, the association of slavery with the functions of the home, and the consequent difficulty of associating love with home. Thus the fulfillment of love was sought outside the home and outside marriage.

A radical reversal in male-female relationships occurred in the eleventh century with the appearance of the troubadours and their love ballads in southern France. In a short time, heroic love was replaced with what is known as "courtly love," in which the theme of pursuit and capture gave way to the image of male supplication and entreaty of the female. Images of force and rape were replaced with refinements of courtship. This led to the formation of "courts of love," where the merits of love were debated and where judgments were usually rendered that true love was attainable only outside of marriage and often only if there was no sexual communion. The form of modern love relationships was influenced and developed against this background.

Romantic love as the door to marriage had to await the evolving freedom and rights of individuals to choose their fate and to determine their own forms of government. That and the emerging freedom and equality of women were the forces that led to modern marriage, and its attendant psychological baggage. (See Morton Hunt, *The Natural History of Love,* and Isidor Schneider, ed., *The World of Love,* vol. 1.)

2. Quoted in Jane Lahr and Lena Tabori, *Love,* p. 189.
3. Michael R. Liebowitz, M.D., *The Chemistry of Love,* pp. 37ff.
4. In contrast to classical views of romantic love, which attribute its source to external forces, modern psychologies of love locate its origin in the human mind. In this book, love is viewed as a single energy that is directed to outside persons or to the self, depending upon need and motivation. Although it is a singular phenomenon, its distinctive forms are represented as stages. However, since the experience of romantic love seems to us to be stimulated by an outside source, namely the loved one, the ancients' belief in the external origins of love can be understood as the objectification of our inner sensations. Now, however, we understand that the external person has no power to activate such passions, but instead is endowed by the unconscious with attributes that appear to give him or her that power. The passions are

self-activated by the association of an internal need-gratifying image with the character makeup of the loved other.

5. Lucius Apuleius, *The Golden Ass,* in Robert Lynd, *Love Through the Ages,* pp. 1165ff.

CHAPTER 5: THE POWER STRUGGLE

1. My first encounter with a full discussion of the unconscious expectations couples bring to marriage was in *Marriage Contracts* by Clifford Sager. Sager has worked out a very detailed analysis of conscious, preconscious, and unconscious contracts.

2. Early-childhood experience also seems to be the source of other beliefs that characterize the power struggle. The intuitive response of parents to childhood stress, especially in the preverbal stage, leads to the belief in the omniscience of spouses: they know what we need without having to ask. We resent our needs not being responded to automatically. Having to ask breaks the illusion that our partners know what we need. Another belief is that they have what we need and can satisfy us if they would. This is called the "illusion of partner omnipotence." Finally, we believe they should always be available to meet our needs and have no needs of their own. This is the belief in partner omnipresence. Their failure to meet our needs creates emotional pain and leads eventually to the belief in the partner as evil and therefore the enemy.

3. The stages of grief in a dying person were worked out by Elisabeth Kübler-Ross and described in her book *On Death and Dying.*

4. The bargaining stage in the power struggle, an expression of the quid pro quo that most couples naturally evolve in their attempt to negotiate their needs, is the stage most couples present to the therapist when they enter therapy. In my opinion, this is the source of earlier methods in marital counseling that attempted to help couples develop contracts and negotiate their conflicts. Therapists responded to what couples were trying to do and sought to help them do it better. They did not recognize it as a stage in the power struggle and unwittingly helped couples stay in it, rather than help them move to the next stage, despair, and to the surrender of their illusions. The surrender of illusions is a precondition for the conscious marriage and precedes the final step of acceptance.

5. This estimate is attributed to Virginia Satir, a well-known family therapist.

CHAPTER 6: BECOMING CONSCIOUS

1. The idea of "becoming conscious" refers to processes common to psychology and the spiritual traditions. Long before Freud's development of his theory of the unconscious, which states that our lives are directed largely by forces not in our consciousness nor under its control, the ancient mystical traditions of the East and the West perceived our ordinary, everyday consciousness as an illusion, a state of "waking sleep." While there are important technical distinctions between the "unconscious" and "waking sleep," both views are in agreement in perceiving that things are not the way they appear and that a fundamental change in mental life is necessary if we are to know the "truth." These changes consist of "insight" and "awakening," respectively.

   Insight brings unconscious contents into consciousness, and awakening gives us direct experience of "reality" that has been hidden behind our symbolic constructions. I use the phrase "becoming conscious" to combine these two processes as they apply to marriage.
2. The Bible, Exodus 12:37ff.

CHAPTER 7: CLOSING YOUR EXITS

1. The no-exist decision is an adaptation of the "escape-hatch" concept developed by Frank Ernst, a transaction analyst, who conceived the idea of the OK Corral (see bibliography). The purpose of this exercise is to engage the rational mind, the new brain, which can make cognitive decisions not to act on impulses and emotions that would be destructive to therapy, to the self, or to a relationship. My experience that couples will make this decision and still not improve led to the discovery that they use many noncatastrophic exits to avoid positive involvement with each other.
2. I first learned about the concepts of graduated change from Kurt Lewin, an analytically oriented social psychologist who pioneered in the area of the social psychology of group process and group change. Graduated change is also commonly used in behavioral psychology and social-learning theory.

CHAPTER 8: CREATING A ZONE OF SAFETY

1. Richard Stuart, *Helping Couples Change*, p. 17.
2. I am greatly indebted to Stuart and to behaviorism in general for the idea of a structured therapeutic change process. I was also influenced

by Transactional Analysis (which talks about giving people permission to want) and by John Whitaker, a Dallas psychiatrist and transactional analyst, who developed the idea of the "want" list.

One key difference between the Reromanticizing exercise and Stuart's Caring Days exercise is that I ask couples to generate their list of caring behaviors by writing down three different kinds of pleasurable transactions: ones they experienced during the romantic stage of their relationship, ones they are currently experiencing in their relationships, and ones that they would like to experience but have never asked for, because of fear of being criticized or rejected. All three kinds of pleasurable transactions tap into unmet childhood needs. The enactment of these behaviors touches childhood issues in the unconscious and creates an environment in which the deeper conflicted issues can later be addressed.

CHAPTER 10: DEFINING YOUR CURRICULUM

1. In earlier versions of this exercise, I did not ask couples like Melanie and Stewart to try to figure out what childhood wounds they were reinjuring. It did not seem necessary in order to benefit from the exercise. All they had to do was identify a chronic criticism, convert it into a fear, then into a desire, and then describe a positive, specific behavior that would satisfy that desire. It seemed very straightforward.

   Now I see it quite differently. I believe that it is important to attach the current frustration to a childhood memory for two reasons. First, it helps the sender know that his or her frustrations have their roots in childhood, not in the relationship. I use the ninety percent formula. Ninety percent of a person's frustrations are repetitions of childhood wounds and ten percent are from the current relationship. The partner's behaviors trigger the memories, but do not create them. Second, linking the present frustrations with the past helps the listening partner know that he or she is not the ultimate cause of the frustrations, but instead the occasion for it. Knowing that the frustrations come from the sender's childhood, the listener can develop compassion and even empathy for his or her partner's pain.

2. Agape is the second word in the Greek language for "love." It is used to express human love, the love of humans for God, and the love of God for humans. It also refers to a love feast that expresses brotherly love. In every case it seems to mean a love for another without regard for conditions—unconditional love. It is not dependent upon the worth or

value of the other, and when it is expressed it carries no obligation. It is an unconditional gift. (See Bauer, *A Greek-English Lexicon,* p. 6.)

In Greek philosophy, agape is one of the forms of love on a continuum with eros and philia. Therefore, it is not another kind of love, but a special way in which love is expressed. In this book, I view agape as the act of directing eros, the life energy, away from oneself and toward the welfare of the other. In that sense it is sacrificial, but what is sacrificed is not the self but preoccupation with the self. Although it is used as a noun, and thus denotes an attitude, it is also used as a verb, and thus denotes the way one acts toward another. The merger of these two senses means that agape can be understood as an attitude that is expressed in behaviors. On this basis, I call it the "power of transformation" that directs eros to the other, thus creating a new quality in relationships, called "philia."

CHAPTER 12: PORTRAIT OF TWO RELATIONSHIPS

1. The focus of this book has been on the power of love for psychological and spiritual healing. Evidence is now being accumulated by research psychologists and physicians on the positive effects of altruistic love on the immune system (McClelland) and on the healing process in general (Siegel). This means that love influences body functions as well as psychological processes such as depression (Weissman). Evidence that marital stress results in psychosomatic symptoms by depressing the immune system (Kiecolt-Glaser) and influences psychological stress such as adolescent suicide, high blood pressure, depression (Folkenberg), and possibly cancer (Levenson) is correlated with evidence that an altruistic lifestyle, a life of loving energy directed to others, improves physical and emotional health (McClelland). The implications emerging from this research indicate the significance of a positive marriage, or the idea of marriage as a passionate friendship, for a general sense of well-being and health. Safety is posited as the invariant and essential component behind mental, physical, emotional, and spiritual health.

2. "Philia" is the root of the English word "filial." Its basic meaning has to do with brotherly love. But in Greek "brotherly" is not limited to and does not necessarily refer to kinship. It also refers to an attitude and a quality of relating in which the feelings of care that are experienced between people who are connected by blood are experienced between people who are not blood-related. Such bonding is a desirable

human condition, because it would remove the reality of the other as strange and therewith all attendant threats from the outside or the other. Philia is thus the basis of friendship and refers to love among equals (see Bauer, p. 866).

To distinguish friend from foe is essential for personal and group survival. This polarity is the basis of personal and group conflict, violence, and war. True peace—that is, peace without fear—exists only among friends. Peace with fear can exist between foes, but it is always unstable. Again, this appears to be an old-brain function—to respond to this perceived distinction in the service of organismic survival. The admonition by Jesus in the New Testament to "love your enemies" collides with this old-brain directive, but it is the highest concept humans have been able to develop to deal with the animal residues of evolution.

It is interesting that, in a research project of "happy" couples, the item ranked first by all couples was "we are each other's best friend" (Lauer and Lauer, "Marriages Made to Last"). This form of love between friends is a love among equals that is created through agape, a new quality of relating.

CHAPTER 13: TEN STEPS TOWARD A CONSCIOUS PARTNERSHIP

1. Craft, Harriet, "A Descriptive Study of the Love or Illusion Workshop," 1984, unpublished manuscript, East Texas University.

Bibliography

Apuleius, Lucius. *The Golden Ass,* in *Love Through the Ages* by Robert Lynd, Coward-McCann, Inc., New York, 1932.

Atkinson, Brent J. *Emotional Intelligence in Couples Therapy: Advances from Neurobiology and the Science of Intimate Relationships,* W. W. Norton & Company, New York, 2005.

Barker, Robert L. *Treating Couples in Crisis,* The Free Press, New York, 1984.

Bauer, W. A. *Greek-English Lexicon of the New Testament and Other Early Christian Literature,* trans. W. F. Arndt and F. W. Gingrich, The University of Chicago Press, Chicago, Illinois, 1957.

Bellah, Robert, Richard Madson, William M. Sullivan, Ann Swidler, and Steven M. Tipton. *Habits of the Heart,* The Perennial Library, New York, 1985.

Bohm, David. *On Dialogue,* ed. Lee Nichol, Routledge, New York, 1996.

Brandon, Nathaniel. *The Psychology of Romantic Love,* J. P. Tarcher, Inc., Los Angeles, California, 1980.

Buber, Martin. *Between Man and Man,* trans. Ronald Gregor Smith, Collier Books/Macmillan Publishing Company, New York, 1965.

Buber, Martin. *I and Thou,* Charles Scribner's Sons, New York, 1958.

Craft, Harriet. "A Descriptive Study of the Love or Illusion Workshop," 1984, unpublished manuscript.

Ellinor, Linda, and Glenna Gerard. *Dialogue: Rediscover the Transforming Power of Conversation,* John Wiley & Sons, Inc., New York, 1998.

Ernst, Frank. "The OK Corral: The Grid for Get-on-With," *Transactional Analysis Journal* 1:4 (October 1971).

Folkenberg, Judy. "Multi-Site Study of Therapies for Depression," *Archives of General Psychiatry* 42 (March 1985).

Freud, Sigmund. "On Narcissism: An Introduction (1914)," in *General Psychological Theory: Papers on Metapsychology,* Collier Books, New York, 1963.

———. "The Instincts and Their Vicissitudes (1915)" in *Collected Papers,* vol. 4, Basic Books, New York, 1959.

Friedman, Maurice. *The Healing Dialogue in Psychotherapy,* Jason Aronson, Inc., New York, 1985.

Fromm, Erich. *The Art of Loving,* Bantam Books, New York, 1956.

Gaylin, Willard. *Rediscovering Love,* Viking Penguin, Inc., New York, 1986.

Gottman, John M., Ph.D., and Joan DeClaire. *The Relationship Cure: A 5 Step Guide for Building Better Connections with Family, Friends and Lovers,* Crown Publishers, New York, 2001.

Greenberg, Leslie S., and Susan M. Johnson. *Emotionally Focused Therapy for Couples,* The Guilford Press, New York, 1988.

Gunzburg, John C. *Healing Through Meeting: Martin Buber's Conversational Approach to Psychotherapy,* Jessica Kingsley Publishers, Bristol, Pennsylvania, 1907, 1997.

Hunt, Morton. *The Natural History of Love,* Alfred A. Knopf, New York, 1959.

Jung, C. G. *The Archetypes and the Collective Unconscious,* trans. R. F. C. Hull, Bollingen Series XX, Princeton University Press, Princeton, New Jersey, 1969.

———. "Marriage as a Psychological Relationship," in *The Portable Jung,* ed. Joseph Campbell, The Viking Press, New York, 1971.

———. *Two Essays in Analytical Psychology,* in *Collected Work, vol. 7.,* trans. R. F. C. Hull, Bollingen Series XX, Princeton University Press, Princeton, New Jersey, 1969.

Kiecolt-Glaser, Janice K. "Marital Quality, Marital Disruption, and Immune Function," *Psychosomatic Medicine,* in press.

Kubler-Ross, Elisabeth. *On Death and Dying,* The Macmillan Company, New York, 1969.

Lahr, Jane, and Lena Tabori. *Love: A Celebration in Art and Literature,* Stewart, Tabori and Chang, Publishers, New York, 1982.

Lauer, Jeanette, and Robert Lauer. "Marriages Made to Last," in *Psychology Today* 19:6 (June 1985).

Levenson, Frederick F. *The Anti-Cancer Marriage: Living Longer Through Loving,* Stein and Day, Publishers, New York.

Liebowitz, Michael, M.D. *The Chemistry of Love,* Little, Brown and Company, Boston, 1983.

Lynd, Robert. *Love Through the Ages: Love Stories of All Nations,* Coward-McCann, Inc., New York, 1932.

Mahler, Margaret. *On Human Symbiosis and the Vicissitudes of Individuation: Infantile Psychosis,* International Universities Press, New York, 1968.

May, Rollo. *Love and Will,* W. W. Norton and Company, Inc., New York, 1969.

McClelland, David C. "Some Reflections on the Two Psychologies of Love," *Journal of Personality* 54:2 (June 1986).

McLean, Paul. "Man of His Animal Brains," *Modern Medicine,* February 3, 1964.

Mitchell, Stephen A. *Relational Concepts in Psychoanalysis: An Integration,* Harvard University Press, Cambridge, Massachusetts, 1988.

Mitchell, Stephen A. *Relationality: From Attachment to Intersubjectivity,* The Analytic Press, Hillsdale, New Jersey, 2000.

Penfield, Wilder. *The Mystery of Mind: A Critical Study of Consciousness and the Human Brain,* Princeton University Press, Princeton, New Jersey, 1975.

Perls, Frederick S., with Abraham Levitsky. "The Rules and Games of Gestalt Therapy," in *Gestalt Therapy Now,* ed. Joan Fagen and Irma Lee Shepherd, Science and Behavior Books, Palo Alto, California, 1970.

Plato. *Symposium,* in *The Portable Plato,* ed. Scott Buchanan, The Viking Press, New York, 1948.

de Quincey, Christian. *Radical Knowing: Understanding Consciousness through Relationship,* Park Street Press, Rochester, Vermont, 2005.

de Rougemont, Denis. *Love in the Western World,* trans. Montgomery Belgion, Doubleday Anchor Books, Doubleday and Company, Garden City, New York, 1957.

Sager, Clifford J. *Marriage Contracts and Couples Therapy: Hidden Forces in Intimate Relationships,* Brunner/Mazel, Publishers, New York, 1976.

Shafir, Rebecca Z., M.A. CCC. *The Zen of Listening: Mindful Communication in the Age of Distraction,* Quest Books, Wheaton, Illinois, 2000.

Scharff, David E., M.D., and Jill Savege Scharff, M.D. *Object Relations Couple Therapy,* Jason Aronson, Inc., Northvale, New Jersey, 1991.

Schneider, Isidor, ed. *The World of Love,* vols. I and II, George Braziller, New York, 1948.

Siegel, Bernard. *Love, Medicine and Miracles: Lessons Learned About Self-Healing from a Surgeon's Experience with Exceptional Patients,* Harper and Row, Publishers, New York, 1986.

Silverman Lloyd H., Frank M. Lachmann, and Robert L. Milich. *The Search for Oneness,* International Universities Press, New York, 1982.

Stolorow, Robert D., and George E. Atwood. *Contexts of Being: The Intersubjective Foundations of Psychological Life,* The Analytic Press, Inc, Hillsdale, New Jersey, 1992.

Stolorow, Robert D., George E. Atwood, and Donna M. Orange. *Worlds Of Experience: Interweaving Philosophical and Clinical Dimensions in Psychoanalysis,* Basic Books, New York, 2002.

Stuart, Richard. *Helping Couples Change: A Social Learning Approach to Marital Therapy,* The Guilford Press, New York, 1980.

Sullivan, Harry Stack. *The Interpersonal Theory of Psychiatry,* W.W. Norton & Company, Inc., New York, 1953.

Weissman, Myrna M. "Advances in Psychiatric Epidemiology: Rates and Risks of Major Depression," *American Journal of Health,* in press.

Wilber, Ken. *Integral Psychology: Consciousness, Spirit, Psychology, Therapy,* Shambhala Publications, Inc., Boston, Massachusetts, 2000.

Yerkovich, Milan, and Kay Yerkovich. *How We Love: A Revolutionary Approach to Deeper Connections in Marriage,* Water Brook Press, Colorado Springs, Colorado, 2006.

About Imago Relationship Therapy

Imago Relationship Therapy, originating in the partnership of Harville Hendrix, Ph.D., and Helen LaKelly Hunt, Ph.D., integrates the seminal interpersonal insights of major Western psychological systems, behavioral sciences, and spiritual disciplines into a uniquely comprehensive theory of primary love relationships. Developed from the exclusive study of couples and the integration of the relational implications of various psychological and spiritual systems, it presents an approach that builds on previous efforts to understand intimate partnerships and extends those efforts to create a relational theory and therapy that mirrors the view that the basic characteristic of the universe is connectedness.

Imago Relationship Therapy is an expression of the new paradigm of relationality which includes and transcends the traditional paradigm of the individual. In the individual paradigm, all things are separate and relationships have to be constructed. The focus is on the intra-psychic. In the relationship paradigm, all things in the universe, from particles to galaxies to persons, constitute an unbroken wholeness. The focus is on the intersubjective or the "between." This means that couples are essentially connected, although they experience themselves as separate. In conflict, they lose their awareness of connection and experience isolation. IRT utilizes a variety of clinical procedures to help couples—and singles desiring an intimate union—understand that the unconscious forces that influence partner selection, and the inevitable power struggle that follows, is an unconscious attempt to restore connections that were ruptured in childhood. The goal of therapy is to help couples achieve a "conscious partnership." This includes assisting them in identifying and interpreting their defenses against intimacy, which precipitate the power struggle, as a paradoxical yearning for connection, and helping couples restore connections within themselves, between themselves, and with the universe. The process of the therapy includes: identifying frustrations rooted in primitive and illusory ideation of one's love partner; recognizing the failure of archaic behavior to gratify needs and achieve self-completion; and perceiving one's partner as an "other" without the encumbrance of one's own unconscious projections. Other aspects of the Imago process involve learning new skills and changing hurtful behavior, in the course of which partners consciously aim to meet one another's needs and thereby restore the lost and denied parts of themselves and recover their wholeness. The core skill is a three-part dialogue that helps couples make contact by breaking out of defensive and symbiotic relating and promoting differentiation from each other, compassion and empathy for each other, and connection and communion with each other. Therapy is ultimately made obsolete as each partner becomes a skilled advocate and "container" for the other's growth process. The Imago process, when consistently applied in any relationship, has the potential to be a transformational journey toward mutual healing, emotional maturation, and spiritual evolution. Creating healthy intimate partnerships and healthy children ultimately transforms society.

Imago Contacts

Imago Relationship Therapy is available in thirty countries from more than 2,000 Imago therapists. If you are interested in working with a couples therapist specifically trained in Imago Relationship Therapy or wish to attend a *Getting the Love You Want* or *Keeping the Love You Find* workshop, visit the Web site www.HarvilleHendrix.com.

Seeking Training in Imago Relationship Therapy

Training in Imago Relationship Therapy is available internationally. For more information on clinical and educational training opportunities, visit the Web site www.HarvilleHendrix.com.

Additional Imago Resources

For additional Imago resources including books, DVDs, audiotapes, videotapes, and other educational opportunities, please contact:

Imago

Imago Relationships International
160 Broadway
Suite 1001—East Building
New York, New York 10038
telephone: (800) 729-1121 *or* (212) 240-7433
Web site: *www.HarvilleHendrix.com*
e-mail: *info@imagorelationships.org*

Meetings with Harville

Living a Life of Dialogue

> All real living is meeting.
> — MARTIN BUBER

 "Meeting" takes place in all of our relationships, the moment when we can turn toward the other and engage in genuine Dialogue. We invite you to "live a life of Dialogue" by visiting the Web site www.HarvilleHendrix.com.

- Discover writings, podcasts, and invitations to special events including live teleseminars with Harville Hendrix.
- Find updates on Harville Hendrix and Helen LaKelly Hunt's workshop and lecture schedule.
- Participate in a community committed to bringing genuine dialogue to all walks of life.
- Explore Imago resources including workshops and educational programs for couples and singles, Certified Imago Therapists, professional training programs for qualified therapists and educators, and related products.
- Teach *Couplehood as a Spiritual Path,* a faith-based educational program for couples, based on the principles of *Getting the Love You Want.*

www.HarvilleHendrix.com

Index

About the Authors

HARVILLE HENDRIX, PH.D., and HELEN LAKELLY HUNT, PH.D., married in 1982 and became partners in life and work. They cocreated Imago Relationship Therapy and developed the concept of "conscious partnership." Their partnership and collaboration has resulted in nine books on intimate relationships and parenting.

Harville is a Clinical Pastoral Counselor who is known internationally for his work with couples. A graduate of Mercer University in Macon, Georgia, in 1957, his alma mater awarded him an honorary doctorate of humane letters in 1989. He holds a bachelor of divinity from Union Theological Seminary in New York and a Ph.D. in psychology and religion from the School of Divinity at the University of Chicago. Dr. Hendrix is the recipient of several honors, including the Outstanding Pastoral Counselor of the Year Award (1995) from the American Baptist Churches, the 1995 Distinguished Contribution Award from the American Association of Pastoral Counselors, and, jointly with Helen, the Distinguished Contributors Award from the Association for Imago Relationship Therapy. He is a Diplomate in the American Association of Pastoral Counselors and has been a clinical member of the American

Group Psychotherapy Association and the International Transactional Analysis Association, and former board member of the Group Psychotherapy Foundation.

Dr. Hendrix began his career as a therapist and educator at the Pastoral Counseling Center of Greater Chicago in 1965 where he was clinical director. In 1968 he became a member of the faculty of Perkins Divinity School at Southern Methodist University in Dallas, Texas. After teaching for nine years, he entered private practice. Following his divorce in 1975, he began a study of couples in order to better understand his own divorce and to search for the ingredients of a successful marriage. Since 1977 he has conducted couples therapy and couples workshops, taught Imago therapy to clinical professionals, lectured on marriage to the public, and written books with Helen on primary relationships.

Helen is nationally known as an activist in the women's movement and holds two master's degrees from Southern Methodist University, Dallas, Texas, as well as a Ph.D. from Union Theological Seminary in New York City. She is the sole author of *Faith and Feminism: A Holy Alliance* and is actively working on two other books. In addition to being Founder and President of the Sister Fund, she is also cofounder of the New York Women's Foundation, the Dallas Women's Foundation, and the Women's Funding Network. Helen has served on the Boards of Directors of the Ms. Foundation for Women, Women and Foundations, and the New York City Women's Agenda. Among Helen's major civic activities have been active memberships on the Childcare Commission for the Mayor of the City of New York. She has been recognized for her leadership in building the women's funding movement, including the following awards: the 2007 Lead Award from Women & Philanthropy, the National Creative Philanthropy Award from the National Network of Women's Funds, Gloria Steinem's Women of Vision and Action Award through the Ms. Foundation for Women, the Equity Leadership Award from Nontraditional

Employment of Women (NEW), the Laura Parsons Pratt Award for Outstanding Achievement on Behalf of Women and Children from the Federation of Protestant Welfare Agencies, and was an Honoree of the Center of the Elimination of Violence in the Family. Helen is honored to be an inductee in the National Women's Hall of Fame, in Seneca Falls, New York.

To make Imago Relationship Therapy available to people outside his practice, in 1984 Harville and Helen founded the Institute for Imago Relationship Therapy (now Imago Relationships International in New York City—a non-profit cofounded with Imago therapists) to train therapists in the Imago process and to develop workshops for couples and singles. The Institute has trained over 2,000 therapists in thirty countries, and there are nearly 200 workshop presenters who conduct workshops around the world. Imago Relationship Therapy has been featured on the *Oprah Winfrey Show* sixteen times, one of which won for her the "most socially redemptive" award for daytime talk shows, and Dr. Hendrix's second show was included in *O* magazine's "Oprah's Top Twenty Shows" in 2005. He has also been featured on many other major television shows, and in countless radio shows, newspapers, and major magazines, and continues to conduct professional trainings and appear as a public lecturer.

In addition to *Getting the Love You Want: A Guide for Couples,* a *New York Times* bestseller which has sold more than two million copies and been read by millions of couples worldwide, Harville is the author of the two other bestselling books, *Keeping the Love You Find: A Personal Guide* (written for singles) and *Giving the Love that Heals: A Guide for Parents,* which he coauthored with Helen. They have also authored and coauthored nine other books and their work has been translated into more than fifty languages. Harville and Helen were also executive editor and producer, respectively, of *Getting the Love You Want: the Home Video,* which has been seen on more than 300 television stations.

Harville and Helen have a blended family of six children, including two from their own marriage. They live and work in New York and New Mexico where they are busy writing new books, giving lectures at various conventions, and planning the expansion of Imago processes into the larger community.

Imago

Ongoing support for your relationship from Imago

Imago Relationships International was cofounded by Harville Hendrix, Ph.D., and Helen LaKelly Hunt, Ph.D., to help couples and individuals create strong and fulfilling relationships. We offer the following:

- Weekend workshops based on *Getting the Love You Want* are available at many locations in the U.S. and internationally. Over 6,000 couples take this workshop each year.
- 1,000 certified Imago therapists are available in more than 25 countries. They can guide you through the Imago process and help you achieve the relationship of your dreams.
- A monthly e-mail newsletter, with stories from couples and a look at Imago in practice
- A range of audio and video programs based on Imago, including "Through Conflict to Connection," an introductory DVD showing three couples using Imago Dialogue, that features Harville Hendrix and Helen LaKelly Hunt
- Information on training programs for mental-health professionals, coaches, and educators that can help you work more effectively with couples and families
- Workshops for individuals, and parenting programs

For information on these and other Imago programs please visit our Web site: www.GettingtheLoveYouWant.com
Phone: 1-800-729-1121   E-mail: Info@ImagoRelationships.org

In addition, you can find information about the Imago program for religious groups by visiting www.CouplehoodasaSpiritual Path.com

Imago Relationships International, 160 Broadway, Suite 1001, East Building, New York, NY 10038